Taste of Home
Favorite Brand Name Recipes
2008

Taste of Home
B O O K S

REIMAN MEDIA GROUP, INC.
Senior Vice President/Editor in Chief: Catherine Cassidy
Vice President, Executive Editor/Books: Heidi Reuter Lloyd
Chief Marketing Officer: Lisa Karpinski
Creative Director: Ardyth Cope
Senior Editor/Books: Mark Hagen
Art Director: Gretchen Trautman
Food Director: Diane Werner, R.D.
Senior Home Economist: Patricia Schmeling
Senior Recipe Editor: Sue A. Jurack

THE READER'S DIGEST ASSOCIATION, INC.
President and Chief Executive Officer: Mary G. Berner
President, RDA Food & Entertaining: Suzanne M. Grimes

Front cover photography by Reiman Photo Studio
Photographer: Jim Wieland
Food Stylist: Suzanne Breckenridge
Set Stylist: Dolores Schaefer

Pictured on the front cover *(clockwise from top left):* Coconut Lemon Torte *(page 200),* Garlic Onion Bread *(page 112)* and Cheesy Stuffed Meatballs & Spaghetti *(page 167).*
Pictured on the back cover *(clockwise from top left):* Szechuan Grilled Flank Steak *(page 164),* Apricot Miniature Muffins *(page 116)* and Pecan Pie Bars *(page 196).*

ISBN-13: 978-1-4127-2724-2
ISBN-10: 1-4127-2724-3

ISSN: 1554-0111

Manufactured in U.S.A.

8 7 6 5 4 3 2 1

Microwave Cooking: Microwave ovens vary in wattage. Use the cooking times as guidelines and check for doneness before adding more time.

Taste of Home
Favorite Brand Name Recipes
2008

America's Most Trusted Brands Make Weeknight Cooking a Breeze!

NEED a home-cooked supper in a hurry? Looking for a fast weeknight feast? Don't fret! With *Taste of Home Favorite Brand Name Recipes 2008*, you have 363 specialties at your fingertips.

Thanks to this latest edition in the popular series of cookbooks, you'll always have time to surprise your family with a hearty meal that's sure to please. From classic chicken favorites and savory pasta dishes to heartwarming casseroles and toasted sandwiches…the perfect homemade meal is always within reach. That's because all of the dishes come together with ingredients that are likely sitting in your cabinet or refrigerator right now.

Simply the Best

Everything in this sensational collection was approved by a home economist from *Taste of Home*…America's No. 1 recipe source. As such, you can rest assured that every item will cook up perfectly each and every time. Best of all, many of the recipes call for the brand names you trust the most—so you know that they are going to be absolutely delicious!

For example, you just can't go wrong when you whip up Turkey and Stuffing Casserole (p. 174). It comes together easily with a can of Campbell's® creamed soup and a package of Pepperidge Farm® seasoned stuffing. You can also consider savory Empanadas (p. 146), which are a breeze to assemble with a jar of ORTEGA® salsa. Or try Sausage-Stuffed Green Peppers (p. 144). The recipe is a weeknight staple that can be made in moments with Prego® Italian sauce.

Flip through this colorful keepsake and you'll also find finger-licking delights from organizations that know how to make the most of their products. Take Grilled T-Bone Steaks with BBQ Rub (p. 153), for instance. The recipe for these mouth-watering steaks comes from the National Cattlemen's Beef Association.

Chicken Caesar Salad

Recipes Worth Celebrating

In addition to must-try main courses, you'll discover refreshing salads, down-home breads and versatile side dishes. Just page through the book and see for yourself! You'll find the perfect dish for any menu or occasion.

Looking for a stress-free appetizer? Consider the recipe for Tuna in Crispy Wonton Cups (p. 11), which calls for a pouch of Starkist Tuna. Want a special item to spruce up celebrations? Try Holiday Fruit Salad (p. 24), featuring refreshing products from DOLE®.

When you need a sweet treat, *Taste of Home Favorite Brand Name Recipes 2008* has you covered. Grab some HERSHEY᠄S Milk Chocolate Chips and REESE'S® Peanut Butter Chips, and bake up a batch of Double Chip Brownies (p. 188). Refreshing Lemon Cake (p. 198) is also a snap to prepare. It can be assembled in no time with only a handful of items, including a box of DUNCAN HINES® cake mix and a container of DUNCAN HINES® frosting.

Pumpkin Pecan Pie

Mexican Steak Tacos

Menu Planning Made Easy

To help you decide what to prepare for dinner, turn to page 213. The general index lists recipes by food category, major ingredient and/or cooking method. It's a timesaving way to create any menu. If you'd like to make something with chicken, for example, see "chicken" in the general index. You'll find dozens of wonderful options to choose from.

The alphabetical index on page 221 is another handy tool. There you can find the dishes you enjoy most by their titles.

Regardless of how you use *Taste of Home Favorite Brand Name Recipes 2008*, we're sure it will become a most-trusted source when preparing the foods you share with your family... each and every day.

Appetizers & Snacks

Cocktail Meatballs

(pictured at left)

1 pound ground beef
1 pound bulk pork or Italian sausage
1 cup finely chopped onion
1 cup cracker crumbs
1 cup finely chopped sweet green pepper
1/2 cup milk
1 egg, beaten
2 teaspoons salt
1 teaspoon Italian seasoning
1/4 teaspoon pepper
1 cup ketchup
3/4 cup packed brown sugar
1/2 cup (1 stick) butter
1/2 cup cider vinegar
1/4 cup water
1/4 cup lemon juice
1 teaspoon yellow mustard
1/4 teaspoon garlic salt

SLOW COOKER DIRECTIONS
1. Preheat oven to 350°F. Combine beef, sausage, onion, crumbs, sweet pepper, milk, egg, salt, Italian seasoning and pepper in large bowl, mixing lightly but thoroughly. Shape mixture into 1-inch balls. Place on racks on 2 nonstick baking sheets. Bake 25 minutes or until meatballs are no longer pink.

2. Meanwhile, place ketchup, brown sugar, butter, vinegar, water, lemon juice, mustard and garlic salt in 4-quart slow cooker; mix well. Cover; cook on HIGH until hot and bubbly.

3. Transfer meatballs to 4-quart slow cooker; carefully stir to coat with sauce. Reduce heat to LOW. Cover and cook 2 hours.
Makes 12 servings

Clockwise from top left: *Cocktail Meatballs, Stuffed Mushroom Caps (p. 12), Hot Crab-Cheddar Spread (p. 16), Chunky Pinto Bean Dip (p. 18)*

BLT Dip

(pictured at right)

1 envelope LIPTON® RECIPE SECRETS® Onion
    Soup Mix*
1 container (8 ounces) sour cream
1 cup HELLMANN'S® or BEST FOODS® Real
    Mayonnaise
1 medium tomato, chopped (about 1 cup)
1/2 cup cooked crumbled bacon (about 6 slices)
    or bacon bits
    Shredded lettuce

Also terrific with LIPTON® RECIPE SECRETS® Golden Onion Soup Mix.

1. In medium bowl, combine all ingredients except
lettuce; chill, if desired.

2. Garnish with lettuce and serve with your favorite
dippers.   *Makes 3 cups dip*

Spinach-Artichoke Party Cups

36 (3-inch) wonton wrappers
 1 jar (about 6 ounces) marinated artichoke
    hearts, drained and chopped
1/2 (10-ounce) package frozen chopped spinach,
    thawed and squeezed dry
 1 cup (4 ounces) shredded Monterey Jack cheese
1/2 cup grated Parmesan cheese
1/2 cup mayonnaise
 1 garlic clove, minced

1. Preheat oven to 300°F. Spray mini (1-3/4-inch)
muffin cups lightly with nonstick cooking spray.
Press 1 wonton wrapper into each cup; spray lightly
with cooking spray. Bake about 9 minutes or until
light golden brown. Remove shells from pan; place
on wire rack to cool. Repeat with remaining wonton
wrappers.*

2. Meanwhile, combine artichoke hearts, spinach,
cheeses, mayonnaise and garlic in medium bowl;
mix well.

3. Fill each wonton cup with about 1-1/2 teaspoons
spinach-artichoke mixture. Place filled cups on
baking sheet. Bake about 7 minutes or until heated
through. Serve immediately.   *Makes 36 appetizers*

*Wonton cups may be prepared up to one week in advance. Cool
completely and store in an airtight container.*

Tip: If you have leftover spinach-artichoke mixture
after filling the wonton cups, place the mixture in a
shallow ovenproof dish and bake it at 350°F until hot
and bubbly. Serve it with bread or crackers.

Grilled Summer Bruschetta

3/4 cup WISH-BONE® 5 Cheese Italian Dressing
 2 medium red, orange and/or yellow bell
    peppers, quartered
 2 medium yellow squash and/or green zucchini,
    quartered lengthwise
 1 tablespoon chopped fresh basil leaves
 1 loaf Italian or French bread (about 15-inches
    long), cut 1/2-inch slices

1. In large shallow nonaluminum baking dish or
plastic bag, pour 1/4 cup Wish-Bone 5 Cheese Italian
Dressing over red peppers and squash; turn to coat.
Cover, or close bag, and marinate in refrigerator
15 minutes.

2. Meanwhile, brush bread with 1/4 cup dressing
and grill or broil until golden. Remove vegetables
from marinade, reserving marinade. Grill or
broil vegetables, turning once and brushing with
reserved marinade, 15 minutes or until vegetables
are tender. Cool vegetables slightly, then coarsely
chop.

3. In medium bowl, combine remaining 1/4 cup
Dressing, basil and, if desired, salt and ground black
pepper to taste. Stir in vegetables and toss to coat.
To serve, spoon vegetable mixture on toasted
bread.   *Makes 30 appetizers*

Margherita Panini Bites

1 loaf (16 ounces) ciabatta or crusty Italian
    bread, cut into 16 (1/2-inch) slices
8 teaspoons prepared pesto
16 fresh basil leaves
8 slices mozzarella cheese
24 thin slices plum tomatoes (about 2 tomatoes)
    Olive oil

1. Preheat indoor grill. Spread each of 8 slices bread
with 1 teaspoon pesto. Top each slice with 2 basil
leaves, 1 slice mozzarella cheese and 3 tomato
slices. Top with remaining bread slices.

2. Brush both sides of sandwiches lightly with oil.
Grill sandwiches 5 minutes or until lightly browned
and cheese is melted.

3. Cut each sandwich into 4 pieces. Serve warm.
                                        Makes 32 panini bites

Pineapple-Scallop Bites

Pineapple-Scallop Bites

(pictured above)

1/2 cup *French's*® Honey Dijon Mustard
1/4 cup orange marmalade
1 cup canned pineapple cubes (24 pieces)
12 sea scallops (8 ounces), cut in half crosswise
12 strips (6 ounces) uncooked turkey bacon, cut in half crosswise*

*Or, substitute thinly sliced regular bacon for turkey bacon.

1. Soak 12 (6-inch) bamboo skewers in hot water 20 minutes. Combine mustard and marmalade in small bowl. Reserve 1/2 cup mustard mixture for dipping sauce.

2. Hold 1 pineapple cube and 1 scallop half together. Wrap with 1 bacon strip. Thread onto skewer. Repeat with remaining pineapple, scallops and bacon.

3. Place skewers on oiled grid. Grill over medium heat 6 minutes or until scallops are opaque, turning frequently and brushing with remaining mustard mixture. Serve hot with reserved dipping sauce.
Makes 12 skewers

Onion & White Bean Spread

1 can (15 ounces) cannellini or great northern beans, rinsed and drained
2 garlic cloves, minced
1/4 cup minced green onions
1/4 cup grated Parmesan cheese
1/4 cup olive oil
1 tablespoon chopped fresh rosemary leaves
Additional olive oil
French bread slices

1. Combine all ingredients except additional olive oil and bread in food processor. Process 30 to 40 seconds or until mixture is almost smooth.

2. Spoon bean mixture into serving bowl. Drizzle additional olive oil over spread just before serving. Serve with bread slices.
Makes 1-1/4 cups spread

Tip: For a more rustic spread, place all ingredients in a medium bowl and mash with a potato masher.

Pepper Cheese Cocktail Puffs

1 sheet frozen puff pastry dough, thawed
1 tablespoon Dijon mustard
1/2 cup (2 ounces) finely shredded Cheddar cheese
1 teaspoon cracked pepper
1 egg
1 tablespoon water

1. Preheat oven to 400°F. Grease baking sheets.

2. Roll out 1 sheet puff pastry dough on well floured surface to 14×10-inch rectangle. Spread half of dough (from 10-inch side) with mustard. Sprinkle with cheese and pepper. Fold dough over filling; roll gently to seal edges.

3. Cut lengthwise into 3 strips; cut each strip diagonally into 1-1/2-inch pieces. Place on prepared baking sheets. Beat egg and water in small bowl; brush onto appetizers.

4. Bake appetizers 12 to 15 minutes or until puffed and deep golden brown. Remove from baking sheets to wire rack; cool. *Makes about 20 appetizers*

Tip: Work quickly and efficiently when using puff pastry. The colder puff pastry is, the better it will puff in the hot oven. This recipe can be easily doubled.

Tuna in Crispy Wonton Cups

(pictured below)

18 wonton skins, each 3-1/4 inches square
    Butter or olive oil cooking spray
1 (3-ounce) STARKIST Flavor Fresh Pouch® Tuna
    (Albacore or Chunk Light)
1/3 cup cold cooked orzo (rice-shaped pasta) or
    cooked rice
1/4 cup southwestern ranch-style vegetable dip
    with jalapeños or other sour cream dip
1/4 cup drained pimiento-stuffed green olives,
    chopped
3 tablespoons sweet pickle relish, drained
    Paprika, for garnish
    Parsley sprigs, for garnish

Cut wontons into circles with 3-inch round cookie cutter. Spray miniature muffin pans with cooking spray. Place one circle in each muffin cup; press to sides to mold wonton to cup. Spray each wonton with cooking spray. Bake in 350°F oven 6 to 8 minutes or until golden brown; set aside.

In small bowl, gently mix tuna, orzo, dip, olives and relish. Refrigerate filling until ready to serve. Remove wonton cups from muffin pan. Use rounded teaspoon to fill each cup; garnish with paprika and parsley.
Makes 18 cups

Tip: These cups can be made one day ahead; store in airtight container. Reheat in 350°F oven 1 to 2 minutes to recrisp.

Everything But The Kitchen Sink

1 cup candy-coated chocolate candies
1 cup SUN•MAID® Raisins
1 cup dry roasted peanuts
1 cup round toasted oat cereal
1 cup miniature pretzel twists

In large self-sealing plastic bag, **PLACE** candy coated chocolate candies, raisins and peanuts. **SEAL** bag and gently **ROTATE** to mix together.

Just before serving, **STIR** in toasted oat cereal and mini pretzel twists.
Makes 5 cups

Tuna in Crispy Wonton Cups

Empanaditas

(pictured at right)

Chicken Filling (recipe follows)
Pastry for double crust 9-inch pie
1 egg yolk mixed with 1 teaspoon water

1. Preheat oven to 375°F. Prepare Chicken Filling.

2. Roll out pastry, one half at a time, on floured board to 1/8-inch thickness; cut into 2-1/2-inch circles. Place about 1 teaspoon Chicken Filling on each circle. Fold dough over to make half moons; seal edges with fork. Prick tops; brush with egg mixture.

3. Place on ungreased baking sheets. Bake 12 to 15 minutes or until golden brown. Serve warm.

Makes about 36 empanaditas

Chicken Filling

1 tablespoon butter
1 cup finely chopped onion
2 cups finely chopped cooked chicken
1/4 cup canned diced green chiles
1 tablespoon capers, rinsed, drained and coarsely chopped
1/4 teaspoon salt
1 cup (4 ounces) shredded Monterey Jack cheese

Melt butter in medium skillet over medium heat. Add onion; cook until tender. Stir in chicken, chiles, capers and salt; cook 1 minute. Remove from heat and let cool; stir in cheese. *Makes about 3 cups*

Stuffed Mushroom Caps

(pictured on page 6)

2 packages (8 ounces each) whole mushrooms
1 tablespoon butter
2/3 cup finely chopped cooked chicken
1/4 cup grated Parmesan cheese
1 tablespoon chopped fresh basil
2 teaspoons lemon juice
1/8 teaspoon onion powder
1/8 teaspoon salt
    Pinch garlic powder
    Pinch pepper
1 package (3 ounces) cream cheese, softened
    Paprika

1. Preheat oven to 350°F. Clean mushrooms; remove stems and finely chop. Arrange mushroom caps on greased baking sheet.

2. Melt butter in medium skillet over medium-high heat; cook chopped mushrooms 5 minutes. Add chicken, Parmesan cheese, basil, lemon juice, onion powder, salt, garlic powder and pepper to skillet. Cook and stir 5 minutes. Remove from heat; stir in cream cheese.

3. Spoon mixture into hollow of each mushroom cap. Bake 10 to 15 minutes or until heated through. Sprinkle with paprika.

Makes about 26 stuffed mushrooms

Savory Onion Crab Cakes over Greens

1 envelope LIPTON® RECIPE SECRETS® Onion Soup Mix
1 cup plain dry bread crumbs
1 can (6 ounces) refrigerated pasteurized crabmeat or 1 package (6 ounces) frozen crabmeat, thawed and drained
1 medium red, orange or yellow bell pepper, finely chopped
2 eggs
2 tablespoons HELLMANN'S® or BEST FOODS® Real Mayonnaise
2 teaspoons red or green cayenne pepper sauce
    All-purpose flour
4 teaspoons BERTOLLI® Olive Oil, divided
8 cups assorted baby greens
    Your favorite vinaigrette dressing

1. In medium bowl, combine soup mix, bread crumbs, crabmeat, bell pepper, eggs, mayonnaise and cayenne pepper sauce. Shape into 12 small patties. Lightly flour both sides.

2. In 12-inch nonstick skillet, heat 2 teaspoons olive oil over medium-high heat and cook 6 crab cakes 3-1/2 minutes or until golden brown, turning once. Remove from skillet and keep warm. Repeat with remaining olive oil and patties.

3. To serve, on 4 plates, arrange baby greens. Arrange 3 crab cakes on each salad and drizzle with dressing. *Makes 4 servings*

Baked Brie

(pictured at right)

1/2 pound Brie cheese, rind removed
1/4 cup chopped pecans
1/4 cup KARO® Dark Corn Syrup

1. Preheat oven to 350°F. Place cheese in shallow oven-safe serving dish. Top with pecans and corn syrup.

2. Bake 8 to 10 minutes or until cheese is almost melted. Serve warm with plain crackers or melba toast. *Makes 8 servings*

Spicy Mustard Kielbasa Bites

1 pound whole kielbasa or smoked Polish sausage
1 cup *French's®* Spicy Brown Mustard
3/4 cup honey
1 tablespoon *Frank's® RedHot®* Original Cayenne Pepper Sauce

1. Place kielbasa on grid. Grill over medium heat 10 minutes or until lightly browned, turning occasionally. Cut into bite-sized pieces; set aside.

2. Combine mustard and honey in large saucepan. Bring to a boil over medium heat. Stir in kielbasa and **Frank's RedHot** Sauce. Cook until heated through. Transfer to serving bowl. Serve with party toothpicks. *Makes 8 servings*

Reuben Dip

2 cans (14 ounces each) sauerkraut, drained
2 cups (8 ounces) shredded Swiss cheese
3 packages (2-1/2 ounces each) corned beef, shredded
1/2 cup (1 stick) butter, melted
1 egg, beaten
Rye cocktail bread or crackers

SLOW COOKER DIRECTIONS
1. Combine all ingredients except rye bread in 3-quart slow cooker. Cover; cook on HIGH 2 hours.

2. Serve with rye cocktail bread or crackers.
Makes 12 servings

Marinated Antipasto Kabobs

1/2 (9-ounce) package spinach three-cheese tortellini or plain tortellini
1 package (9 ounces) frozen artichoke hearts, thawed
20 small mushrooms, stems removed
1 large sweet red pepper, cut into 20 pieces
1/2 cup white balsamic or white wine vinegar
1/4 cup grated Parmesan cheese
1/4 cup minced fresh basil
2 tablespoons Dijon mustard
1 tablespoon olive oil
1/2 teaspoon sugar
1/4 teaspoon pepper
20 cherry tomatoes

1. Cook tortellini according to package directions. Drain well. Cool slightly; cover and refrigerate until ready to assemble kabobs.

2. Cook artichokes according to package directions; drain. Immediately add artichokes to bowl of ice water to stop cooking process. Let stand 1 to 2 minutes; drain well. Place artichokes in large resealable food storage bag. Add mushrooms and sweet pepper.

3. Combine vinegar, cheese, basil, mustard, oil, sugar and pepper in small bowl; mix well. Add to vegetable mixture; seal bag. Turn bag over several times to coat ingredients evenly. Refrigerate several hours or overnight, turning bag occasionally.

4. Remove vegetables from marinade. Arrange vegetables on skewers alternately with tortellini and tomatoes; place on serving platter.
Makes 20 kabobs

Tip: Don't clean mushrooms until just before you're ready to use them (they will absorb water and become mushy). Wipe them with a damp paper towel or rinse them under cold running water and blot dry.

Baked Brie

Spicy Cocoa Glazed Pecans

Spicy Cocoa Glazed Pecans

(pictured above)

    1/4 cup plus 2 tablespoons sugar, divided
    1 cup warm water
1-1/2 cups pecan halves or pieces
    1 tablespoon HERSHEY'S Cocoa
    3 to 4 teaspoons chili powder
    1/8 to 1/4 teaspoon cayenne pepper

1. Heat oven to 350°F. Lightly spray shallow baking pan with vegetable oil spray.

2. Stir together 1/4 cup sugar and warm water, stirring until sugar dissolves. Add pecans; let soak 10 minutes. Drain water and discard.

3. Stir together remaining 2 tablespoons sugar, cocoa, chili powder and cayenne pepper in medium bowl. Add pecans; toss until all the cocoa mixture coats the pecans. Spread coated pecans on prepared pan.

4. Bake 10 to 15 minutes or until pecans start to glisten and appear dry. Stir occasionally while baking. Cool completely. Store in cool, dry place. Serve as a snack with beverages or sprinkle in salads.   *Makes 1-1/2 cups coated pecans*

Ortega® Hot Poppers

    1 can (3-1/2 ounces) ORTEGA® Whole
      Jalapeños, drained
    1 cup (4 ounces) shredded Cheddar cheese
    1 package (3 ounces) cream cheese, softened
1/4 cup chopped fresh cilantro
1/2 cup all-purpose flour
    2 eggs, lightly beaten
    2 cups cornflake cereal, crushed
      Vegetable oil
      ORTEGA Salsa, any variety
      Sour cream

CUT jalapeños lengthwise into halves; remove seeds.

BLEND Cheddar cheese, cream cheese and cilantro in small bowl. Place 1 to 1-1/2 teaspoons cheese mixture into each jalapeño half; chill for 15 minutes or until cheese is firm.

DIP each jalapeño half in flour; shake off excess. Dip in eggs; coat with cornflake crumbs.

ADD vegetable oil to 1-inch depth in medium skillet; heat over high heat for 1 minute. Fry jalapeños turning frequently with tongs, until golden brown on all sides. Remove from skillet; drain on paper towels. Serve with salsa and sour cream.
Makes 8 servings

Hot Crab-Cheddar Spread

(pictured on page 6)

    1 (8-ounce) container crabmeat, drained and
      shredded
    8 ounces CABOT® Mild or Sharp Cheddar, grated
      (about 2 cups)
1/2 cup mayonnaise
1/4 teaspoon Worcestershire sauce

1. Preheat oven to 350°F.

2. In medium bowl, mix together all ingredients thoroughly. Transfer to small (1-quart) baking dish. Bake for 25 to 35 minutes, or until lightly browned on top and bubbling at edges. Serve with crackers or bread toasts.   *Makes 8 to 10 servings*

Zesty Crab Cakes with Red Pepper Sauce

(pictured below)

- 1/2 pound raw medium shrimp, shelled and deveined
- 2/3 cup heavy cream
- 1 egg white
- 3 tablespoons *Frank's® RedHot®* Original Cayenne Pepper Sauce
- 1 tablespoon *French's®* Worcestershire Sauce
- 1/4 teaspoon seasoned salt
- 1 pound crabmeat or imitation crabmeat, flaked (4 cups)
- 1 red or yellow bell pepper, minced
- 2 green onions, minced
- 1/4 cup minced fresh parsley
- 1-1/2 cups fresh bread crumbs
- 1/2 cup corn oil
- Red Pepper Sauce (recipe follows)

1. Place shrimp, cream, egg white, **Frank's RedHot** Sauce, Worcestershire and seasoned salt in food processor. Process until mixture is puréed. Transfer to large bowl.

2. Add crabmeat, bell pepper, onions and parsley. Mix with fork until well blended.

3. Shape crabmeat mixture into 12 (1/2-inch-thick) patties, using about 1/4 cup mixture for each. Coat both sides in bread crumbs.

4. Heat oil in large nonstick skillet. Add crab cakes; cook until browned on both sides. Drain on paper towels. Serve with Red Pepper Sauce.

Makes about 12 crab cakes

Red Pepper Sauce

- 1 jar (7 ounces) roasted red peppers, drained
- 1/4 cup mayonnaise
- 3 tablespoons *Frank's® RedHot®* Original Cayenne Pepper Sauce
- 2 tablespoons minced onion
- 1 tablespoon *French's®* Spicy Brown Mustard
- 1 tablespoon minced parsley
- 1 clove garlic

Place all ingredients in blender or food processor. Cover; process until smooth. *Makes 1 cup sauce*

Zesty Crab Cakes with Red Pepper Sauce

Saucy Mini Franks

(pictured at right)

1/2 cup *French's®* Honey Mustard
1/2 cup chili sauce or ketchup
1/2 cup grape jelly
  1 tablespoon *Frank's®* RedHot® Original
    Cayenne Pepper Sauce
  1 pound mini cocktail franks or 1 pound
    cooked meatballs

1. Combine mustard, chili sauce, grape jelly and
Frank's RedHot Sauce in large saucepan.

2. Add cocktail franks. Simmer and stir 5 minutes
or until jelly is melted and franks are hot.

Makes about 6 servings

Toasted Ravioli
with Fresh Tomato-Basil Salsa

  1 package (about 9 ounces) refrigerated cheese
    ravioli
    Olive oil cooking spray
3/4 cup plain dry bread crumbs
  2 tablespoons grated Parmesan cheese
  1 teaspoon dried basil
  1 teaspoon dried oregano
1/4 teaspoon pepper
  2 egg whites
    Fresh Tomato-Basil Salsa (recipe follows)

1. Cook ravioli according to package directions.
Rinse under cold running water until ravioli are
cool; drain well.

2. Preheat oven to 375°F. Spray large nonstick
baking sheet with cooking spray.

3. Combine bread crumbs, cheese, basil, oregano
and pepper in medium bowl.

4. Beat egg whites lightly in shallow dish. Add
ravioli; toss lightly to coat. Transfer ravioli, a few
at a time, to crumb mixture; toss to coat evenly.
Arrange on prepared baking sheet. Repeat with
remaining ravioli. Spray tops of ravioli with
cooking spray.

5. Bake 12 to 14 minutes or until crisp. Meanwhile,
prepare Fresh Tomato-Basil Salsa; serve with ravioli.

Makes 8 servings

Fresh Tomato-Basil Salsa

  1 pound fresh tomatoes, peeled and seeded
1/2 cup loosely packed fresh basil leaves
  1 small onion
  1 teaspoon red wine vinegar
1/4 teaspoon salt

Process all ingredients in food processor until finely
chopped but not smooth.

Makes about 1 cup salsa

Chunky Pinto Bean Dip

(pictured on page 6)

  2 cans (15 ounces each) pinto beans, rinsed
    and drained
  1 can (14-1/2 ounces) diced tomatoes with
    mild green chiles
  1 cup chopped onion
2/3 cup chunky salsa
  1 tablespoon vegetable oil
1-1/2 teaspoons minced garlic
  1 teaspoon ground coriander
  1 teaspoon ground cumin
1-1/2 cups (6 ounces) shredded Mexican cheese
    blend or Cheddar cheese
1/4 cup chopped fresh cilantro
    Blue corn or other tortilla chips
    Assorted raw vegetables

SLOW COOKER DIRECTIONS
1. Combine beans, tomatoes, onion, salsa, oil, garlic,
coriander and cumin in 3-quart slow cooker.

2. Cover; cook on LOW 5 to 6 hours or until onion
is tender.

3. Partially mash bean mixture with potato masher.
Stir in cheese and cilantro. Serve with chips and
vegetables at room temperature.

Makes about 5 cups dip

Mexican Tortilla Stacks

(pictured at right)

1/2 cup ORTEGA® Salsa, any variety, divided
1/2 cup finely chopped cooked chicken
1/4 cup sour cream
   8 (8-inch) ORTEGA Soft Flour Tortillas
1/2 cup prepared guacamole
1/3 cup ORTEGA Refried Beans
   6 tablespoons (1-1/2 ounces) shredded
      Cheddar cheese
      Sour cream and chopped fresh cilantro

HEAT oven to 350°F. Mix 1/4 cup salsa, chicken and sour cream in small bowl.

PLACE 2 tortillas on ungreased cookie sheet; spread with salsa-chicken mixture. Spread 2 more tortillas with guacamole and place on top of salsa-chicken mixture.

MIX refried beans with remaining 1/4 cup salsa; spread onto 2 more tortillas and place on top of guacamole. Top each stack with remaining 2 tortillas; sprinkle with cheese.

BAKE 8 to 10 minutes until cheese is melted and filling is hot.

TOP with sour cream and cilantro. Cut each stack into 8 wedges.   *Makes 16 servings*

Note: Prepared guacamole can be found in the refrigerated or frozen food sections at most supermarkets.

Hot Artichoke Dip

   1 cup mayonnaise
   1 cup sour cream
1/4 cup grated Parmesan cheese
1/4 cup chopped roasted red peppers
   1 can (14 ounces) artichoke hearts, drained and
      chopped
1-1/3 cups *French's*® French Fried Onions, divided
      Assorted crackers or bagel chips

1. Preheat oven to 375°F. Combine mayonnaise, sour cream, cheese, roasted peppers, artichokes and *2/3 cup* French Fried Onions. Spoon into 9-inch pie plate or 1-quart shallow baking dish.

2. Bake 25 minutes or until hot. Top with remaining onions and bake 5 minutes or until onions are golden. Serve with assorted crackers or bagel chips.
                                   Makes 3 cups

Ranch Style Shrimp and Bacon Appetizers

      Ranch Style Barbecue Sauce (recipe follows)
   30 large peeled, deveined shrimp
1/2 pound thick-cut bacon
   10 wooden skewers*

*To prevent wooden skewers from burning while grilling or broiling, soak in water about 20 minutes before using.

1. Prepare Ranch Style Barbecue Sauce.

2. Wrap each shrimp with 1/2 bacon strip. Thread 3 wrapped shrimp onto each wooden skewer.

3. Grill or broil shrimp skewers until bacon is cooked and shrimp is no longer translucent, but has turned pink. Baste with barbecue sauce. Return to heat to warm sauce. Serve with additional barbecue sauce, if desired.   *Makes 10 shrimp skewers*

Ranch Style Barbecue Sauce

1/4 cup vegetable or olive oil
1/2 cup minced onion
   2 garlic cloves, minced
   2 tablespoons lemon juice
   1 tablespoon ground pepper
   1 teaspoon dry mustard
   1 teaspoon paprika
1/2 teaspoon salt
1/2 teaspoon hot pepper sauce
1-1/2 cups ketchup
   1 cup HEATH® BITS 'O BRICKLE™ Toffee Bits
1/4 cup cider vinegar
   3 tablespoons sugar
1-1/2 tablespoons HERSHEY'S Cocoa

1. Heat oil in large saucepan over medium heat; add onion and garlic. Cook until tender. Stir in lemon juice, pepper, mustard, paprika, salt and hot pepper sauce. Simmer for 5 minutes; reduce heat.

2. Stir in ketchup, toffee bits, vinegar, sugar and cocoa. Simmer 15 minutes. Refrigerate leftovers.
                               Makes 3 cups sauce

Helpful Hint

Use 2 skewers to keep the food from rotating when turning. Thread the pieces onto one skewer, then run another through the pieces parallel to the first.

Mexican Tortilla Stacks

Salads

Tropical Curried Chicken Salad

(pictured at left)

2/3 cup prepared olive oil vinaigrette salad dressing
1/4 cup *French's®* Worcestershire Sauce
1/4 cup honey
  2 tablespoons *Frank's® RedHot®* Cayenne Pepper Sauce
  2 teaspoons curry powder
  2 cloves garlic, minced
  1 pound boneless skinless chicken breasts
  8 cups washed and torn watercress and Boston lettuce
1/4 cup coarsely chopped unsalted cashew nuts
1/2 cup shredded coconut, toasted

1. Place salad dressing, Worcestershire, honey, *Frank's RedHot* Sauce, curry powder and garlic in blender or food processor. Cover; process until well blended. Reserve 1/2 cup curry mixture to dress salad.

2. Place chicken in large resealable plastic food storage bag. Pour remaining curry mixture over chicken. Seal bag; marinate in refrigerator 30 minutes.

3. Heat electric grill pan or barbecue grill. Grill chicken 10 to 15 minutes or until no longer pink in center. Arrange salad greens on large serving platter. Cut chicken into thin slices. Arrange over greens. Top with nuts and coconut. Serve with reserved dressing. *Makes 4 servings*

Helpful Hint

To be sure chicken stays juicy, use tongs or a spatula to turn chicken pieces during cooking. Piercing them with a fork allows delicious juices to escape which can make the chicken dry.

Clockwise from top left: *Tropical Curried Chicken Salad, Gazpacho Shrimp Salad (p. 24), Spicy Citrus Slaw (p. 26), BLT Salad with Bow Ties & Cheddar (p. 34)*

Crunchy Mexican Side Salad

(pictured at right)

3 cups romaine and iceberg lettuce blend
1/2 cup grape tomatoes, halved
1/2 cup peeled and diced jicama
1/4 cup sliced olives
1/4 cup ORTEGA® Sliced Jalapeños, quartered
2 tablespoons ORTEGA Taco Sauce
1 tablespoon vegetable oil
1/8 teaspoon salt
     Crushed ORTEGA Taco Shells

TOSS together lettuce, tomatoes, jicama, olives and jalapeños in large bowl.

COMBINE taco sauce, oil and salt in small bowl. Stir with a fork until blended.

POUR dressing over salad; toss gently to coat. Top with taco shells, if desired.   *Makes 4 servings*

Note: ORTEGA Sliced Jalapeños are available in a 12-ounce jar. They are pickled, adding great flavor and crunch to this salad.

Tip: Jicama is a root vegetable with a thick brown skin and crunchy, sweet flesh. It may be eaten raw or cooked. It can be purchased in most supermarkets or Mexican markets. Canned, sliced water chestnuts may be substituted.

Gazpacho Shrimp Salad

(pictured on page 22)

8 cups mixed torn salad greens
1 large tomato, chopped
1 small ripe avocado, peeled, seeded and diced
1/2 cup thinly sliced unpeeled cucumber
1/2 cup chunky salsa
1 tablespoon balsamic vinegar
1 tablespoon olive oil
1 garlic clove, minced
8 ounces large cooked shrimp, peeled and deveined
1/2 cup coarsely chopped fresh cilantro

Combine greens, tomato, avocado and cucumber in large bowl. Combine salsa, vinegar, oil and garlic in small bowl. Add dressing to salad greens; toss well. Transfer to dinner plates. Top salads with shrimp. Drizzle dressing over salads. Sprinkle with cilantro.
Makes 4 servings

Holiday Fruit Salad

3 packages (3 ounces each) strawberry flavor gelatin
3 cups boiling water
2 ripe DOLE® Bananas
1 package (16 ounces) DOLE® Frozen Whole Strawberries. sliced
1 can (20 ounces) DOLE® Crushed Pineapple
1 package (8 ounces) cream cheese, softened
1 cup dairy sour cream or plain yogurt
1/4 cup sugar
     Crisp DOLE® Lettuce leaves

• In large bowl, dissolve gelatin in boiling water. Slice bananas into gelatin mixture. Add frozen strawberries and undrained crushed pineapple. Reserve half of the mixture at room temperature. Pour remaining mixture into 13×9-inch pan. Refrigerate 1 hour or until firm.

• In mixer bowl, beat cream cheese with sour cream and sugar; spread over chilled layer. Gently spoon reserved gelatin mixture on top. Refrigerate until firm, about 2 hours.

• Cut into squares; serve on lettuce-lined salad plates. Garnish with additional pineapple and mint leaves, if desired.   *Makes 12 servings*

Mandarin Chicken Salad

1/2 cup WISH-BONE® Ranch Dressing
1/4 cup orange marmalade
1-1/4 pounds boneless, skinless chicken breasts, cooked and sliced (about 3 cups)
1/4 small red onion, thinly sliced (about 1/4 cup)
1 package (10 to 12 ounces) mixed salad greens (about 4 cups)
1 can (11 ounces) mandarin oranges, drained
1/2 cup seasoned croutons

1. In large bowl, blend dressing and marmalade.

2. Add chicken, red onion and salad greens; toss to coat.

3. Gently fold in oranges and croutons.
Makes 4 servings

Crunchy Mexican Side Salad

Cranberry Crunch Gelatin

(pictured at right)

2 cups boiling water
2 packages (3 ounces each) cherry gelatin
1 can (16 ounces) whole berry cranberry sauce
1-1/2 cups miniature marshmallows
1 cup coarsely chopped walnuts

1. Stir boiling water into gelatin in medium bowl 2 minutes until completely dissolved. Chill until slightly set, about 2 hours.

2. Fold in remaining ingredients. Pour into 6-cup gelatin mold. Cover; refrigerate at least 4 hours or until set. Remove from mold.

Makes 8 servings

Fresh Pepper Pasta Salad

5 tablespoons olive oil, divided
4 sweet red or yellow peppers, seeded and cut into strips
2 garlic cloves, cut into thin slices
3 tablespoons balsamic vinegar
1/2 teaspoon salt
1/2 teaspoon pepper
8 ounces wagon wheel pasta
3/4 cup fresh basil leaves
1-1/2 cups canned garbanzo beans or chickpeas, rinsed and drained
1/2 cup grated Parmesan cheese
1/3 cup chopped walnuts
1/4 cup sliced pimiento-stuffed green olives

1. Heat 2 tablespoons oil in large nonstick skillet over medium heat. Add half pepper strips and garlic; cook and stir 2 minutes. Cover; cook 10 minutes or until very soft, stirring occasionally.

2. Place cooked peppers in food processor or blender. Add remaining 3 tablespoons oil, vinegar, salt and pepper. Cover; process until smooth. Cool.

3. Cook pasta according to package directions. Rinse with cold water; drain. Place in large bowl. Add remaining pepper strips and dressing; toss to coat. Cool slightly. Stack basil with largest leaves on bottom; roll up. Slice roll into 1/4-inch-thick slices; separate into strips. Add basil, garbanzo beans, cheese, walnuts and olives to pasta mixture; toss to blend. Serve at room temperature or chilled.

Makes 8 cups

Spinach Salad with Grilled Chicken Thighs

1-1/4 cups WISH-BONE® Italian or Robusto Italian Dressing
1/3 cup finely chopped, drained sun-dried tomatoes packed in oil
4 tablespoons grated Parmesan cheese
1-1/2 pounds boneless, skinless chicken thighs
1 cup sliced baby portobellas, cremini and/or white mushrooms
1/2 small red onion, thinly sliced
1 package (10 ounces) fresh spinach leaves, trimmed, rinsed and patted dry

1. For marinade, combine Wish-Bone Italian Dressing, tomatoes and 2 tablespoons cheese. In large, shallow nonaluminum baking dish or plastic bag, pour 1/2 cup marinade over chicken; turn to coat. Cover, or close bag, and marinate in refrigerator, turning occasionally, up to 3 hours. Refrigerate remaining marinade.

2. Remove chicken from marinade, discarding marinade. Grill or broil chicken, turning once and brushing frequently with 1/4 cup refrigerated marinade, until chicken is thoroughly cooked. To serve, slice chicken. Arrange chicken, mushrooms and onion over spinach; drizzle with remaining refrigerated marinade. Sprinkle with remaining 2 tablespoons cheese and, if desired, cracked pepper.

Makes 4 servings

Spicy Citrus Slaw

(pictured on page 22)

1 cup HELLMANN'S® or BEST FOODS® Canola Real Mayonnaise
1 can (11 ounces) mandarin oranges, drained (reserve 2 tablespoons syrup)
2 teaspoons apple cider vinegar
1 tablespoon chopped fresh cilantro (optional)
Hot pepper sauce to taste
1/2 teaspoon salt
1 bag (16 ounces) coleslaw mix

In large bowl, combine Hellmann's or Best Foods Canola Real Mayonnaise, reserved syrup, vinegar, cilantro, hot pepper sauce and salt. Stir in coleslaw mix and oranges. Chill, if desired.

Makes 4 cups

Cranberry Crunch Gelatin

Roast Beef and Pasta Salad

(pictured below)

9 ounces uncooked radiatore pasta
6 ounces lean cooked roast beef
1 can (15 ounces) kidney beans, rinsed and drained
1 can (15 ounces) whole baby corn, rinsed and drained
1 can (10 ounces) diced tomatoes and green chilies, undrained
1 cup cherry tomato halves
1/2 cup sliced black olives (optional)
1/4 cup olive oil
2 tablespoons minced fresh parsley
1 tablespoon minced fresh oregano

1. Cook pasta according to package directions; drain. Rinse in cold water; drain.

2. Slice beef into thin strips. Combine pasta, beef and remaining ingredients in large bowl. Toss to coat. *Makes 6 servings*

Roast Beef and Pasta Salad

Spicy Orzo and Black Bean Salad

2 tablespoons olive oil
2 tablespoons minced jalapeño pepper,* divided
1 teaspoon chili powder
6 cups water
3/4 cup uncooked orzo pasta
1 cup frozen mixed vegetables
1 can (15 ounces) black beans, rinsed and drained
2 thin slices red onion
1/4 cup chopped fresh cilantro
1/4 cup lime juice
1/4 cup lemon juice
4 cups washed and torn spinach leaves
2 tablespoons crumbled blue cheese

*Jalapeño peppers can sting and irritate the skin, so wear rubber gloves when handling peppers and do not touch your eyes.

1. Combine oil, 1 tablespoon jalapeño and chili powder in medium bowl; set aside.

2. Bring water and remaining 1 tablespoon jalapeño to a boil in large saucepan. Add orzo. Cook 10 to 12 minutes or until tender; drain. Rinse in cold water; drain.

3. Place frozen vegetables in small microwavable dish. Cover; microwave on HIGH 3 minutes or until hot. Cover; let stand 5 minutes.

4. Add orzo, vegetables, black beans, onion, cilantro, lime juice and lemon juice to olive oil mixture; toss to coat. Divide spinach evenly among serving plates. Top with orzo and bean mixture. Sprinkle with blue cheese. *Makes 4 servings*

Classic Coleslaw

1 cup HELLMANN'S® or BEST FOODS® Real Mayonnaise
3 tablespoons lemon juice
2 tablespoons sugar
1 teaspoon salt
6 cups shredded cabbage
1 cup shredded carrots
1/2 cup chopped green bell pepper

In large bowl, combine Hellmann's or Best Foods Real Mayonnaise, lemon juice, sugar and salt. Stir in cabbage, carrots and green pepper. Chill, if desired. *Makes 6 cups*

Tip: Also terrific with Hellmann's® or Best Foods® Canola Real Mayonnaise.

*Grilled Shrimp Salad
with Hot Bacon Vinaigrette*

Grilled Shrimp Salad with Hot Bacon Vinaigrette

(pictured above)

4 strips bacon, chopped
1/2 cup prepared Italian or vinaigrette salad dressing
1/3 cup *French's®* Honey Dijon Mustard or *French's®* Honey Mustard
2 tablespoons water
8 cups mixed salad greens
1 cup diced yellow bell peppers
1 cup halved cherry tomatoes
1/2 cup pine nuts
1 pound jumbo or extra large shrimp, shelled with tails left on

1. Cook bacon until crisp in medium skillet. Whisk in salad dressing, mustard and water; keep warm over very low heat.

2. Place salad greens, bell peppers, tomatoes and pine nuts in large bowl; toss. Arrange on salad plates.

3. Cook shrimp in an electric grill pan or barbecue grill 3 minutes until pink. Arrange on salads, dividing evenly. Serve with dressing. *Makes 4 servings*

Cashew Chicken Stir-Fry Salad

2/3 cup hoisin sauce
3 tablespoons *Frank's® RedHot®* Cayenne Pepper Sauce
2 tablespoons vegetable oil, divided
1 pound boneless skinless chicken, cut into small cubes
1 red or green bell pepper, cut into 1/2-inch chunks
1 can (8 ounces) pineapple chunks, drained
1/2 cup cashew nuts
1 bag (12 ounces) broccoli slaw or coleslaw mix

1. Combine hoisin sauce, *Frank's RedHot* Sauce and 1 tablespoon oil; set aside.

2. Heat remaining oil in large nonstick skillet or wok. Stir-fry chicken, bell pepper, pineapple and cashews until chicken is browned.

3. Pour sauce mixture over chicken. Toss to coat and remove from heat. Place slaw in serving bowls. Spoon stir-fry over slaw. *Makes 4 servings*

Couscous Turkey Salad

(pictured at right)

1-1/2 cups chicken broth
3/4 cup uncooked couscous
1-1/2 cups chopped cooked turkey
1 cup shredded carrots (2 medium carrots)
1 stalk celery, trimmed and finely chopped
1 green onion, trimmed and chopped
2 tablespoons toasted pine nuts*
Salad greens

DRESSING
2 tablespoons jellied cranberry sauce
2 tablespoons vegetable oil
4 teaspoons balsamic vinegar
1/2 teaspoon curry powder**
1/4 teaspoon salt
1/4 teaspoon pepper

Toast pine nuts in skillet over medium-high heat about 2 minutes or until fragrant, stirring constantly.

**Curry powder is a blend of spices. Taste varies from brand to brand. Start with 1/2 teaspoon curry powder for a mildly flavored dressing, then adjust to taste.*

1. For salad, place chicken broth in small saucepan. Bring to a boil. Stir in couscous. Cover; remove from heat. Let stand, covered, 5 minutes. Fluff couscous with fork; chill.

2. Meanwhile, combine turkey, carrots, celery, green onion and pine nuts in large bowl. Spoon in couscous.

3. For dressing, stir together cranberry sauce, oil, vinegar, curry powder, salt and pepper. Pour over salad. Toss well. Serve on bed of greens.
Makes 4 servings

Savory Chicken Salad

1/3 cup HELLMANN'S® or BEST FOODS® Canola
     Real Mayonnaise
1/4 cup mango chutney
2 cups diced cooked chicken
1/2 cup halved red grapes
1/2 cup finely chopped celery
2 tablespoons finely chopped red onion

1. In blender or mini food processor, process Hellmann's or Best Foods Canola Real Mayonnaise and mango chutney until smooth.

2. In medium bowl, combine remaining ingredients with mayonnaise mixture. Season, if desired,

with salt and ground pepper. Serve on lettuce and garnish with toasted sliced almonds. Chill, if desired.
Makes 4 to 6 servings

Tip: Also terrific with Hellmann's® or Best Foods® Real Mayonnaise, Hellmann's® or Best Foods® Light Mayonnaise or Hellmann's® or Best Foods® Reduced Fat Mayonnaise Dressing.

Grilled Chicken Caesar Salad

1 pound boneless skinless chicken breasts
1/2 cup extra-virgin olive oil
3 tablespoons lemon juice
2 teaspoons anchovy paste
2 garlic cloves, minced
1/2 teaspoon salt
1/2 teaspoon pepper
6 cups torn romaine lettuce leaves
4 plum tomatoes, quartered
1/4 cup grated Parmesan cheese
1 cup garlic croutons

1. Place chicken in large resealable food storage bag. Combine oil, lemon juice, anchovy paste, garlic, salt and pepper in small bowl. Reserve 1/3 cup marinade. Cover; refrigerate until serving. Pour remaining marinade over chicken in bag. Seal bag; turn to coat. Marinate in refrigerator at least 1 hour or up to 4 hours, turning occasionally.

2. Combine lettuce, tomatoes and cheese in large bowl. Cover; refrigerate until serving.

3. Prepare grill for direct cooking. Drain chicken, pouring marinade into small saucepan. Bring marinade to a rolling boil; boil 1 minute.

4. Place chicken on grid over medium heat. Grill chicken, covered, 10 to 12 minutes or until chicken is no longer pink in center, turning once. Brush chicken with cooked marinade on both sides the last 5 minutes of grilling. Discard remaining marinade. Cool chicken slightly.

5. Slice warm chicken widthwise into 1/2-inch-wide strips; add chicken and croutons to lettuce mixture in bowl. Drizzle with 1/3 cup reserved marinade; toss to coat well.
Makes 4 servings

Note: Chicken can also be refrigerated until cold before slicing.

Couscous Turkey Salad

SPAM™ Tostada Salad

(pictured at right)

8 (7-inch) flour tortillas
1 tablespoon vegetable oil
1 (12-ounce) can SPAM® Classic, cut into
    1/2-inch strips
1 onion, cut into wedges
4 cups torn romaine lettuce
2 tomatoes, chopped
1 (2-1/4-ounce) can sliced ripe olives, drained
1 cup (4 ounces) shredded Monterey Jack cheese
CHI-CHI'S® Salsa

In large skillet over medium-high heat, cook tortillas in hot oil 2 to 3 minutes or until crisp; set aside. In same skillet, cook SPAM® and onion 7 to 10 minutes or until SPAM® is browned. Meanwhile, toss together lettuce, tomatoes, olives and cheese. Place SPAM™ mixture on top of tortillas. Top with lettuce mixture. Serve with salsa. *Makes 4 servings*

Butterflied Shrimp and Vermicelli Salad

1/4 small yellow onion
    3 tablespoons tarragon vinegar or white
        wine vinegar
    2 tablespoons sugar
1/2 teaspoon salt
1/2 teaspoon dry mustard
1/4 cup extra-virgin olive oil
1/4 cup vegetable oil
    1 teaspoon celery seeds
    1 pound medium raw shrimp, peeled and
        deveined
    8 ounces uncooked vermicelli pasta, broken
        into 2-inch lengths
    1 cup finely chopped celery
    1 cup seedless grapes, halved
    1 jar (4 ounces) sliced pimientos, drained
    3 tablespoons mayonnaise
    2 oranges, peeled and cut into sections *or*
        1 cup mandarin orange slices
    1 head Bibb lettuce, torn
    5 green onions, sliced

1. To prepare dressing, place onion and vinegar in food processor; process until onion is finely chopped. Add sugar, salt and mustard; process until mixture is blended.

2. With motor running, slowly pour olive oil and vegetable oil through feed tube; process until smooth. Add celery seeds; process until mixture is blended. Set aside.

3. Place amount of water for cooking pasta according to package in large saucepan. Bring to a boil. Add half the shrimp; simmer 1 minute or until shrimp turn pink and opaque. Remove shrimp with slotted spoon; place in large bowl. Repeat with remaining shrimp.

4. Add pasta to cooking water. Cook according to package directions. Rinse under cold water; drain. Add pasta, celery, grapes, pimientos, mayonnaise and dressing to shrimp. Toss to coat. Gently stir in orange segments. Chill several hours or overnight. Serve on lettuce-lined plates. Sprinkle with green onions. *Makes 5 servings*

Waldorf Chicken Salad

1/3 cup lemon juice
1/4 cup honey
1/4 cup vegetable oil
    2 tablespoons Dijon mustard
    1 tablespoon poppy seeds
1/2 teaspoon grated lemon peel
    12 dried apricots, sliced (moist pack preferable)
    2 cups cubed cooked chicken or turkey
    2 apples, cored and diced
    1 cup diced celery
1/3 cup toasted sliced almonds
1/4 cup minced green onions

Stir together lemon juice, honey, oil, mustard, poppy seeds and lemon peel in large bowl. Add apricots and let stand 30 minutes. Add chicken and toss lightly. Refrigerate until ready to serve.

To serve, add apples, celery, almonds and green onions to chicken mixture; toss to coat.
Makes 6 servings

Favorite recipe from **National Honey Board**

Marinated Antipasto

(pictured at right)

1/4 cup extra-virgin olive oil
2 tablespoons balsamic vinegar
1 garlic clove, minced
1/2 teaspoon sugar
1/2 teaspoon salt
1/4 teaspoon pepper
1 pint (2 cups) cherry tomatoes
1 can (14 ounces) quartered water-packed
artichoke hearts, drained
8 ounces small balls or cubes fresh mozzarella
cheese
1 cup drained pitted kalamata olives
1/4 cup sliced fresh basil
Lettuce leaves

1. Whisk together oil, vinegar, garlic, sugar, salt and
pepper in medium bowl. Add tomatoes, artichokes,
mozzarella, olives and basil; toss to coat. Let stand
at least 30 minutes.

2. Line platter with lettuce. Arrange tomato mixture
over lettuce; serve at room temperature.

Makes about 5 cups

Serving Suggestion: Serve antipasto with
toothpicks as an appetizer or spoon over Bibb
lettuce leaves for a first-course salad.

BLT Salad
with Bow Ties & Cheddar

(pictured on page 22)

2 cups (4 ounces) bow-tie or corkscrew-shaped
pasta
1 package (9 ounces) DOLE® Organic Salad
Blend Romaine & Radicchio or Baby
Spinach Salad
1 cup cherry, pear or baby Roma tomatoes,
halved
3/4 cup (3 ounces) Cheddar cheese, diced
5 strips bacon, cooked, drained and crumbled
or 1/3 cup packaged bacon bits
1/3 cup ranch salad dressing

• Cook pasta according to package directions. Drain
well and rinse in cool water. Drain again.

• Toss together salad blend, pasta, tomatoes,
cheese, and bacon in large bowl. Pour dressing over
salad; toss to evenly coat.   *Makes 3 to 4 servings*

Creamy Red Potato Salad

3 pounds red bliss or new potatoes, cut into
3/4-inch chunks
1/2 cup WISH-BONE® Italian Dressing
3/4 cup HELLMANN'S® or BEST FOODS® Real
Mayonnaise
1/2 cup sliced green onions
2 tablespoons snipped fresh dill
1 teaspoon Dijon mustard
1 teaspoon lemon juice
1/8 teaspoon ground pepper

1. In 4-quart saucepot, cover potatoes with water;
bring to a boil over medium-high heat. Reduce heat
and simmer uncovered 10 minutes or until potatoes
are tender; drain and cool slightly.

2. In large salad bowl, thoroughly combine all
ingredients except potatoes. Add potatoes and toss
gently. Serve chilled or at room temperature.

Makes 10 servings

Note: Recipe can be halved.

Tip: Also terrific with Wish-Bone® Robusto Italian
Dressing.

Sassy Chicken Pasta Salad

12 ounces uncooked rotini pasta
2 cups cubed cooked chicken
1 cup sliced yellow squash
1 cup green salsa
1 cup coarsely chopped marinated artichoke
hearts
1/3 cup chopped green onions
1/4 cup sliced black olives
1 tablespoon chopped drained pimiento
1/4 teaspoon pepper
Lettuce leaves

1. Cook pasta according to package directions. Rinse
in cold water; drain. Combine pasta with remaining
ingredients except lettuce in large bowl; toss well.
Cover and refrigerate 6 hours or overnight.

2. To serve, line serving platter with lettuce leaves.
Top with pasta mixture.   *Makes 4 servings*

Marinated Antipasto

Garden Salad Jumbo Shells

Garden Salad Jumbo Shells

(pictured above)

15 jumbo pasta shells
2 cups (12 ounces) HORMEL® CURE 81® ham, cut into thin strips
1 cup shredded zucchini
1/2 cup finely chopped red bell pepper
2 tablespoons grated Parmesan cheese
3 tablespoons CARAPELLI® Extra Virgin Olive Oil
3 tablespoons red wine vinegar
1 clove garlic, minced
1/2 teaspoon Italian seasoning
1/2 teaspoon sugar
1/4 teaspoon salt
1/8 teaspoon pepper

Cook pasta according to package directions. In large bowl, combine ham, zucchini, bell pepper and cheese. In small bowl, whisk together oil, vinegar, garlic, Italian seasoning, sugar, salt and pepper. Pour over ham mixture; toss. Spoon ham mixture into each pasta shell. Place the shells, filled side up, in a serving dish. Cover and chill several hours or overnight. *Makes 5 servings*

Balsamic Oranges with Pecans on Mixed Greens

2 medium oranges
1/3 cup WISH-BONE® Balsamic Vinaigrette Dressing
1/4 teaspoon salt
8 cups lightly packed mixed salad greens (about 12 ounces)
1/2 cup chopped pecans, toasted
3 slices bacon, crisp-cooked and crumbled (optional)

1. From the oranges, grate enough peel to equal 1 teaspoon; set aside. Remove remaining peel and pith (white layer) from oranges.

2. Over medium bowl, with sharp knife, cut between membranes of oranges to remove segments, reserving juice. Toss segments and their juice with Wish-Bone Balsamic Vinaigrette Dressing, orange peel and salt.

3. Just before serving, toss greens, orange mixture, pecans and bacon. *Makes 4 servings*

Three-Pepper Tuna Salad

2 cups thinly sliced zucchini
1/2 cup sweet red pepper strips
1/2 cup sweet green pepper strips
1/2 cup sweet yellow pepper strips
1 cup cherry tomatoes, halved
1 can (6 ounces) solid albacore tuna packed in water, drained and flaked
1/4 cup chopped green onions
1/4 cup chopped fresh basil
2 tablespoons red wine vinegar
1 tablespoon olive oil
1/2 teaspoon minced garlic
1/4 teaspoon dried marjoram
1/8 teaspoon pepper

1. Pour 3/4 cup water into medium saucepan. Add zucchini and pepper strips. Cook vegetables about 10 minutes or until crisp-tender; drain. Transfer to serving bowl. Add tomatoes, tuna, green onions and basil.

2. Combine vinegar, oil, garlic, marjoram and pepper in jar with tight-fitting lid; shake well. Pour dressing over vegetable mixture; toss to coat. *Makes 4 servings*

Chicken Caesar Salad

(pictured below)

6 ounces chicken tenders
1/4 cup plus 1 tablespoon Caesar salad dressing, divided
Pepper
4 cups (about 5 ounces) prepared Italian salad mix (romaine and radicchio)
1/2 cup croutons, divided
2 tablespoons grated Parmesan cheese

1. Cut chicken tenders in half lengthwise and widthwise. Heat 1 tablespoon salad dressing in large nonstick skillet. Add chicken; cook and stir over medium heat 3 to 4 minutes or until chicken is cooked through. Remove chicken from skillet. Season with pepper; let cool.

2. Combine salad mix, 1/4 cup croutons, remaining 1/4 cup salad dressing and Parmesan cheese in serving bowl; toss to coat. Top with chicken and remaining 1/4 cup croutons.   *Makes 2 servings*

Sweet Dijon Pasta Salad

8 ounces uncooked tricolor rotini pasta
3/4 cup plain yogurt
1/4 cup mayonnaise
2 tablespoons honey
1 tablespoon Dijon mustard
1/4 teaspoon ground cumin
1/4 teaspoon salt
1 can (15 ounces) black beans, rinsed and drained
1 medium tomato, chopped
1/2 cup shredded carrot
1/4 cup chopped green onions

1. Cook pasta according to package directions; drain. Rinse with cold water; drain.

2. Combine yogurt, mayonnaise, honey, mustard, cumin and salt in small bowl until well blended.

3. Combine pasta, beans, tomato, carrot and green onions in medium bowl. Add yogurt mixture; toss to coat. Cover; refrigerate until serving.
Makes 6 servings

Chicken Caesar Salad

Mandarin Orange Mold

(pictured at right)

> 1-3/4 cups boiling water
> 2 packages (3 ounces each) orange flavor gelatin
> 3 cups ice cubes
> 1 can (15.25 ounces) DOLE® Tropical Mixed Fruit, drained
> 1 can (11 ounces) DOLE® Mandarin Oranges, drained

• Stir boiling water into gelatin in large bowl at least 2 minutes until completely dissolved. Add ice cubes. Stir until ice is melted and gelatin is thickened. Stir in fruit salad and mandarin oranges. Spoon into 6-cup mold.

• Refrigerate 4 hours or until firm. Unmold.* Garnish as desired. *Makes 12 servings*

To unmold, dip mold in warm water about 15 seconds. Gently pull gelatin from around edges with moist fingers. Place moistened serving plate on top of mold. Invert mold and plate. Holding mold and plate together, shake slightly to loosen. Gently remove mold.

Oriental Chicken and Spinach Salad

> 1/3 cup peanut oil
> 1/4 cup honey
> 1/4 cup soy sauce
> 2 teaspoons Worcestershire sauce
> 1 teaspoon dark sesame oil
> 3 boneless skinless chicken breasts (about 12 ounces), cut into 2-inch strips
> 1 cup baby carrots, cut widthwise into 1/4-inch slices
> 3 cups coarsely chopped bok choy (stems and leaves)
> 3 cups spinach, torn into bite-size pieces
> 1 cup canned bean sprouts
> 1/4 cup dry roasted peanuts

1. To prepare dressing, combine peanut oil, honey, soy sauce, Worcestershire sauce and sesame oil in small bowl; whisk until well blended.

2. Heat 2 tablespoons dressing in large nonstick skillet over medium heat. Add chicken and carrots; cook and stir about 5 minutes or until chicken is cooked through. Remove from skillet and let cool.

3. Heat another 2 tablespoons dressing in same skillet. Add bok choy; cook and stir about 1 minute or just until wilted.

4. Place spinach on individual plates. Arrange bok choy over spinach. Top with chicken, carrots and bean sprouts. Sprinkle with peanuts; serve with remaining dressing. *Makes 4 servings*

BLT Chicken Salad for Two

> 2 boneless skinless chicken breasts
> 1/4 cup mayonnaise or salad dressing
> 1/2 teaspoon pepper
> 4 large lettuce leaves
> 1 large tomato, seeded and diced
> 3 slices crisp-cooked bacon, crumbled
> 1 hard-cooked egg, sliced
> Additional mayonnaise or salad dressing (optional)

1. Prepare grill for direct cooking.

2. Brush chicken with mayonnaise; sprinkle with pepper. Grill over medium coals 5 to 7 minutes per side or until no longer pink in center. Cool slightly; cut into thin strips.

3. Arrange lettuce leaves on serving plates. Top with chicken, tomato, bacon and egg. Spoon additional mayonnaise over top, if desired. *Makes 2 servings*

Helpful Hint

For tender hard-cooked eggs, simmer, never boil eggs. Simmering also helps prevent the greenish ring that forms around the yolk. Immediately run cold water over eggs until completely cooled. If eggs are not to be consumed within a few hours, refrigerate in the shell.

Mandarin Orange Mold

Tarragon Tuna Pasta Salad

(pictured at right)

1/2 cup mayonnaise
1/2 teaspoon dried tarragon or thyme, crushed
3 cups chilled cooked mostaccioli or elbow macaroni
2 stalks celery, sliced
1 can (6 ounces) solid white tuna in water, drained and broken into bite-sized pieces
1 can (14-1/2 ounces) DEL MONTE® Peas and Carrots, drained

1. In large bowl, combine mayonnaise and tarragon. Add pasta, celery and tuna. Gently stir in peas and carrots.

2. Line serving plates with lettuce, if desired. Top with salad. Garnish, if desired.   *Makes 4 servings*

Thai Chicken Fettuccine Salad

3 boneless skinless chicken breasts (about 1 pound)
6 ounces uncooked fettuccine
1 cup salsa
1/4 cup chunky peanut butter
2 tablespoons orange juice
2 tablespoons honey
1 teaspoon soy sauce
1/2 teaspoon ground ginger
2 tablespoons vegetable oil
Lettuce or savoy cabbage leaves (optional)
1/4 cup coarsely chopped fresh cilantro
1/4 cup peanuts
1/4 cup thin sweet red pepper strips, cut into halves

1. Cut chicken into 1-inch pieces; set aside. Cook pasta according to package directions; drain.

2. While pasta is cooking, combine salsa, peanut butter, orange juice, honey, soy sauce and ginger in small saucepan. Cook and stir over low heat until blended and smooth. Reserve 1/4 cup salsa mixture.

3. Place pasta in large bowl. Pour remaining salsa mixture over pasta; toss gently to coat.

4. Heat oil in large skillet over medium-high heat. Add chicken; cook and stir about 5 minutes until chicken is browned on the outside and cooked through. Add reserved 1/4 cup salsa mixture; mix well.

5. Arrange pasta on lettuce-lined platter, if desired. Place chicken mixture on pasta. Top with cilantro, peanuts and pepper strips. Refrigerate until mixture is cooled to room temperature.
Makes 4 servings

Fruit Salad with Orange Ginger Dressing

1/4 cup orange juice
2 tablespoons honey
1/4 teaspoon ground ginger
1 can (20 ounces) DOLE® Pineapple Chunks, drained
3 cups watermelon, honeydew or cantaloupe chunks
1/2 cup blueberries

• Stir together orange juice, honey and ginger in small bowl.

• Combine pineapple chunks, watermelon and blueberries in bowl. Pour dressing over salad. Toss to evenly coat. Cover; refrigerate 15 minutes to allow flavors to blend   *Makes 4 to 6 servings*

Spinach & Tomato Salad

1 can (15 ounces) kidney beans, rinsed and drained
1 bag (7 ounces) baby spinach
2 medium tomatoes, cut into wedges
1 small cucumber, halved and thinly sliced
1/2 small onion, thinly sliced
1 cup seasoned croutons
1/4 cup bacon bits or crumbled crisp-cooked bacon
1/2 cup red wine vinaigrette

1. Combine beans, spinach, tomatoes, cucumber, onion, croutons and bacon in medium bowl; toss gently.

2. Pour vinaigrette over salad; toss to coat evenly.
Makes 4 servings

Tarragon Tuna Pasta Salad

Southwestern Chicken Salad

(pictured at right)

1 cup LAWRY'S® Louisiana Red Pepper
    Marinade with Lemon Juice
4 boneless, skinless chicken breasts (about
    1-1/4 pounds)
6 cups torn lettuce
1/2 red onion, thinly sliced
1 large tomato, cut into wedges
1 avocado, thinly sliced
    WISHBONE® Ranch Dressing

In large resealable plastic bag, pour 3/4 cup
LAWRY'S® Louisiana Red Pepper Marinade with
Lemon Juice over chicken; turn to coat. Close
bag and marinate in refrigerator 30 minutes.

Remove chicken from Marinade, discarding
Marinade. Grill or broil chicken, turning once
and brushing frequently with remaining 1/4 cup
Marinade, 10 minutes or until chicken is thoroughly
cooked. Let cool slightly, then slice. On serving
platter, arrange lettuce, then top with chicken,
onion, tomato and avocado. Drizzle with Dressing.

Makes 4 servings

Layered Southwest Salad

    Creamy Ranch-Style Dressing (recipe follows)
1 jicama (3/4 pound), peeled and cut into
    8 wedges
1 can (15 ounces) black beans, rinsed and
    drained
2/3 cup salsa
1/2 cup diced red onion
10 ounces spinach, stemmed and chopped
1 package (10 ounces) frozen corn, cooked,
    drained and cooled
4 large hard-cooked eggs, peeled and sliced
1-1/2 cups (6 ounces) shredded Cheddar cheese

1. Prepare Creamy Ranch-Style Dressing.

2. Cut jicama wedges widthwise into 1/8-inch-thick
slices. Combine beans, salsa and onion in medium
bowl. Layer half of spinach, jicama, bean mixture,
corn, eggs and Creamy Ranch-Style Dressing in large
salad bowl. Repeat first 5 layers beginning with
spinach and ending with eggs; sprinkle with cheese.
Drizzle with remaining dressing.

3. Cover; refrigerate 1 to 2 hours before serving.

Makes 6 servings

Creamy Ranch-Style Dressing

2/3 cup cottage cheese
1/2 cup buttermilk
1 tablespoon white wine vinegar
1 garlic clove
1/2 teaspoon salt
1/2 teaspoon ground cumin
1/2 teaspoon dried oregano
1/2 teaspoon pepper

Combine all ingredients in blender. Cover; process
until smooth. Cover; refrigerate 1 hour.

Makes 1-1/4 cups dressing

Blushing Cranberry & Pear Turkey Salad

1/2 cup HELLMANN'S® or BEST FOODS® Real
    Mayonnaise
1/2 cup whole berry cranberry sauce or cranberry
    relish
4 cups torn romaine lettuce leaves
2 cups baby spinach leaves
2 cups diced cooked turkey
1 medium pear, cored and thinly sliced
1/4 cup toasted chopped pecans
1/4 cup thinly sliced red onion

1. In medium bowl, combine Hellmann's or Best
Foods Real Mayonnaise and cranberry sauce; set
aside.

2. In large bowl, combine romaine, spinach and
turkey. Just before serving, toss with mayonnaise
mixture. Top with pear slices, pecans and onion.
Garnish, if desired, with dried cranberries.

Makes 4 servings

Note: Recipe can be doubled.

Southwestern Chicken Salad

Side Dishes

Creamy Green Beans

(pictured at left)

    4 tablespoons butter, divided
    2 cups coarsely chopped mushrooms
1/3 cup diced celery
1/3 cup diced onion
1/3 cup grated carrot
    2 cups whipping cream
    1 cup chicken broth
    1 teaspoon salt
1/2 teaspoon pepper
    8 cups frozen French-cut green beans, thawed
        and well drained
1/2 cup canned French fried onions

1. Melt 2 tablespoons butter in medium saucepan over medium heat. Add mushrooms; cook and stir 2 to 3 minutes or until mushrooms are softened. Remove mushrooms from saucepan; set aside.

2. Melt remaining 2 tablespoons butter in same pan; add celery, onion and carrot. Cook and stir 5 minutes or until onion is translucent. Stir in cream, broth, salt and pepper. Bring to a boil. Reduce heat; simmer until mixture thickens slightly, about 12 to 15 minutes.

3. Preheat oven to 325°F.

4. Place thawed green beans in 2-quart casserole. Pour mushroom mixture over green beans; stir. Sprinkle with French fried onions; bake 25 minutes or until hot.

Makes 8 servings

Clockwise from top left: *Creamy Green Beans, Sweet Potato-Cranberry Bake (p. 56), Summer Squash and Pepper Sauté (p. 48), Grilled Vegetable Platter (p. 46)*

Twice Baked Potatoes

(pictured at right)

> 3 hot baked potatoes, split lengthwise
> 1/2 cup sour cream
> 2 tablespoons butter or margarine
> 1-1/3 cups *French's*® French Fried Onions, divided
> 1 cup (4 ounces) shredded Cheddar cheese, divided
> Dash paprika (optional)

1. Preheat oven to 400°F. Scoop out inside of potatoes into medium bowl, leaving thin shells. Mash potatoes with sour cream and butter until smooth. Stir in *2/3 cup* French Fried Onions and 1/2 cup cheese. Spoon mixture into shells.

2. Bake 20 minutes or until heated through. Top with remaining cheese, onions and paprika, if desired. Bake 2 minutes or until cheese melts.

Makes 6 servings

Tip: To bake potatoes quickly, microwave on HIGH 10 to 12 minutes until tender.

Variation: For added Cheddar flavor, substitute *French's*® **Cheddar French Fried Onions** for the original flavor.

Country Garden Stir-Fry with Herbed Butter

> 1/2 pound green beans, trimmed
> 4 carrots, sliced 1/8 inch thick
> 2 cups fresh cauliflower florets
> 1/4 cup (1/2 stick) butter, softened
> 1 tablespoon lemon juice
> 1 tablespoon finely chopped fresh parsley
> 1/2 teaspoon salt

1. Place 1/3 cup water in large nonstick skillet or wok. Add beans, carrots and cauliflower. Bring to a boil. Reduce heat; cover tightly and simmer 8 to 10 minutes or until crisp-tender.

2. Meanwhile, in small bowl, whisk together butter, lemon juice, parsley and salt; set aside.

3. Uncover vegetables; increase heat to medium-high. Cook until all liquid has evaporated, stirring gently.

4. Remove from heat; toss gently with butter mixture.

Makes 4 servings

Grilled Vegetable Platter

(pictured on page 44)

> 2 pounds assorted fresh vegetables (zucchini, summer squash, eggplant, bell pepper, asparagus, red onion and/or mushrooms), thickly sliced
> 1/3 cup BERTOLLI® Extra Virgin Olive Oil
> 1/2 to 1 tablespoon LAWRY'S® Seasoned Salt

In large resealable plastic bag, combine all ingredients; toss to coat. Grill vegetables, turning once, until vegetables are tender.

Makes 6 servings

Variation: To roast vegetables, prepare vegetables as above. In broiler pan, without the rack, arrange in single layer. Roast at 450°, turning once, 20 minutes or until vegetables are tender.

Broccoli with Red Pepper and Shallots

> 2 heads broccoli (about 2-1/4 pounds), cut into florets and stalks cut into 1-inch pieces
> 2 teaspoons butter
> 1 large sweet red pepper, cut into short thin strips
> 3 large shallots (3 ounces) *or* 1 small onion, thinly sliced
> 1/2 teaspoon salt
> 1/4 teaspoon pepper
> 1/4 cup sliced almonds, toasted

1. Bring 2 quarts water to a boil in large saucepan over high heat. Add broccoli; boil, uncovered, 3 to 5 minutes or until bright green and tender. Drain and rinse with cold water; drain well.

2. Melt butter in large nonstick skillet over medium heat. Add sweet pepper and shallots. Cook 3 minutes, stirring occasionally. Add broccoli. Cook 4 to 6 minutes, stirring occasionally. Sprinkle with salt and pepper; mix well. Sprinkle with almonds.

Makes 6 servings

Twice Baked Potatoes

Delicious Corn Soufflé

(pictured below)

3 tablespoons flour
1 tablespoon sugar
1/2 teaspoon pepper
3 eggs
2 cups frozen corn kernels, thawed
    and drained
1 can (14-3/4 ounces) cream-style corn
1 cup (4 ounces) shredded Mexican cheese
    blend or Monterey Jack cheese
1 jar (2 ounces) chopped pimientos, drained
1/3 cup milk

1. Preheat oven to 350°F. Spray 8-inch round baking dish with nonstick cooking spray.

2. Combine flour, sugar and pepper in large bowl. Add eggs; beat with electric mixer at high speed until smooth. Stir in corn kernels, cream-style corn, cheese, pimientos and milk.

3. Bake, uncovered, 55 minutes or until set. Let stand 15 minutes before serving.

Makes 6 servings

Delicious Corn Soufflé

Summer Squash and Pepper Sauté

(pictured on page 44)

1 tablespoon olive oil
2 medium yellow summer squash (1/2 pound),
    thinly sliced
2 medium zucchini (1/2 pound), thinly sliced
2 medium bell peppers (green, red or orange),
    cut into thin strips
1 teaspoon chopped fresh rosemary leaves *or*
    1/2 teaspoon dried rosemary
1-1/3 cups *French's®* French Fried Onions
    Salt and pepper to taste

1. Heat oil in large nonstick skillet over medium-high heat. Add squash, zucchini, bell peppers and rosemary. Cook and stir 5 minutes or until vegetables are crisp-tender.

2. Add French Fried Onions. Cook and stir until onions are golden. Season with salt and pepper.

Makes 8 servings

Roast Herbed Sweet Potatoes with Bacon & Onions

3 thick slices applewood-smoked or peppered
    bacon, diced
2 pounds sweet potatoes, peeled and cut into
    2-inch chunks
2 medium onions, cut into 8 wedges
1 teaspoon salt
1 teaspoon dried thyme
1/4 teaspoon pepper

1. Preheat oven to 375°F. Cook bacon in large skillet until crisp. Remove from heat. Transfer bacon to paper towels; set aside. Add potatoes and onions to drippings in skillet; toss until coated. Stir in salt, thyme and pepper.

2. Spread mixture in single layer in ungreased 15×10×1-inch jelly-roll pan or shallow roasting pan. Bake 40 to 50 minutes or until golden brown and tender. Transfer vegetables to serving bowl; sprinkle with bacon.

Makes 10 to 12 servings

Swiss Vegetable Casserole

Swiss Vegetable Casserole

(pictured above)

1 can (10-3/4 ounces) Campbell's®
    Condensed Cream of Mushroom Soup
    (Regular, 98% Fat Free or 25% Less Sodium)
1/3 cup sour cream
1/4 teaspoon ground black pepper
1 bag (16 ounces) frozen vegetable combination
    (broccoli, cauliflower, carrots), thawed
1 can (2.8 ounces) French fried onions
    (1-1/3 cups)
1/2 cup shredded Swiss cheese

1. Stir the soup, sour cream, black pepper, vegetables, **2/3 cup** of the onions and **1/4 cup** of the cheese in a 2-quart casserole. **Cover.**

2. Bake at 350°F. for 40 minutes or until the vegetables are tender. Stir the vegetable mixture.

3. Sprinkle the remaining onions and cheese over the vegetable mixture. Bake for 5 minutes more or until the onions are golden brown.

Makes 8 servings

Time-Saving Tip: To thaw the vegetables, cut off one corner of bag, microwave on HIGH for 5 minutes.

Eggplant Italiano

2 tablespoons olive oil, divided
2 medium onions, halved and thinly sliced
2 stalks celery, cut into 1-inch pieces
1-1/4 pounds eggplant, cut into 1-inch cubes
1 can (14-1/2 ounces) diced tomatoes, drained
1/2 cup pitted black olives, cut widthwise in half
2 tablespoons balsamic vinegar
1 tablespoon sugar
1 tablespoon drained capers
1 teaspoon dried oregano or basil
    Salt and pepper

1. Heat wok or large skillet over medium-high heat 1 minute. Add 1 tablespoon oil to wok; heat 30 seconds. Add onions and celery; stir-fry about 2 minutes or until tender. Move onions and celery up side of wok. Reduce heat to medium.

2. Add remaining 1 tablespoon oil to wok; heat 30 seconds. Add eggplant; stir-fry about 4 minutes or until tender. Add tomatoes; mix well. Cover and cook 10 minutes.

3. Stir olives, vinegar, sugar, capers and oregano into eggplant mixture. Season with salt and pepper.

Makes 6 servings

Roasted Asparagus with Chavrie®-Dijon Sauce

(pictured at right)

1-1/2 pound fresh asparagus spears, trimmed, cleaned
2 teaspoons extra-virgin olive oil
1 package (5.3 ounces) CHAVRIE® goat cheese, plain
1 tablespoon whipping cream
1 teaspoon Dijon mustard
2 tablespoons capers, drained

Blanch asparagus for 1-1/2 minutes. Heat oven to 400°F. Arrange asparagus in single layer in shallow baking pan. Drizzle with olive oil. Bake 5 minutes or until desired doneness.

In small microwavable bowl, mix *Chavrie®*, cream and mustard. Microwave on HIGH 30 seconds. Stir; microwave another 30 seconds or until warm. Stir in capers. Serve sauce with asparagus.

Makes 6 servings

Tex-Mex Spiced Cocoa Vegetable Rub

2 tablespoons Tex-Mex Spiced Rub (recipe follows)
1 yellow pepper, cored and seeded
1 red pepper, cored and seeded
1 large red onion
1 mango, firm but not hard, peeled
1 yellow squash
1 zucchini
15 grape tomatoes
1 large portobello mushroom, sliced lengthwise
3/4 cup vinaigrette dressing, purchased or prepared

1. Heat oven to 450°F.

2. Cut yellow pepper, red pepper, onion, mango, yellow squash and zucchini into 1-inch pieces. Place in large bowl. Add tomatoes and mushroom.

3. Pour vinaigrette dressing and spice mix over vegetables; toss.

4. Spread vegetables in shallow baking pan. Bake 20 to 30 minutes or until vegetables are fork tender.

Makes 6 servings

Tex-Mex Spiced Rub

1/2 cup HEATH® BITS 'O BRICKLE™ Toffee Bits
1/2 cup HERSHEY'S Cocoa
1/2 cup chili powder
1/4 cup paprika
1 tablespoon ground cumin
1 tablespoon ground coffee
2 teaspoons salt
2 teaspoons dried oregano leaves
1 teaspoon garlic powder
1 teaspoon red pepper flakes

1. Place toffee bits in food processor or blender. Cover; process until toffee bits are very fine.

2. Combine toffee and remaining ingredients in medium bowl; blend well. Place in airtight container.*

Makes 6 servings

*Store in cool dry place for up to 4 months.

Grilled Sweet Potato Packets with Pecan Butter

4 sweet potatoes (about 8 ounces each), peeled and cut into 1/4-inch-thick slices
1 large sweet or Spanish onion, thinly sliced and separated into rings
3 tablespoons vegetable oil
1/3 cup butter, softened
2 tablespoons light brown sugar
1/4 teaspoon salt
1/4 teaspoon ground cinnamon
1/4 cup chopped pecans, toasted

1. Prepare grill for direct cooking.

2. Alternately place potato slices and onion rings on four 14×12-inch sheets of heavy-duty foil. Brush tops and sides with oil to prevent drying.

3. Double fold sides and ends of foil to seal packets. Place foil packets on grid. Grill packets, on covered grill, over medium coals 25 to 30 minutes or until potatoes are fork-tender.

4. Meanwhile, to prepare Pecan Butter, combine butter, brown sugar, salt and cinnamon in small bowl. Stir in pecans. Carefully open packets; top each with dollop of Pecan Butter.

Makes 4 servings

Roasted Asparagus with Chavrie®-Dijon Sauce

Salsa Macaroni & Cheese

(pictured at right)

1 jar (1 pound) RAGÚ® Cheesy! Double Cheddar
  Sauce
1 cup prepared mild salsa
8 ounces elbow macaroni, cooked and drained

1. In 2-quart saucepan, heat Double Cheddar Sauce over medium heat. Stir in salsa; heat through.

2. Toss with hot macaroni. Serve immediately.

Makes 4 servings

Roasted Vegetables with Noodles

  5 tablespoons soy sauce, divided
  3 tablespoons peanut or vegetable oil
  2 tablespoons rice vinegar
  2 garlic cloves, minced
1/2 pound large mushrooms
  4 ounces shallots (2 to 3)
  1 medium zucchini, cut in half lengthwise then
    widthwise into 1-inch pieces
  1 medium yellow crookneck squash, cut in
    half lengthwise then widthwise into 1-inch
    pieces
  1 sweet red pepper, cut into 1-inch pieces
  1 sweet yellow pepper, cut into 1-inch pieces
  2 small Asian eggplants, cut into 1/2-inch slices
    or 2 cups cubed eggplant
  8 ounces Chinese egg noodles or vermicelli,
    cooked, drained and kept warm
  1 tablespoon toasted sesame oil

1. Preheat oven to 425°F. Combine 2 tablespoons soy sauce, peanut oil, vinegar and garlic in small bowl.

2. Combine vegetables in shallow roasting pan (do not line pan with foil). Toss with soy sauce mixture to coat well.

3. Roast vegetables 20 minutes or until browned and tender, stirring well after 10 minutes.

4. Place noodles in large bowl. Toss noodles with remaining 3 tablespoons soy sauce and sesame oil.

5. Toss roasted vegetables with noodle mixture; serve warm or at room temperature.

Makes 6 servings

Apple Brown Rice Stuffing

  1 pound BOB EVANS® Savory Sage or
    Original Recipe Roll Sausage
  3 cups cooked brown rice
  2 tablespoons olive oil
  1 medium apple, peeled, cored and sliced
  1 medium onion, chopped
  2 ribs celery, chopped
  4 medium mushrooms, sliced
1/3 cup raisins
1/2 teaspoon poultry seasoning
1/4 teaspoon dried thyme leaves
1/4 teaspoon black pepper
1/4 cup apple juice
1/3 cup sliced almonds
1/3 cup crushed wheat cereal squares or
    other dry cereal

Preheat oven to 350°F. Crumble and cook sausage in large skillet until browned. Drain off any drippings and transfer sausage to large bowl. Stir in rice. Add olive oil to same skillet with apple, onion, celery, mushrooms, raisins, poultry seasoning, thyme and pepper; cook and stir until vegetables are crisp-tender. Stir into sausage mixture. Add apple juice to moisten. Spread almonds and crushed cereal on baking sheet; bake 10 minutes. Add to sausage mixture and toss lightly. Place in 9-inch round greased casserole dish and bake 30 minutes or until heated through. Refrigerate leftovers.

Makes 6 servings

Note: Apple Brown Rice Stuffing may also be used as stuffing for poultry or pork.

Helpful Hint

Cooked brown rice has a slightly chewy texture and a delicious nut-like flavor. 1 cup uncooked brown rice cooked in 2-1/4 cups liquid for 40 to 45 minutes makes about 3 to 4 cups cooked rice. Parboiled brown rice cooks in about 30 minutes. Use packaged ready-to-serve brown rice if you are in a hurry.

Salsa Macaroni & Cheese

Bean Pot Medley

Bean Pot Medley

(pictured above)

1 can (15 ounces) black beans, rinsed and
  drained
1 can (15 ounces) red kidney beans, rinsed and
  drained
1 can (15 ounces) great northern beans, rinsed
  and drained
1 can (15 ounces) black-eyed peas, rinsed and
  drained
1 can (8-1/2 ounces) baby lima beans, rinsed
  and drained
1-1/2 cups ketchup
1 cup chopped onion
1 cup chopped sweet red pepper
1 cup chopped sweet green pepper
1/2 cup packed brown sugar
1/2 cup water
2 to 3 teaspoons cider vinegar
1 teaspoon dry mustard
2 bay leaves
1/8 teaspoon pepper

SLOW COOKER DIRECTIONS

1. Combine beans, ketchup, onion, sweet peppers, brown sugar, water, vinegar, mustard, bay leaves and pepper in 4-quart slow cooker; mix well.

2. Cover; cook on LOW 6 to 7 hours or until onion and sweet peppers are tender.

3. Remove and discard bay leaves.

Makes 8 servings

Cheddar Stuffed Tomatoes

4 large ripe tomatoes
2 tablespoons CABOT® Salted Butter
1/2 cup finely chopped onion
2 teaspoons minced garlic
2 cups fresh bread crumbs (about 4 slices firm
  white bread)
1 cup grated CABOT® Sharp or Extra Sharp
  Cheddar*
1/4 cup chopped fresh parsley
1/4 teaspoon salt
1/4 teaspoon ground black pepper

1. Place rack in upper third of oven and preheat oven to 400°F. Lightly butter shallow baking dish large enough to hold 8 tomato halves.

2. Pull off stems and cut tomatoes in half widthwise. With teaspoon, scoop out and discard seeds. Lightly salt interiors and set upside-down on paper towels to drain.

3. Meanwhile, melt butter in skillet over medium heat. Add onion and garlic and stir until onion is translucent, about 5 minutes.

4. Increase heat to medium-high, add bread crumbs and continue stirring until crumbs are golden, about 5 minutes longer.

5. Transfer crumb mixture to bowl and stir in cheese, parsley, salt and pepper. Spoon mixture into tomato halves and set in prepared dish.

6. Bake for about 15 minutes, or until tomatoes are tender and filling is lightly browned on top.

Makes 8 halves

Kentucky Cornbread & Sausage Stuffing

(pictured below)

1/2 pound BOB EVANS® Original Recipe Roll
    Sausage
  3 cups fresh bread cubes, dried or toasted
  3 cups crumbled prepared cornbread
  1 large apple, peeled and chopped
  1 small onion, chopped
  1 cup chicken or turkey broth
  2 tablespoons minced fresh parsley
  1 teaspoon salt
  1 teaspoon rubbed sage or poultry seasoning
1/4 teaspoon black pepper

Crumble sausage into small skillet. Cook over medium heat until browned, stirring occasionally. Place sausage and drippings in large bowl. Add remaining ingredients; toss lightly. Use to stuff chicken loosely just before roasting. Or, place stuffing in greased 13×9-inch baking dish. Add additional broth for moister stuffing, if desired. Bake in 350°F oven 30 minutes. Leftover stuffing should be removed from bird and stored separately in refrigerator. Reheat thoroughly before serving.

Makes enough stuffing for 5-pound chicken, 8 side-dish servings

Serving suggestion: Double this recipe to stuff 12- to 15-pound turkey.

Mashed Maple Sweet Potatoes

  3 cans (15 ounces each) PRINCELLA® or
    SUGARY SAM® Cut Sweet Potatoes, drained
  4 tablespoons butter
1/4 cup half-and-half
  3 tablespoons maple syrup
    Salt and black pepper to taste

Preheat oven to 350°F. In medium mixing bowl, combine all ingredients; beat with an electric mixer on medium speed until well blended. Transfer mixture to a greased 9-inch square casserole dish; smooth the surface. Cover and bake for 30 minutes.

Makes 5 to 7 servings

Kentucky Cornbread & Sausage Stuffing

Confetti Rice Pilaf

(pictured at right)

1 tablespoon I CAN'T BELIEVE IT'S NOT
    BUTTER!® Spread
1 cup regular or converted rice
1 cup fresh or drained canned sliced mushrooms
2 medium carrots, diced
1 envelope LIPTON® RECIPE SECRETS® Savory
    Herb with Garlic Soup Mix*
2-1/4 cups water

*Also terrific with LIPTON® RECIPE SECRETS® Golden Onion, Onion
Mushroom or Onion Soup Mix.*

1. In 12-inch skillet, melt spread over medium-high
heat and cook rice, stirring frequently, until golden.
Stir in mushrooms, carrots and soup mix blended
with water. Bring to a boil over high heat.

2. Reduce heat to low and simmer covered,
20 minutes or until rice is tender.

Makes 6 servings

Broccoli in Cheese Sauce

1 bag (16 ounces) frozen broccoli florets
1 medium sweet red or yellow pepper, cut
    into 1-inch pieces
1 can (10-3/4 ounces) condensed Cheddar
    cheese soup, undiluted
1/4 cup chopped onion
1/4 cup milk
1-1/2 teaspoons Worcestershire sauce
1/8 teaspoon pepper

1. Preheat oven to 375°F.

2. Combine broccoli and sweet pepper in 8-inch
square baking dish.

3. Combine soup, onion, milk, Worcestershire and
pepper in medium bowl. Pour over broccoli mixture.

4. Bake 25 to 30 minutes or until vegetables are
tender. Transfer mixture to serving bowl.

Makes 6 servings

Sweet Potato-Cranberry Bake

(pictured on page 44)

1 can (40 ounces) whole sweet potatoes, drained
1-1/3 cups *French's®* French Fried Onions, divided
2 cups fresh cranberries
2 tablespoons packed brown sugar
1/3 cup honey

Preheat oven to 400°F. In 1-1/2-quart casserole, layer
sweet potatoes, *2/3 cup* French Fried Onions and
1 cup cranberries. Sprinkle with brown sugar; drizzle
with *half* the honey. Top with remaining cranberries
and honey. Bake, covered, at 400°F for 35 minutes or
until heated through. Gently stir casserole. Top with
remaining *2/3 cup* onions; bake, uncovered, 1 to
3 minutes or until onions are golden brown.

Makes 4 to 6 servings

Fresh Vegetable Casserole

8 small new potatoes
8 baby carrots
1 small head cauliflower, broken into florets
4 stalks asparagus, cut into 1-inch pieces
3 tablespoons butter
3 tablespoons all-purpose flour
2 cups milk
  Salt
  Pepper
3/4 cup shredded Cheddar cheese
  Chopped fresh cilantro or parsley

1. Preheat oven to 350°F. Steam vegetables until
crisp-tender. Arrange vegetables in buttered 2-quart
baking dish.

2. To make sauce, melt butter in medium saucepan
over medium heat. Stir in flour until smooth.
Gradually whisk in milk. Bring to a boil. Cook and
stir 2 minutes or until thick and bubbly. Season with
salt and pepper. Add cheese, stirring until cheese
is melted. Pour sauce over vegetables and sprinkle
with cilantro.

3. Bake 15 minutes or until heated through.

Makes 4 to 6 servings

Honey Mustard-Orange Roasted Vegetables

(pictured at right)

    6 cups assorted cut-up vegetables (red or
        green bell peppers, zucchini, red onions
        and carrots)
    2 tablespoons olive oil
    1 teaspoon minced garlic
  1/4 cup *French's®* Honey Mustard
    2 tablespoons orange juice
    1 teaspoon grated orange peel

1. Preheat oven to 450°F. Toss vegetables with oil, garlic and *1 teaspoon salt* in roasting pan.

2. Bake, uncovered, 20 minutes or until tender.

3. Toss vegetables with mustard, juice and orange peel just before serving. Serve over pasta or with bread, if desired. *Makes 6 servings*

Potatoes au Gratin

  1-1/2 pounds small red potatoes
      6 tablespoons butter, divided
      3 tablespoons all-purpose flour
    1/2 teaspoon salt
    1/4 teaspoon white pepper
  1-1/2 cups milk
      1 cup (4 ounces) shredded Cheddar cheese
      4 green onions, thinly sliced
    3/4 cup cracker crumbs

1. Preheat oven to 350°F. Spray 1-quart round baking dish with nonstick cooking spray.

2. Place potatoes in 2-quart saucepan; add enough water to cover potatoes. Bring to a boil over high heat. Cook, uncovered, about 10 minutes or until partially done. Potatoes should still be firm in center. Drain; rinse in cold water until potatoes are cool. Drain; set aside.

3. Meanwhile, melt 4 tablespoons butter in medium saucepan over medium heat. Add flour, salt and pepper, stirring until smooth. Gradually add milk, stirring constantly until sauce is thickened. Add cheese, stirring until melted.

4. Cut potatoes widthwise into 1/4-inch-thick slices. Layer 1/3 of potatoes in prepared dish. Top with 1/3 of onions and 1/3 of cheese sauce. Repeat layers twice, ending with cheese sauce.

5. Melt remaining 2 tablespoons butter. Combine cracker crumbs and butter in small bowl. Sprinkle evenly over top of casserole. Bake, uncovered, 35 to 40 minutes or until hot and bubbly and potatoes are tender. *Makes 4 to 6 servings*

Success Waldorf Dressing

    1 box SUCCESS® Long Grain & Wild Rice Mix
    3 strips bacon
  1/2 cup chopped celery
    1 medium red apple, chopped
    1 medium green apple, chopped
  1/2 cup chopped walnuts
  1/2 cup raisins
    2 tablespoons honey
    2 tablespoons lemon juice

Prepare rice mix according to package directions.

Meanwhile, cook bacon in skillet until crisp. Remove bacon and crumble. Cook and stir celery in same skillet until tender. Add remaining ingredients. Fold in cooked rice. Top with crumbled bacon.
Makes 4 to 6 servings

Speedy Spanish Rice

    1 can (14-1/2 ounces) stewed tomatoes or
        pasta-ready tomatoes with spices
    1 can (10-1/2 ounces) condensed chicken broth
    1 can (11 ounces) Mexican-style whole kernel
        corn, drained
  1-1/3 cups *French's®* French Fried Onions, divided
  1-1/3 cups uncooked instant rice

Combine tomatoes, broth and corn in large saucepan. Bring to a full boil. Stir in *2/3 cup* French Fried Onions and rice. Remove from heat. Cover; let stand 5 minutes or until all liquid is absorbed. Fluff rice with fork before serving. Sprinkle with remaining *2/3 cup* onions. *Makes 4 to 6 servings*

Tip: For extra-crispy French Fried Onions, place onions on microwavable dish. Microwave on HIGH 1 minute or until onions are golden.

*Honey Mustard-Orange
Roasted Vegetables*

Winter Squash Gratin

(pictured at right)

1-1/2 cups grated CABOT® Sharp Cheddar (about 6 ounces)
1-1/2 cups fresh bread crumbs (about 3 slices firm white bread)
   2 tablespoons CABOT® Salted Butter
   2 cups chopped onions
   1 teaspoon sugar
  1/2 teaspoon salt
  1/2 teaspoon dried thyme leaves, crumbled
  1/4 teaspoon ground black pepper
   2 pounds dry-fleshed winter squash, such as Buttercup, Hubbard or Kabocha, peeled and seeded
 3/4 to 1 cup chicken broth

1. Preheat oven to 375°F. Combine cheese and bread crumbs in bowl and set aside.

2. In large skillet over medium heat, melt butter. Add onions and sugar. Stir often until onions are golden, about 10 minutes. Stir in salt, thyme and pepper, then transfer mixture to 1-1/2-quart baking dish.

3. Cut squash into smaller chunks and cut these chunks into 1/8-inch-thick slices. Add to onions and stir together well.

4. Pour 3/4 cup of chicken broth evenly over squash. Cover dish tightly with lid or foil and bake for about 70 minutes, or until squash is tender and broth is nearly all absorbed. If squash appears dry, add remaining 1/4 cup broth.

5. Sprinkle squash with reserved bread crumb mixture. Bake until topping is golden, about 20 minutes longer. *Makes 8 servings*

Mexican Corn Custard Bake

   1 can (11 ounces) Mexican-style whole kernel corn, drained
 1/4 cup all-purpose flour
   1 jar (16 ounces) chunky medium salsa, divided
   5 eggs, beaten
 1/2 cup sour cream
1-1/3 cups *French's*® French Fried Onions, divided
   1 cup (4 ounces) shredded Monterey Jack cheese with jalapeño peppers or Cheddar cheese

Preheat oven to 375°F. Grease 9-inch deep-dish pie plate. Combine corn and flour in large bowl. Stir in 3/4 cup salsa, eggs, sour cream and *2/3 cup* French

Fried Onions; mix until well blended. Pour into prepared pie plate. Cover; bake 45 minutes or until custard is set.

Pour remaining salsa around edge of dish. Sprinkle with cheese and remaining *2/3 cup* onions. Bake, uncovered, 3 minutes or until onions are golden. Cut into wedges to serve. *Makes 6 servings*

Green Beans and Tomatoes Provençal

   1 pound fresh green beans, trimmed
 1/4 cup FILIPPO BERIO® Olive Oil
   1 clove garlic, crushed
   Salt and freshly ground black pepper
   3 shallots, sliced
   3 tomatoes, cored and cut crosswise in half
 1/4 cup dry bread crumbs
   2 tablespoons chopped fresh Italian parsley
   1 tablespoon chopped fresh thyme *or* 1 teaspoon dried thyme leaves
   Additional fresh Italian parsley (optional)

Preheat oven to 400°F. Steam green beans 6 minutes; place in 13×9-inch dish. In small bowl, combine olive oil and garlic; drizzle 1 tablespoon olive oil mixture over beans. Season to taste with salt and pepper.

In large nonstick skillet, heat remaining olive oil mixture over medium heat until hot. Add shallots; cook and stir 2 minutes. Add tomatoes; cook 1 minute, turning halfway through cooking time.

Place tomatoes, cut side up, and shallots on top of beans. In small bowl, combine bread crumbs, 2 tablespoons parsley and thyme. Sprinkle over top of tomatoes and beans. Drizzle with oil remaining in skillet. Bake 15 to 20 minutes or until golden brown. Garnish with additional parsley, if desired.

Makes 6 servings

Winter Squash Gratin

Saucy Vegetable Casserole

(pictured at right)

2 bags (16 ounces each) frozen mixed vegetables
   (broccoli, cauliflower, carrots), thawed
2 cups *French's®* French Fried Onions, divided
1 package (16 ounces) pasteurized process
   cheese, cut into 1/4-inch slices

1. Preheat oven to 350°F. Combine vegetables and
1 cup French Fried Onions in shallow 3-quart baking
dish. Top evenly with cheese slices.

2. Bake 15 minutes or until hot and cheese is almost
melted; stir. Top with remaining *1 cup* onions and
bake 5 minutes or until onions are golden.
Makes 8 servings

Variation: For added Cheddar flavor, substitute
***French's®* Cheddar French Fried Onions** for the
original flavor.

Apricot-Glazed Beets

1 pound beets
1 tablespoon cornstarch
1 cup apricot nectar
2 tablespoons cider vinegar or red wine vinegar
8 dried apricot halves, cut into strips
1/4 teaspoon salt

1. Cut tops off beets, leaving at least 1 inch of stems
(do not trim root ends). Scrub beets under running
water with soft vegetable brush, being careful not to
break skins. Place beets in medium saucepan; cover
with water. Bring to a boil over high heat; reduce
heat. Cover and simmer about 20 minutes or until
just barely firm when pierced with fork. Transfer to
plate; cool. Rinse pan.

2. Combine cornstarch and apricot nectar in
saucepan until smooth. Add vinegar; stir until
smooth. Add apricot strips and salt. Cook over
medium heat until mixture thickens.

3. Cut roots and stems from beets on plate.*
Peel, halve and cut beets into 1/4-inch-thick slices.
Add beet slices to apricot mixture; toss gently to
coat. Transfer to warm serving dish.
Makes 4 servings

*Do not cut beets on cutting board; the juice will stain the board.

Rustic Potatoes au Gratin

1 can (10-3/4 ounces) condensed Cheddar
   cheese soup, undiluted
1 package (8 ounces) cream cheese, softened
1/2 cup milk
1 garlic clove, minced
1/4 teaspoon ground nutmeg
1/8 teaspoon pepper
2 pounds baking potatoes, cut into
   1/4-inch-thick slices
1 small onion, thinly sliced
Paprika

SLOW COOKER DIRECTIONS

1. Combine soup, cream cheese, milk, garlic, nutmeg
and pepper in large bowl; beat until smooth.

2. Layer one fourth of potatoes and one fourth of
onion in 3-quart slow cooker. Top with one fourth
of soup mixture. Repeat layers 3 times, using
remaining potatoes, onion and soup mixture.

3. Cover; cook on LOW 6-1/2 to 7 hours or until
potatoes are tender and most of liquid is absorbed.
Sprinkle with paprika.
Makes 6 servings

Orange-Spice Glazed Carrots

1 pound baby carrots
1/3 cup orange marmalade
2 tablespoons butter
2 teaspoons Dijon mustard
1/2 teaspoon grated fresh gingerroot

Bring 1 inch lightly salted water in large saucepan
to a boil over high heat; add carrots. Return to a
boil. Reduce heat to low. Cover and simmer 10 to
12 minutes for fresh carrots (8 to 10 minutes for
frozen carrots) or until crisp-tender. Drain well;
return carrots to pan. Stir in marmalade, butter,
mustard and gingerroot. Simmer, uncovered, over
medium heat 3 minutes or until carrots are glazed,
stirring occasionally.*
Makes 6 servings

**At this point, carrots may be transferred to a microwavable casserole
dish with lid. Cover and refrigerate up to 8 hours before serving. To
reheat, microwave on HIGH 4 to 5 minutes or until hot.*

Note: Recipe can be doubled.

Onion-Roasted Potatoes

(pictured at right)

1 envelope LIPTON® RECIPE SECRETS® Onion Soup Mix*
4 medium all-purpose potatoes, cut into large chunks (about 2 pounds)
1/3 cup BERTOLLI® Olive Oil

*Also terrific with LIPTON® RECIPE SECRETS® Onion Mushroom, Golden Onion or Savory Herb with Garlic Soup Mix.

1. Preheat oven to 450°F. In 13×9-inch baking or roasting pan, combine all ingredients.

2. Bake uncovered, stirring occasionally, 40 minutes or until potatoes are tender and golden brown.
Makes 4 servings

Herbed Mushroom Vegetable Medley

4 ounces button or cremini mushrooms
1 medium sweet red or yellow pepper, cut into 1/4-inch-wide strips
1 medium zucchini, cut widthwise into 1/4-inch-thick slices
1 medium yellow squash, cut widthwise into 1/4-inch-thick slices
3 tablespoons butter, melted
1 tablespoon chopped fresh thyme *or* 1 teaspoon dried thyme
1 tablespoon chopped fresh basil *or* 1 teaspoon dried basil
1 tablespoon chopped fresh chives or green onion tops
1 garlic clove, minced
1/4 teaspoon salt
1/4 teaspoon pepper

1. Prepare grill for direct cooking.

2. Cut thin slice from base of mushroom stems with paring knife; discard. Thinly slice mushroom stems and caps. Combine mushrooms, sweet pepper, zucchini and squash in large bowl. Combine butter, thyme, basil, chives, garlic, salt and pepper in small bowl. Pour over vegetable mixture; toss to coat well.

3. Transfer mixture to 20×14-inch sheet of heavy-duty foil; wrap. Place foil packet on grid. Grill packet on covered grill over medium coals 20 to 25 minutes or until vegetables are fork-tender. Open packet carefully to serve.
Makes 4 servings

Apple & Carrot Casserole

6 large carrots, sliced
4 large apples, peeled, cored and sliced
1/4 cup plus 1 tablespoon all-purpose flour
1 tablespoon brown sugar
1/2 teaspoon ground nutmeg
1 tablespoon butter
1/2 cup orange juice
1/2 teaspoon salt (optional)

1. Preheat oven to 350°F. Cook carrots in boiling water in large saucepan 5 minutes; drain. Layer carrots and apples in large casserole.

2. Combine flour, brown sugar and nutmeg in small bowl; sprinkle over top. Dot with butter; pour orange juice over flour mixture. Sprinkle with salt, if desired. Bake 30 minutes or until carrots are tender.
Makes 6 servings

Cheddary Garlic Mashed Potatoes

4 cups hot mashed potatoes
1 can (10-3/4 ounces) condensed cream of chicken soup
1-1/2 cups shredded Cheddar cheese, divided
1/8 teaspoon garlic powder
1-1/2 cups *French's®* French Fried Onions

1. Preheat oven to 375°F. Heat mashed potatoes, soup, 1 cup cheese and garlic powder in saucepan over medium heat. Stir until cheese melts.

2. Spoon potato mixture into 2-quart baking dish. Top with 1/2 cup cheese and French Fried Onions.

3. Bake 5 to 10 minutes or until hot and onions are golden.
Makes 6 to 8 servings

Soups

Southwestern Turkey Stew

(pictured at left)

1 tablespoon vegetable oil
1 small onion, finely chopped
1 garlic clove, minced
2 cups chicken broth
2 cups cooked smoked turkey breast, cut into
    1/2-inch pieces
2 cups frozen corn kernels
1 can (14-1/2 ounces) diced tomatoes
1 package (about 6 ounces) red beans and rice mix
1 to 2 canned chipotle peppers in adobo sauce,*
    drained and minced
Chopped green onion (optional)

Canned chipotle peppers can be found in the Mexican section of most supermarkets or gourmet food stores.

1. Heat oil in large nonstick skillet over medium-high heat. Add onion and garlic; cook and stir 3 minutes or until onion is translucent.

2. Add broth; bring to a boil. Stir in turkey, corn, tomatoes, bean mix and chipotle pepper. Reduce heat to low. Cover; cook 10 to 12 minutes or until rice is tender. Let stand 3 minutes. Garnish with green onion.   *Makes 4 servings*

Substitutions: Use 1 can (14-1/2 ounces) diced tomatoes with jalapeño peppers in place of diced tomatoes. Or, use 1/4 teaspoon chipotle chili powder and 1 minced jalapeño pepper in place of the chipotle peppers.

Clockwise from top left: *Southwestern Turkey Stew, Curried Vegetable-Rice Soup (p. 82), Cheesy Mexican Soup (p. 86), Groundnut Soup with Ginger and Cilantro (p. 68)*

Potato & Spinach Soup with Gouda

(pictured at right)

9 medium Yukon Gold potatoes, peeled and cubed (about 6 cups)
2 cans (14-1/2 ounces each) chicken broth
1/2 cup water
1 small red onion, finely chopped
5 ounces baby spinach leaves
1/2 teaspoon salt
1/4 teaspoon cayenne pepper
1/4 teaspoon pepper
2-1/2 cups shredded smoked Gouda cheese, divided
1 can (12 ounces) evaporated milk
1 tablespoon olive oil
4 garlic cloves, cut into thin slices
Coarsely chopped fresh parsley

SLOW COOKER DIRECTIONS

1. Combine potatoes, broth, water, onion, spinach, salt, cayenne and pepper in 4-quart slow cooker. Cover; cook on LOW 10 hours or on HIGH 4 to 5 hours or until potatoes are tender.

2. Turn slow cooker to HIGH. Slightly mash potatoes in slow cooker; add 2 cups Gouda and evaporated milk. Cover; cook on HIGH 15 to 20 minutes or until cheese is melted.

3. Heat oil in small skillet over low heat. Cook and stir garlic 2 minutes or until golden brown; set aside. Pour soup into bowls; sprinkle with remaining Gouda cheese. Add spoonful of garlic to center of each bowl; sprinkle with parsley.

Makes 8 to 10 servings

Lentil Soup

2 tablespoons olive oil
1 medium onion, chopped
1 medium carrot, chopped
3 quarts chicken broth
1 jar (1 pound 10 ounces) RAGÚ® Light Pasta sauce
1-1/2 cups uncooked lentils, rinsed and drained
2 cups coarsely shredded fresh spinach or escarole

1. In 6-quart saucepot, heat olive oil over medium-high heat and cook onion and carrot, stirring occasionally, 4 minutes or until vegetables are golden.

2. Stir in broth, Pasta Sauce and lentils. Bring to a boil over high heat. Reduce heat to low and simmer, stirring occasionally, 30 minutes or until lentils are tender. Stir in spinach and cook an additional 10 minutes or until spinach is tender.

Makes 3-1/2 quarts soup

Groundnut Soup with Ginger and Cilantro

(pictured on page 66)

1 tablespoon vegetable oil
1-1/2 cups chopped onions
1 garlic clove, minced
2 teaspoons chili powder
1 teaspoon ground cumin
1/4 teaspoon crushed red pepper flakes
8 ounces sweet potatoes, peeled and cut into 1/2-inch cubes
3 cups chicken broth
1 can (14-1/2 ounces) diced tomatoes
1 medium carrot, cut into 1/2-inch pieces
2 teaspoons sugar
1 cup salted peanuts
1 tablespoon grated fresh gingerroot
1/4 cup chopped fresh cilantro

1. Heat oil in large saucepan over medium-high heat. Add onions; cook and stir 4 minutes or until translucent. Add garlic, chili powder, cumin and pepper flakes. Cook and stir 15 seconds.

2. Add sweet potatoes, broth, tomatoes, carrots and sugar. Bring to a boil over high heat. Reduce heat. Cover; simmer 25 minutes or until vegetables are tender, stirring occasionally. Remove from heat. Stir in peanuts and gingerroot. Cool slightly.

3. Working in batches, process soup in blender or food processor until smooth. Return to saucepan. Heat over medium-high heat 2 minutes or until heated through. Sprinkle cilantro over each serving.

Makes 4 servings

Potato & Spinach Soup with Gouda

Black & White Mexican Bean Soup

(pictured at right)

>   1 tablespoon vegetable oil
>   1 cup chopped onion
>   1 clove garlic, minced
>   1/4 cup flour
>   1 package (1.25 ounces) ORTEGA® Taco
>   Seasoning Mix
>   2 cups milk
>   1 can (14-1/2 ounces) chicken broth
>   1 package (16 ounces) frozen corn
>   1 can (15 ounces) great northern beans, rinsed
>   and drained
>   1 can (15 ounces) black beans, rinsed and
>   drained
>   1 can (4 ounces) ORTEGA Diced Green Chiles
>   2 tablespoons chopped fresh cilantro

HEAT oil in large pan or Dutch oven over medium-high heat. Add onion and garlic; cook until onion is tender.

STIR in flour and taco seasoning mix; gradually stir in milk until blended. Add remaining ingredients except cilantro.

BRING to a boil, stirring constantly. Reduce heat to low; simmer for 15 minutes or until thickened, stirring occasionally.

STIR in cilantro.   *Makes 6 servings*

Tip: To save time, substitute 1/2 teaspoon bottled minced garlic for garlic clove.

Cajun Clam Chowder

>   6 slices bacon, diced
>   1/2 pound red potatoes, diced
>   2 medium onions, chopped
>   2 stalks celery, sliced
>   3 tablespoons flour
>   1 can (10 ounces) whole baby clams
>   2 cans (14-1/2 ounces each) DEL MONTE®
>   Stewed Tomatoes - Original Recipe
>   1 bottle (8 ounces) clam juice
>   1/4 to 1/2 teaspoon hot pepper sauce

1. Cook bacon in Dutch oven until slightly crisp. Drain reserving 3 tablespoons drippings. Add potatoes, onions and celery; cook over medium-high heat until tender-crisp, about 10 minutes.

2. Sprinkle with flour; cook 1 to 2 minutes. Drain clams reserving liquid. Add reserved liquid, tomatoes, clam juice and 1 cup water to vegetables.

3. Cook 20 to 25 minutes or until potatoes are tender. Stir in clams and hot pepper sauce; heat through.   *Makes 6 servings*

Italian Vegetable Soup

>   1 tablespoon olive oil
>   1 cup chopped red onion (1 medium onion)
>   1 cup chopped sweet red pepper (1 medium
>   pepper)
>   3 cans (14-1/2 ounces each) chicken broth
>   1 bag (16 ounces) frozen Italian vegetables or
>   mixed vegetables
>   1 can (15 ounces) chickpeas, rinsed and drained
>   1 can (14-1/2 ounces) diced tomatoes
>   1 teaspoon dried oregano
>   1/2 teaspoon salt
>   1/2 teaspoon pepper
>   1 cup uncooked wagon wheel pasta
>   1 cup cooked diced chicken

1. Heat oil in Dutch oven. Add onion and sweet pepper. Cook and stir over medium-high heat 3 minutes or until onion is tender. Stir in broth, frozen vegetables, chickpeas, tomatoes, oregano, salt and pepper. Bring to a boil over high heat.

2. Stir in pasta and chicken. Reduce heat to medium and cook at low boil 15 minutes or until pasta and vegetables are tender.   *Makes 6 servings*

Tip: For convenient school lunches, cool soup and pack into six freezer containers. Label and freeze. Transfer soup from freezer to refrigerator the night before. In the morning, heat soup in microwave until piping hot. Preheat vacuum container with boiling water; drain and dry. Pour into vacuum container and seal. If desired, sprinkle each serving of soup with 1 tablespoon grated Parmesan cheese before packing. For adults, add a tablespoon of extra-virgin olive oil.

Black & White Mexican Bean Soup

Lamb Meatball & Bean Soup

(pictured below)

1 pound ground lamb
1/4 cup chopped onion
1 garlic clove, minced
1 teaspoon ground cumin
1/2 teaspoon salt
2 cups chicken broth
1-1/2 cups frozen chopped broccoli
1 large tomato, chopped
1 can (15 ounces) garbanzo beans or
    black-eyed peas, rinsed and drained
1/2 teaspoon dried thyme
    Salt and pepper

1. Combine lamb, onion, garlic, cumin and salt; mix lightly. Shape into 1-inch balls.* Brown meatballs in large skillet over medium-high heat, turning occasionally.

2. Meanwhile, bring broth to a boil in large saucepan. Add broccoli and tomato; return to a boil. Reduce heat; cover.

3. When meatballs are browned, remove from skillet. Add to broth with beans and thyme; simmer 5 minutes. Season with salt and pepper.

Makes 4 to 6 servings

Lamb Meatball & Bean Soup

*To quickly shape uniform meatballs, place meat mixture on cutting board; pat evenly into large square, 1 inch thick. With sharp knife, cut meat into 1-inch squares; shape each square into a ball.

Tex-Mex Cheddar Cheese Soup

2 cans (10-3/4 ounces each) condensed Cheddar
    cheese or cream of chicken soup
2 cups milk
1 cup half and half
2 cups shredded Cheddar cheese
1 can (4 ounces) green chilies, finely chopped
1 teaspoon ground cumin
2 cups *French's®* French Fried Onions

1. Combine soup, milk and cream in large saucepan. Heat over medium-high heat until hot. Stir in cheese, chilies and cumin. Cook until cheese melts, stirring constantly.

2. Place French Fried Onions on microwave-safe dish. Microwave on HIGH 1 minute or until golden.

3. Spoon soup into bowls. Garnish with sour cream and fresh cilantro if desired. Top with onions.

Makes 6 servings

Asparagus Lemon Soup

1 pound DOLE® Fresh Asparagus, trimmed and
    chopped
1 cup chopped DOLE® Celery
3 cups chicken broth
1/2 cup whipping cream
1/2 teaspoon grated lemon peel
2 tablespoons fresh lemon juice
1/16 teaspoon white pepper

• Combine asparagus, celery and chicken broth in large saucepan. Heat to boiling. Reduce heat to low; cook 10 minutes. Cool.

• Pour asparagus mixture into blender or food processor container. Cover; blend until smooth. Stir in whipping cream, lemon juice, lemon peel and pepper. Pour soup into saucepan. Heat until warm (do not boil).

Makes 5 servings

Tip: Soup can be served cold. Cover; refrigerate about 3 hours or until chilled.

A-B-C Minestrone

A-B-C Minestrone

(pictured above)

1 tablespoon olive oil
1 medium onion, chopped
2 medium carrots, chopped
1 small zucchini, chopped
1/2 teaspoon dried Italian seasoning
4 cups chicken broth
1 jar (1 pound 10 ounces) RAGÚ® Old World Style® Pasta Sauce
1 can (15.5 ounces) cannellini or white kidney beans, rinsed and drained
1 cup alphabet pasta

1. In 4-quart saucepan, heat olive oil over medium heat and cook onion, carrots and zucchini, stirring frequently, 5 minutes or until vegetables are tender. Add Italian seasoning and cook, stirring occasionally, 1 minute. Add broth and Pasta Sauce and bring to a boil. Stir in beans and pasta. Cook, stirring occasionally, 10 minutes or until pasta is tender.

2. Serve, if desired, with chopped parsley and grated Parmesan cheese. *Makes 8 servings*

Oyster Chowder

4 slices thick-cut bacon, diced
1-1/4 cups chopped onion
1 pint fresh shucked oysters, drained, liquor reserved
1 can (14-1/2 ounces) chicken or vegetable broth
1-1/4 cups diced peeled potato
1 cup whipping cream or half-and-half cream
Salt and pepper
Sliced green onions

1. Cook bacon in large saucepan over medium heat until crisp, stirring frequently. Transfer bacon to paper towel with slotted spoon; set aside. Drain off all but about 2 tablespoons drippings. Add onion to skillet; cook and stir 5 minutes or until tender.

2. Add oyster liquor, broth and potato to onion; increase heat to high. Cover; simmer 5 minutes or until potato is tender but firm. Stir in oysters and cream; cook 5 minutes more or until edges of oysters begin to curl. Season with salt and pepper. Ladle into bowls; top with reserved bacon and green onions. *Makes 4 servings*

Creamy Chicken and Veggie Soup

(pictured at right)

2 cans (10-3/4 ounces each) condensed cream of chicken soup, undiluted
2-3/4 cups chicken broth
3 medium Yukon gold potatoes, peeled and diced
1 cup finely chopped green onions, divided
2 cups cooked diced chicken
1 package (10 ounces) frozen green peas and carrots
1/4 cup half-and-half cream or whole milk

1. Place soup, broth, potatoes and 1/2 cup green onions in large saucepan. Bring to a boil over high heat. Reduce heat; cover and simmer 15 minutes or until potatoes are tender.

2. Stir in chicken, peas and carrots and half-and-half. Cook until peas and carrots are heated through. Sprinkle with remaining 1/2 cup green onions.

Makes 6 servings

Chicken Tortilla Soup

4 (6-inch) CHI-CHI'S® flour tortillas, cut into thin strips
3 cups water
3 HERB-OX® chicken flavored bouillon cubes
1 (1-1/4-ounce) package CHI-CHI'S® taco seasoning mix
1 (16-ounce) jar CHI-CHI'S® salsa
2 (10-ounce) cans HORMEL® chunk breast of chicken, drained and flaked
1 (15-ounce) can black beans, drained and rinsed
1 (11-ounce) can corn with red and green bell peppers
Sour cream, if desired

Place tortilla strips onto baking pan. Lightly spray strips with nonstick cooking spray. Bake at 400°F until crisp about 10 minutes. Meanwhile, in large saucepan, combine water, bouillon, taco seasoning mix and salsa. Bring mixture to a boil. Reduce heat and simmer for 5 minutes. Add chunk chicken, black beans and corn. Heat until warmed through, about 10 minutes. Ladle into warm bowls and top with tortilla crisps and sour cream, if desired.

Makes 6 servings

Cuban-Style Black Bean Soup

2 teaspoons olive oil
1 small onion, chopped
1 cup thinly sliced carrots
2 jalapeño peppers,* seeded and minced
2 garlic cloves, minced
1 can (15 ounces) black beans, undrained
1 can (14-1/2 ounces) vegetable or chicken broth
1/4 cup sour cream
1/4 cup chopped fresh cilantro
4 lime wedges

Jalapeño peppers can sting and irritate the skin, so wear rubber gloves when handling peppers and do not touch your eyes.

1. Heat oil in large saucepan over medium heat. Add onion, carrots, jalapeños and garlic; cook 5 minutes, stirring frequently.

2. Add beans and broth; bring to a boil. Cover; reduce heat and simmer 15 to 20 minutes or until vegetables are very tender.

3. Ladle soup into shallow bowls; top with sour cream and cilantro. Serve with lime wedges.

Makes 4 servings

Note: Soup will be chunky. If desired, purée soup with a hand-held immersion blender or in food processor.

Simple Turkey Soup

2 pounds ground turkey, cooked and drained
1 can (28 ounces) whole tomatoes, undrained
2 cans (14-1/2 ounces each) beef broth
1 bag (16 ounces) frozen mixed soup vegetables (such as carrots, beans, okra, corn or onion), thawed
1/2 cup uncooked barley
1 teaspoon salt
1 teaspoon dried thyme
1/2 teaspoon ground coriander
Pepper

SLOW COOKER DIRECTIONS
Combine all ingredients in 4-quart slow cooker. Add water to cover. Cover and cook on HIGH 3 to 4 hours.

Makes 8 servings

Two-Cheese Potato and Cauliflower Soup

(pictured at right)

1 tablespoon butter
1 cup chopped onion
2 garlic cloves, minced
5 cups milk
1 pound Yukon gold potatoes (peeled or unpeeled), diced
1 pound cauliflower florets
1-1/2 teaspoons salt
1/8 teaspoon cayenne pepper
1-1/2 cups (6 ounces) shredded sharp Cheddar cheese
1/3 cup crumbled blue cheese

1. Melt butter in saucepan over medium-high heat. Add onion; cook and stir 4 minutes or until translucent. Add garlic; cook and stir 15 seconds. Add milk, potatoes, cauliflower, salt and cayenne; bring to a boil. Reduce heat; cover tightly and simmer 15 minutes or until potatoes are tender. Cool slightly.

2. Working in batches, process soup in blender or food processor until smooth. Return to saucepan over medium heat. Heat 2 to 3 minutes or until heated through. Remove from heat; add cheeses. Stir until melted.   *Makes 4 to 6 servings*

Noodle Soup Parmigiano

3 cups water
1/2 pound boneless, skinless chicken breast halves, cut into 1/2-inch pieces
1 cup chopped fresh tomatoes *or*
    1 can (8 ounces) whole peeled tomatoes, undrained and chopped
1 pouch LIPTON® Soup Secrets Noodle Soup Mix with Real Chicken Broth
1/2 teaspoon LAWRY'S® Garlic Powder with Parsley (optional)
1/2 cup shredded mozzarella cheese (about 2 ounces)
    Grated Parmesan cheese (optional)

In medium saucepan, combine all ingredients except cheeses; bring to a boil. Reduce heat and simmer uncovered, stirring occasionally, 5 minutes or until chicken is thoroughly cooked. To serve, spoon into bowls; sprinkle with cheeses.   *Makes 5 servings*

Mediterranean Lentil Soup

2 tablespoons olive oil
1 large onion, diced
1 stalk celery, chopped
2 garlic cloves, minced
1 can (28 ounces) plum tomatoes, drained and chopped
1-1/2 cups dried lentils, soaked in cold water 1 hour, drained and rinsed*
1 tablespoon tomato paste
1-1/2 teaspoons dried thyme
6 cups beef broth
2 bay leaves

VINAIGRETTE
3/4 cup packed fresh basil
1/3 cup olive oil
2 tablespoons chopped fresh parsley
2 tablespoons red wine vinegar
    Salt and pepper

*Add 1 to 2 hours to cooking time if lentils are not soaked.

SLOW COOKER DIRECTIONS

1. Heat 2 tablespoons oil in large saucepan over medium heat. Add onion, celery and garlic; cook and stir 5 minutes. Stir in tomatoes, lentils, tomato paste and thyme. Combine lentil mixture, broth and bay leaves in 3-quart slow cooker.

2. Cover; cook on LOW 8 hours or on HIGH 4 hours or until lentils are soft.

3. Meanwhile, prepare vinaigrette. Combine basil, 1/3 cup oil, parsley and vinegar in blender or food processor. Blend until smooth. Stir vinaigrette into soup just before serving. Discard bay leaves. Season with salt and pepper.   *Makes 4 to 6 servings*

Variation: Place all soup ingredients except vinaigrette in slow cooker without precooking; mix well. Cover; cook on LOW 8-1/2 hours or on HIGH 4-1/2 hours.

Helpful Hint

Sprinkle chopped fresh herbs, grated citrus peel, sliced green onions or minced jalapeños over soup just before serving to enhance the flavor.

Two-Cheese Potato and Cauliflower Soup

Winter's Best Bean Soup

(pictured at right)

6 ounces bacon, diced
10 cups chicken broth
3 cans (15 ounces each) great northern beans,
    rinsed and drained
1 can (14-1/2 ounces) diced tomatoes
1 large onion, chopped
2 cups frozen sliced or diced carrots
2 teaspoons bottled minced garlic
1 fresh rosemary sprig *or* 1 teaspoon dried
    rosemary
1 teaspoon pepper

SLOW COOKER DIRECTIONS
1. Cook bacon in medium skillet over medium-high heat until just cooked; drain and transfer to 4-quart slow cooker. Add remaining ingredients.

2. Cover; cook on LOW 8 hours or until beans are tender. Remove rosemary sprig before serving.
Makes 8 to 10 servings

Serving Suggestion: Place slices of toasted Italian bread in bottom of individual soup bowls. Drizzle with olive oil. Pour soup over bread and serve.

Creamy Roasted Garlic & Potato Chowder

2 cups milk
1-1/2 cups water
1 tablespoon HERB-OX® chicken flavored
    bouillon
1 cup refrigerated diced potatoes
1/2 cup frozen whole kernel corn, thawed
1/4 cup light roasted garlic flavored cream cheese
1-1/4 cups instant mashed potato flakes
1/4 cup finely shredded Cheddar cheese
1/4 cup sliced green onions
1/4 cup crumbled HORMEL® fully cooked bacon
    or HORMEL® bacon bits

In saucepan, bring milk, water, bouillon and refrigerated potatoes to a boil. Reduce heat and simmer for 5 to 8 minutes or until potatoes are tender. Stir in corn, cream cheese and instant potato flakes. Heat over low heat until warmed through. Ladle chowder into bowls. Top with cheese, green onions and bacon. *Makes 4 servings*

Chicken Tortellini Soup

1 can (48 ounces) chicken broth
1 package (9 ounces) refrigerated cheese and
    spinach tortellini or three-cheese tortellini
1 package (about 6 ounces) refrigerated fully
    cooked chicken breast strips, cut into
    bite-size pieces
2 cups coarsely chopped baby spinach leaves
4 to 6 tablespoons grated Parmesan cheese
1 tablespoon chopped fresh chives *or*
    2 tablespoons sliced green onion

1. Bring chicken broth to a boil in large saucepan over high heat. Add tortellini. Reduce heat to medium; cook 5 minutes. Stir in chicken and spinach.

2. Reduce heat to low; cook 3 minutes or until chicken is hot. Sprinkle with Parmesan cheese and chives. *Makes 4 servings*

Beef, Barley & Onion Soup

2 pounds beef stew meat (1/2-inch cubes)
3 large carrots, cut into 1/2-inch-thick slices
2 large ribs celery, cut into 1/2-inch-thick slices
4 cans (14-1/2 ounces each) beef broth
1/2 teaspoon dried oregano leaves
1/2 teaspoon salt
1/4 teaspoon ground pepper
1/2 cup quick cooking barley
2 cups *French's*® French Fried Onions, divided

SLOW COOKER DIRECTIONS
1. Combine beef, carrots, celery, broth and seasonings in 4-quart slow cooker. Cover and cook on LOW setting for 7 hours (or on HIGH setting for 3-1/2 hours) until meat and vegetables are tender.

2. Stir in barley. Cover and cook on LOW setting for 1 hour (or on HIGH setting for 1/2 hour) until barley is tender. Stir in *1 cup* French Fried Onions. Spoon soup into serving bowls; sprinkle with remaining onions. *Makes 8 servings*

Note: Cook times vary depending on type of slow cooker used. Check manufacturer's recommendations for cooking beef and barley.

Thick and Creamy Succotash Soup

(pictured at right)

2 strips bacon
1 small onion, chopped
1 stalk celery, chopped
2 tablespoons all-purpose flour
3 cups chicken broth
1-1/2 cups frozen corn kernels
1 cup frozen baby lima beans, thawed
1 bay leaf
1/4 teaspoon salt
1/4 teaspoon pepper
1/4 teaspoon hot pepper sauce
1/2 cup whipping cream

1. Cook bacon in Dutch oven over medium heat until crisp and browned. Drain on paper towel. Crumble; set aside.

2. Add onion and celery to bacon drippings in Dutch oven; cook and stir 5 minutes or until tender. Stir in flour; cook to a thin paste. Stir in chicken broth. Bring to a boil; cook and stir until slightly thickened.

3. Add corn, beans, bacon, bay leaf, salt, pepper and hot pepper sauce. Reduce heat to low. Simmer 15 minutes. Stir in cream. Remove bay leaf before serving. *Makes 6 servings*

Tip: If prepared in advance, cover and refrigerate up to one day. To serve at your host's home, reheat over low heat. Or, wrap covered Dutch oven in several layers of aluminum foil and overwrap with thick towel or newspapers to keep finished dish warm when transporting.

Curried Turkey Noodle Soup

Nonstick cooking spray
3/4 pound turkey breast tenderloin, cut into bite-size pieces
5 cups water
2 packages (3 ounces each) chicken-flavored ramen noodles
1 tablespoon curry powder
1/8 teaspoon salt
1 cup sliced celery
1 apple, cored and chopped (1-1/2 cups)
1/4 cup dry roasted peanuts

1. Spray large nonstick saucepan with cooking spray; heat over medium-high heat. Add turkey; cook and stir 3 to 4 minutes or until no longer pink. Remove turkey to bowl; set aside.

2. Add water, flavor packets from noodles, curry powder and salt to saucepan. Bring to boil. Reduce heat and simmer, covered, 5 minutes.

3. Break up noodles; gently stir noodles and celery into saucepan. Bring mixture to a boil. Reduce heat and simmer, uncovered, 5 minutes.

4. Stir in turkey and apple; cook until heated through. Ladle into soup bowls. Sprinkle with peanuts. *Makes 5 servings*

Sausage and Chicken Gumbo

1 tablespoon canola oil
1 sweet red pepper, chopped
1 pound boneless skinless chicken thighs, trimmed and cut into 1-inch pieces
1 package (12 ounces) andouille or spicy chicken sausage, sliced 1/2 inch thick
1/2 cup chicken broth
1 can (28 ounces) crushed tomatoes with roasted garlic
1/4 cup finely chopped green onions
1 bay leaf
1/2 teaspoon dried basil
1/2 teaspoon pepper
1/4 to 1/2 teaspoon crushed red pepper flakes
6 lemon wedges (optional)

1. Heat oil in large saucepan. Add sweet pepper; cook and stir over medium-high heat 2 to 3 minutes. Add chicken; cook and stir about 2 minutes or until browned. Add sausage; cook and stir 2 minutes or until browned. Add broth; scrape up any browned bits from bottom of saucepan.

2. Add tomatoes, green onions, bay leaf, basil, pepper and red pepper flakes. Simmer 15 minutes. Remove and discard bay leaf. Garnish each serving with lemon wedge. *Makes 6 servings*

Zippy Beef Alphabet Soup with Parmesan Toasts

beef is not pink, breaking up into 3/4-inch crumbles. Season with 1/2 teaspoon salt and 1/4 teaspoon pepper.

2. Add water, broth, beans, tomatoes and pasta; bring to a boil. Reduce heat; cover and simmer 5 minutes. Stir in broccoli; return to a boil. Reduce heat; cover and simmer 3 to 5 minutes or until broccoli is crisp-tender and pasta is tender. Season with salt and pepper, as desired.

3. Meanwhile prepare Parmesan Toasts. Cut out shapes from bread slices with cookie cutters. Place on baking sheet sprayed with nonstick cooking spray. Brush cutouts lightly with oil and sprinkle evenly with cheese. Bake in 350°F oven 6 to 8 minutes or until lightly toasted.

4. Serve soup with toasts; sprinkle with additional cheese, if desired.   *Makes 4 servings*

Favorite recipe from **National Cattlemen's Beef Association on behalf of The Beef Checkoff**

Curried Vegetable-Rice Soup

(pictured on page 66)

    1 package (16 ounces) frozen Asian-blend
        vegetable medley, such as broccoli,
        cauliflower, sugar snap peas and sweet red
        peppers
    1 can (14-1/2 ounces) vegetable broth
3/4 cup uncooked instant brown rice
    2 teaspoons curry powder
1/2 teaspoon salt
1/2 teaspoon hot pepper sauce or to taste
    1 can (14 ounces) unsweetened coconut milk
    1 tablespoon lime juice

1. Combine vegetables and broth in large saucepan. Cover; bring to a boil over high heat. Stir in rice, curry powder, salt and hot pepper sauce; reduce heat to medium-low. Cover and simmer 8 minutes or until rice is tender, stirring once.

2. Stir in coconut milk; cook 3 minutes or until heated through. Remove from heat. Stir in lime juice. Ladle into bowls and serve immediately.
          Makes 4 servings

Zippy Beef Alphabet Soup with Parmesan Toasts

(pictured above)

    1 pound ground beef (95% lean)
1/2 teaspoon salt
1/4 teaspoon pepper
    2 cups water
    1 can (14 to 14-1/2 ounces) ready-to-serve
        beef broth
    1 can (15-1/2 ounces) Great Northern beans,
        undrained
    1 can (14-1/2 ounces) Italian-style diced
        tomatoes, undrained
    1 cup uncooked alphabet pasta
    2 cups small broccoli florets
        Salt and pepper

PARMESAN TOASTS:
    3 slices whole wheat bread
        Olive oil for brushing
    2 tablespoons grated or shredded Parmesan
        cheese

1. Heat oven to 350°F. Brown ground beef in stockpot over medium heat 8 to 10 minutes or until

Kielbasa & Chicken Gumbo

(pictured below)

6 slices bacon
1 pound BOB EVANS® Kielbasa Sausage, cut
    into 1-inch pieces
1/2 pound boneless skinless chicken breasts, cut
    into 1-inch chunks
1/4 cup all-purpose flour
1 can (12 ounces) tomato juice
1 cup water
1 can (28 ounces) whole tomatoes, undrained
2 cubes chicken bouillon
1 can (8 ounces) tomato sauce
1-1/2 cups sliced fresh okra *or* 1 package
    (10 ounces) frozen cut okra, thawed
1 medium onion, coarsely chopped
1 medium green bell pepper, coarsely chopped
2 bay leaves
1/2 teaspoon salt
1/2 teaspoon ground red pepper
1/8 teaspoon ground allspice
1 pound uncooked medium shrimp, peeled and
    deveined
Hot cooked rice (optional)

Cook bacon in large Dutch oven over medium-high heat until crisp. Remove bacon; drain and crumble on paper towel. Set aside. Cook and stir kielbasa and chicken in drippings over medium heat until chicken is lightly browned. Remove kielbasa and chicken; set aside. Drain off all but 3 tablespoons drippings from Dutch oven. Add flour to drippings; cook over medium heat 12 to 15 minutes or until a reddish-brown roux forms, stirring constantly. Gradually stir in tomato juice and water until smooth. Add tomatoes with juice and bouillon, stirring well to break up tomatoes. Add reserved kielbasa, chicken, tomato sauce, okra, onion, green pepper, bay leaves, salt, red pepper and allspice; mix well. Bring to a boil over high heat. Reduce heat to low; simmer, covered, 1 hour, stirring occasionally. Add shrimp and simmer, covered, 10 minutes more or until shrimp turn pink and opaque. Remove and discard bay leaves. Stir in reserved bacon. Serve hot over rice, if desired. Refrigerate leftovers.   *Makes 10 servings*

Kielbasa & Chicken Gumbo

Chile Pepper Corn Cream Chowder

(pictured at right)

2 tablespoons butter
1 cup chopped onion
1/2 cup thinly sliced celery
1 package (16 ounces) frozen corn
12 ounces red potatoes, diced
4 cups milk
2 Anaheim or poblano chile peppers, seeded and diced*
6 ounces cream cheese, cubed
2 teaspoons salt
3/4 teaspoon pepper

Chile peppers can sting and irritate the skin, so wear rubber gloves when handling and do not touch eyes.

Melt butter in large saucepan over medium-high heat. Add onion and celery. Cook and stir 5 minutes or until onion is translucent. Add corn, potatoes, milk and chile peppers. Bring to a boil. Reduce heat; cover and simmer 10 to 15 minutes or until potatoes are tender. Remove from heat. Add cream cheese, salt and pepper. Stir until cheese has melted.

Makes 4 to 6 servings

Minute Minestrone

1 tablespoon vegetable oil
1 medium onion, chopped
1 clove garlic, minced
1 can (46 ounces) vegetable juice
1/2 teaspoon Italian seasoning (more or less to taste)
1 can (15 ounces) VEG•ALL® Original Mixed Vegetables, undrained
1 can (14.5 ounces) ALLENS® Cut Italian Green Beans, undrained
1 can (15.5 ounces) TRAPPEY'S® Great Northern Beans, drained and rinsed
3/4 cup uncooked pasta shells, cooked according to package instructions
1 can (13.5 ounces) POPEYE® Chopped Spinach, drained
Grated Parmesan cheese

In large pan, heat vegetable oil. Add onion and garlic; heat 2 minutes. Stir in vegetable juice and Italian seasoning; bring to a boil. Cover, reduce heat, and simmer 10 minutes. Add VEG•ALL®, beans, pasta, and spinach. Cover; simmer 10 minutes. Sprinkle with cheese before serving.

Makes 8 servings

Vegetable and Red Lentil Soup

1 can (14-1/2 ounces) vegetable broth
1 can (14-1/2 ounces) diced tomatoes
2 medium zucchini or yellow summer squash (or 1 of each), diced
1 sweet red or yellow pepper, diced
1/2 cup thinly sliced carrots
1/2 cup red lentils, rinsed and sorted*
1/2 teaspoon salt
1/2 teaspoon sugar
1/4 teaspoon pepper
2 tablespoons chopped fresh basil or thyme
1/2 cup croutons or shredded cheese

If you have difficulty finding red lentils, substitute brown lentils instead.

SLOW COOKER DIRECTIONS

Combine broth, tomatoes, zucchini, sweet pepper, carrots, lentils, salt, sugar and pepper in 3-quart slow cooker. Cover; cook on LOW 8 hours or on HIGH 4 hours or until lentils and vegetables are tender. Ladle into shallow bowls; top with basil and croutons.

Makes 4 servings

Chilled Avocado Soup

3 small onion slices, each 1/4 inch thick, divided
1 can (14-1/2 ounces) chicken broth
1/2 cup plain yogurt
1 tablespoon plus 1-1/2 teaspoons lemon juice
1 large ripe avocado, halved and pitted
3 to 5 drops hot pepper sauce
Salt
White pepper
1/4 cup finely chopped tomato
1/4 cup finely chopped cucumber
Fresh cilantro sprigs

1. Place 1 onion slice, broth, yogurt and lemon juice in blender or food processor; process until well blended. Remove pulp from avocado; spoon into blender. Process until smooth. Pour into bowl. Add hot pepper sauce, salt and pepper. Finely chop remaining 2 onion slices; add to soup. Stir in tomato and cucumber.

2. Cover and refrigerate 2 hours or up to 24 hours. Serve cold. Garnish with cilantro. *Makes 6 servings*

Portuguese Potato & Greens Soup

(pictured at right)

2 tablespoons olive oil
1 cup chopped onion
1 cup chopped carrots
2 garlic cloves, minced
1 pound new red potatoes, unpeeled, cut
    into 1-inch pieces
2 cups water
1 can (14-1/2 ounces) chicken broth
1/4 teaspoon salt
1/2 pound chorizo sausage, casings removed
1/2 pound kale
    Salt and pepper

1. Heat oil in large saucepan over medium heat. Add onion, carrots and garlic; cook and stir 5 to 6 minutes or until lightly browned. Add potatoes, water, chicken broth and 1/4 teaspoon salt. Bring to a boil. Reduce heat to low. Cover; simmer 10 to 15 minutes or until potatoes are tender. Cool slightly.

2. Meanwhile, heat large nonstick skillet over medium heat. Crumble chorizo into skillet. Cook and stir 5 to 6 minutes or until sausage is cooked through. Drain sausage on paper towels.

3. Wash kale; remove tough stems. Slice into thin shreds.

4. Add sausage and kale; cook, uncovered, 4 to 5 minutes over medium heat until heated through. Kale should be bright green and slightly crunchy. Season with salt and pepper. *Makes 4 servings*

Cheesy Mexican Soup

(pictured on page 66)

1 cup chopped onion
1 tablespoon vegetable oil
2 cups milk
1 can (about 14 ounces) chicken broth
1 container (13 ounces) ORTEGA® Salsa
    & Cheese Bowl
1 can (7 ounces) ORTEGA Diced Green Chiles
4 ORTEGA Taco Shells, crushed
1/4 cup chopped cilantro

COOK and stir onion in oil in large saucepan over medium-high heat for 4 to 6 minutes until tender. Reduce heat to medium-low.

STIR in milk, chicken broth, Salsa & Cheese and green chiles; cook for 5 to 7 minutes until hot, stirring frequently.

MICROWAVE crushed taco shells on HIGH (100%) 30 to 45 seconds. Cool. Serve soup sprinkled with cilantro and crushed taco shells.

Makes 8 servings

Tip: If you can't find a 7-ounce can of ORTEGA® Diced Green Chiles, use two 4-ounce cans.

Corn & Red Pepper Soup

2 tablespoons butter
2 cups coarsely chopped sweet red peppers
1 medium onion, thinly sliced
1 can (14-1/2 ounces) chicken broth
1 package (10 ounces) frozen corn*
1/2 teaspoon ground cumin
1/2 cup sour cream
    Salt
    White pepper

Cut raw kernels from 4 large ears of yellow or white corn to substitute for frozen corn.

1. Melt butter in 3-quart saucepan over medium heat. Add sweet peppers and onion; cook until tender. Add broth, corn and cumin.

2. Bring to a boil over high heat. Reduce heat to low. Cover and simmer 20 minutes or until corn is tender. Cool slightly.

3. Working in batches, process soup into blender or food processor until smooth. Pour into sieve set over bowl; press mixture with rubber spatula to extract all liquid. Discard pulp.** Return liquid to pan; whisk in sour cream until evenly blended. Season with salt and white pepper. Cook over low heat until heated through; do not boil.

Makes 4 servings

**Omit straining, if desired. Return processed soup to pan; whisk in sour cream. Proceed as above.

Greek Lemon and Rice Soup

(pictured at right)

> 2 tablespoons butter
> 1/3 cup minced green onions
> 6 cups chicken broth
> 2/3 cup uncooked long grain white rice
> 4 eggs
>   Juice of 1 lemon
> 1/8 teaspoon white pepper
>   Fresh mint
>   Lemon peel

1. Melt butter in 3-quart saucepan over medium heat. Add green onions. Cook and stir about 3 minutes or until green onions are tender.

2. Stir in broth and rice. Bring to a boil over medium-high heat. Reduce heat to low; simmer, covered, 20 to 25 minutes or until rice is tender.

3. Beat eggs in medium bowl with wire whisk until well beaten. Add lemon juice and 1/2 cup broth mixture to bowl. Gradually pour egg mixture into broth mixture in saucepan, stirring constantly. Cook and stir over low heat 2 to 3 minutes or until broth mixture thickens enough to lightly coat spoon. *Do not boil.*

4. Stir in pepper. Garnish with mint and lemon peel.

Makes 6 to 8 servings

Curried Sweet Potato Soup

> 1 tablespoon olive oil
> 1 small onion, chopped
> 1 tablespoon finely chopped fresh ginger
> 1 teaspoon curry powder
> 1 teaspoon ground cinnamon
> 1/4 teaspoon ground cumin
> 1 pinch cayenne pepper
> 1 tablespoon sugar
> 1 quart ALLENS® Chicken Broth
> 3 cans (15 ounces each) PRINCELLA® or
>   SUGARY SAM® Cut Sweet Potatoes, drained
>   Salt and pepper to taste
> 1 tablespoon fresh lime juice
> 2 tablespoons plain yogurt
> 1 tablespoon chopped fresh cilantro

In large saucepan, add olive oil; sauté onion and ginger over medium heat until soft. Add curry powder, cinnamon, cumin and cayenne pepper; cook for 1 minute. Add sugar, chicken broth, and

sweet potatoes to spice mixture; cook until heated through. Working in batches, purée mixture in a blender until smooth. Season to taste with salt and pepper. Stir in lime juice just before serving. Top with yogurt and chopped cilantro.

Makes 4 servings

Creamy Roasted Poblano Soup

> 6 large poblano chile peppers
> 1 tablespoon olive oil
> 3/4 cup chopped onion
> 1/2 cup thinly sliced celery
> 1/2 cup thinly sliced carrots
> 1 garlic clove, minced
> 2 cans (14-1/2 ounces each) chicken broth
> 1 package (8 ounces) cream cheese, cubed
>   Salt

1. Preheat oven to 350°F. Line baking sheet or broiler pan with foil. Place whole chile peppers on foil; broil 5 to 6 inches from heat source 16 minutes or until blistered and beginning to char, turning occasionally. Place peppers in medium bowl; cover bowl with plastic wrap. Let stand 20 to 30 minutes.

2. Heat oil in large saucepan over medium-high heat. Add onion, celery, carrots and garlic. Cook and stir 4 minutes or until onions are translucent. Add broth. Increase heat to high; bring to a boil. Reduce heat. Cover; simmer 12 minutes or until celery is tender. Set aside.

3. Remove stems, seeds and skins from broiled peppers. Briefly run peppers under running water to help remove skins and seeds, if necessary. (This removes some smoky flavor, so work quickly.) Add peppers to broth.

4. Working in 1-cup batches, process broth mixture and cream cheese in food processor or blender until smooth. Return to saucepan. Heat over medium heat 2 to 3 minutes or until heated through. Season with salt.

Makes 4 servings

Sandwiches

Curried Chicken Salad Sandwiches

(pictured at left)

1 (2- to 3-pound) whole roasted chicken*
1-1/4 cups halved seedless red grapes
1/2 cup diced Granny Smith apple
1/2 cup sliced almonds, toasted
1/3 cup golden raisins
1/3 cup dried cranberries
1/4 cup unsweetened shredded coconut
1/4 cup finely diced red onion
1 stalk celery, diced
3/4 cup mayonnaise
1 tablespoon curry powder
1 tablespoon lime juice
2 teaspoons honey
Salt and pepper
10 croissants
10 leaves red leaf lettuce
20 slices tomato

You can substitute 3-1/2 cups diced cooked chicken.

1. Remove skin and bones from chicken; dice meat. Combine chicken, grapes, apple, almonds, raisins, cranberries, coconut, onion and celery in large bowl; set aside.

2. Combine mayonnaise, curry powder, lime juice and honey in medium bowl. Add mayonnaise mixture to chicken mixture; stir until well blended. Season with salt and pepper.

3. Cut croissants in half horizontally. For each sandwich, line bottom half of 1 croissant with 1 leaf lettuce; top with about 3/4 cup chicken salad and 2 slices tomato. Cover with top half of croissant.   *Makes 10 sandwiches*

Clockwise from top left: *Stromboli Sticks (p. 102), Curried Chicken Salad Sandwich, Philadelphia Hero (p. 97), Spinach & Roasted Pepper Panini (p. 96)*

Fiesta Chicken Sandwich

(pictured at right)

    Olive oil
1/2 medium onion, sliced
1/2 medium sweet red pepper, sliced
    6 ounces chicken tenders, cut in half lengthwise
       and widthwise
1/2 cup guacamole
    6 slices (1 ounce each) pepper jack cheese
    1 package (10 ounces) 8-inch mini pizza crusts

1. Heat 1 tablespoon oil in large nonstick skillet over medium-high heat. Add onion and sweet pepper; cook and stir 3 to 4 minutes or until crisp-tender. Remove vegetables with slotted spoon; set aside. Add chicken to skillet; cook and stir 4 minutes or until chicken is cooked through. Remove from skillet; wipe out skillet with paper towel.

2. Layer guacamole, chicken, vegetables and cheese evenly on one pizza crust; top with remaining pizza crust. Brush outsides of sandwich lightly with oil.

3. Heat same skillet over medium heat. Add sandwich; cook 4 to 5 minutes per side or until cheese melts and sandwich is golden brown. Cut into wedges to serve.   *Makes 2 servings*

Barbecued Beef Sandwiches

    1 boneless beef chuck shoulder roast (about
       3 pounds)
    2 cups ketchup
    1 medium onion, chopped
1/4 cup cider vinegar
1/4 cup dark molasses
    2 tablespoons Worcestershire sauce
    2 garlic cloves, minced
1/2 teaspoon salt
1/2 teaspoon dry mustard
1/2 teaspoon pepper
1/4 teaspoon garlic powder
1/4 teaspoon crushed red pepper flakes
    Sesame seed buns, split

SLOW COOKER DIRECTIONS

1. Cut roast in half; place in 4-quart slow cooker. Combine remaining ingredients, except buns in large bowl. Pour sauce mixture over roast. Cover; cook on LOW 8 to 10 hours or on HIGH 4 to 5 hours.

2. Remove roast from sauce; cool. Trim and discard excess fat from beef. Shred meat using two forks.

3. Let sauce stand 5 minutes to allow fat to rise. Skim off fat.

4. Return shredded meat to slow cooker. Stir meat to evenly coat with sauce. Adjust seasonings. Cover; cook 15 to 30 minutes or until heated through.

5. Spoon filling into sandwich buns and top with additional sauce, if desired.   *Makes 12 servings*

Sausage & Peppers Subs with Creamy Italian Spread

1/2 cup HELLMANN'S® or BEST FOODS® Real
    Mayonnaise
    2 tablespoons grated Parmesan cheese
    1 tablespoon finely chopped fresh basil leaves
    1 tablespoon white wine vinegar, apple cider
       vinegar or white balsamic vinegar
    1 clove garlic, finely chopped
    1 pound sweet or hot Italian sausage links
    2 large red or orange bell peppers, cut into
       1-inch pieces
    1 large sweet onion, cut into 1-inch pieces
    4 medium hoagie rolls, split

1. In small bowl, combine Hellmann's or Best Foods Real Mayonnaise, cheese, basil, vinegar and garlic. Reserve 1/4 cup.

2. On skewers, thread sausage. On separate skewers, alternately thread red peppers and onion. Grill or broil sausage and vegetables, brushing vegetables with remaining mayonnaise mixture, until sausage is done and vegetables are tender.

3. Meanwhile, brush reserved mayonnaise mixture on both sides of rolls. Grill or broil, turning once, until toasted. To serve, arrange cooked sausage and vegetable skewers on grilled rolls; remove skewers.

Makes 4 servings

Fiesta Chicken Sandwich

Barbecue Steak Sandwiches with Smothered Onions

(pictured at right)

1 tablespoon vegetable oil
8 to 12 slices (about 1 pound) minute steaks
1 large Vidalia or other sweet onion, sliced
3/4 cup *CATTLEMEN'S®* Authentic Smoke House Barbecue Sauce
1/4 cup *French's®* Worcestershire Sauce or *Frank's® RedHot®* Cayenne Pepper Sauce
8 slices Jack or American cheese
4 sub or hero rolls, split

1. Heat oil in large nonstick skillet until very hot. Cook steaks 5 minutes until browned, turning once; remove from skillet.

2. Sauté onion in same skillet until tender. Add barbecue sauce and Worcestershire. Heat through.

3. Spoon saucy onions on bottoms of rolls, dividing evenly. Arrange 2 or 3 pieces steak on each sandwich and top with 2 slices cheese. Close rolls.

Makes 4 servings

Tip: Substitute 1 pound deli roast beef but do not cook meat.

Chipotle Chicken Quesadillas

1 package (8 ounces) cream cheese, softened
1 cup (4 ounces) shredded Mexican blend cheese
1 tablespoon minced chipotle peppers in adobo sauce
5 (10-inch) burrito-size flour tortillas
5 cups shredded cooked chicken (about 1-1/4 pounds)
Nonstick cooking spray
Guacamole, sour cream and salsa

1. Combine cheeses and chipotle peppers in large bowl.

2. Spread 1/3 cup cream cheese mixture over half of tortilla. Top with about 1 cup chicken. Fold over tortilla. Repeat with remaining tortillas.

3. Heat large nonstick skillet over medium-high heat. Spray outside surface of each tortilla with nonstick cooking spray. Cook each tortilla 4 to 6 minutes or until lightly browned, turning once during cooking.

4. Cut into wedges to serve. Serve with guacamole, sour cream and salsa. *Makes 5 servings*

Tip: Chipotle peppers in adobo sauce can be found in small cans in the Mexican food section of your grocery store.

Italian Sausage & Pepper Pita Wraps

1 cup marinara sauce
1/2 teaspoon dried basil
1/4 teaspoon dried oregano
4 (6-inch) hot or mild Italian sausages (about 1-1/4 pounds)
1 sweet green pepper, cut lengthwise into quarters
1 onion, cut into thick slices
4 rounds pita bread
1 tablespoon olive oil
1 cup (4 ounces) shredded Italian blend cheese or mozzarella cheese

1. Prepare grill for direct cooking.

2. Combine marinara sauce, basil and oregano in small saucepan. Simmer over medium-low heat until heated through, about 5 minutes; keep warm.

3. Place sausage links on grid over medium heat; arrange sweet pepper and onion around sausages. Grill, covered, 7 minutes. Turn sausages and vegetables; grill 8 to 9 minutes or until sausages are cooked through and vegetables are crisp-tender.

4. Brush pita rounds on one side with oil. Place on grid; grill until soft, turning once.

5. Cut sausages in half lengthwise. Cut sweet pepper into strips and separate onion slices into rings. Divide sausages, sweet pepper and onion among pitas. Top with sauce and cheese. Fold pitas in half.

Makes 4 servings

Barbecue Steak Sandwich with Smothered Onions

Cuban Sandwich

Spinach & Roasted Pepper Panini

(pictured on page 90)

1 loaf (12 ounces) focaccia
1-1/2 cups spinach leaves
1 jar (about 7 ounces) roasted red peppers, drained
4 ounces fontina cheese, thinly sliced
3/4 cup thinly sliced red onion
Olive oil

1. Place focaccia on cutting board; cut in half horizontally. Layer bottom half with spinach, peppers, cheese and onion. Cover with top half of focaccia. Brush outsides of sandwich very lightly with olive oil. Cut sandwich into 4 equal pieces.

2. Heat large nonstick skillet over medium heat. Add sandwiches; press down lightly with spatula. Cook sandwiches 4 to 5 minutes per side or until cheese melts and sandwiches are golden brown.

Makes 4 servings

Note: Focaccia can be found in the bakery section of most supermarkets. It is often available in different flavors, such as tomato, herb, cheese or onion.

Cuban Sandwiches

(pictured above)

6 tablespoons *French's® Classic Yellow® Mustard* or *French's® Sweet 'n Zesty Mustard*
4 Portuguese or Kaiser rolls, split in half
8 ounces thinly sliced ham
8 ounces thinly sliced deli roast pork
8 ounces sandwich-style dill pickles
4 ounces thinly sliced Swiss or Muenster cheese

1. Spread mustard on cut sides of rolls. Layer ham, pork, pickles and cheese on bottoms of rolls. Cover with top halves of rolls. With bottom of a heavy skillet, press sandwiches firmly down on work surface to compress bread and filling.

2. Preheat an electric grill pan for 5 minutes. Place sandwiches on pan and close cover. Cook 6 minutes, turning halfway during cooking. Cut in half and serve hot. *Makes 4 servings*

Tip: If you don't have an electric grill pan, use a nonstick skillet to cook sandwiches. Place a heavy skillet on top of sandwiches to press down during cooking.

Spicy Chicken Stromboli

1 cup broccoli florets
1 can (10 ounces) diced chicken
1-1/2 cups (6 ounces) shredded Monterey Jack cheese with jalapeño peppers
1/4 cup chunky salsa
2 green onions, chopped
1 can (10 ounces) refrigerated pizza dough

1. Preheat oven to 400°F. Coarsely chop broccoli. Combine broccoli, chicken, cheese, salsa and green onions in small bowl.

2. Unroll pizza dough. Pat into 15×10-inch rectangle. Sprinkle broccoli mixture evenly over top. Starting with long side, tightly roll up jelly-roll style. Pinch seam to seal. Place on baking sheet, seam side down.

3. Bake 15 to 20 minutes or until golden brown. Transfer to wire rack to cool slightly. Slice and serve warm. *Makes 6 servings*

Serving Suggestion: Serve with salsa on the side for dipping or pour salsa on top of slices for a boost of added flavor.

BelGioioso® Asiago and Sweet Pepper Sandwiches

(pictured below)

2 tablespoons olive oil
1 red bell pepper, sliced into strips
1 yellow bell pepper, sliced into strips
1 medium onion, thinly sliced
1 teaspoon dried thyme
  Salt and pepper
4 ounces BELGIOIOSO® Asiago Cheese, thinly
  sliced
4 crusty Italian sandwich rolls, sliced open
  lengthwise

Heat olive oil in large skillet. Add red and yellow bell peppers and cook over medium heat about 6 minutes. Add onion and cook until vegetables are softened. Stir in thyme. Salt and pepper to taste.

Layer BelGioioso Asiago Cheese on bottom half of rolls and top with vegetable mixture. Serve immediately. *Makes 4 servings*

Philadelphia Heroes

(pictured on page 90)

1 package (approximately 1 pound)
  JOHNSONVILLE® Italian Sausage
  Links, casings removed or 1 package
  JOHNSONVILLE® Italian Ground Sausage,
  browned and drained
2 teaspoons olive oil
1 medium onion, sliced
3/4 cup red pepper, sliced
3/4 cup green pepper, sliced
1 cup Italian-style tomato sauce
6 hoagie buns, split
1-1/2 cups (6 ounces) shredded cheddar cheese

Heat oil in large saucepan. Add onion, red pepper and green pepper. Cook 2 to 3 minutes or until vegetables are crisp-tender. Add cooked sausage and tomato sauce; cook 2 to 3 minutes or until hot.

Spoon sausage mixture into hoagie buns; top with cheese. Broil 1 to 2 minutes or until cheese is melted. If desired, top with pepperoncini and black olives. *Makes 8 servings*

BelGioioso® Asiago and Sweet Pepper Sandwich

Chicken & Spinach Muffuletta

(pictured at right)

>   6 boneless skinless chicken breasts
>   Salt and pepper
>   1 tablespoon olive oil
> 1/4 cup prepared pesto
> 1/4 cup chopped pitted black olives
> 1/4 cup chopped pitted green olives
>   1 round loaf (16 ounces) Hawaiian or French
>   bread
>   2 cups spinach leaves
>   4 ounces sliced mozzarella cheese

1. Season chicken with salt and pepper. Heat oil in large skillet over medium heat. Add chicken; cook 4 minutes on each side or until no longer pink in center. Cut chicken into strips.

2. Combine pesto and olives in small bowl. Cut bread in half horizontally. Spread bottom half of bread with pesto mixture. Top with spinach, chicken strips, cheese and top half of bread. Cut into wedges. *Makes 6 servings*

Apple Monte Cristos

>   4 ounces Gouda cheese, shredded
>   1 ounce cream cheese, softened
>   2 teaspoons honey
> 1/2 teaspoon ground cinnamon
>   4 slices cinnamon raisin bread
>   1 small apple, cored and thinly sliced
> 1/4 cup milk
>   1 egg, beaten
>   1 tablespoon butter
>   Powdered sugar

1. Combine Gouda cheese, cream cheese, honey and cinnamon in small bowl; stir until well blended. Spread cheese mixture evenly on all bread slices. Layer apple slices evenly over cheese on 2 bread slices; top with remaining bread slices.

2. Combine milk and egg in shallow bowl; stir until well blended. Dip sandwiches in egg mixture, turning to coat well.

3. Melt butter in large nonstick skillet over medium heat. Add sandwiches; cook 4 to 5 minutes per side or until cheese melts and sandwiches are golden brown. Sprinkle with powdered sugar. *Makes 2 sandwiches*

Ham and Cheese Strudels with Mustard Sauce

>   2 cups (12 ounces) diced HORMEL®
>   CURE 81® ham
>   1 cup shredded Swiss cheese
>   1 cup sliced fresh mushrooms
>   1 egg, beaten
> 1/4 cup chopped green onions
>   8 sheets frozen phyllo dough, thawed
> 1/2 cup butter or margarine, melted
>   Mustard Sauce (recipe follows)

Heat oven to 350°F. In bowl, combine ham, cheese, mushrooms, egg and green onion. Brush 1 sheet phyllo dough with butter. Keep remaining phyllo sheets covered with a dampened towel to prevent drying. To assemble, fold phyllo sheet in half widthwise; brush with butter. Fold in half widthwise again; brush with butter. Place 1/3 cup ham mixture in center of sheet. Fold long sides up and over filling, overlapping slightly. Fold into thirds from narrow edge. Place strudel, seam side down, on baking sheet. Cover with dampened towel to prevent drying. Repeat with remaining phyllo sheets, ham mixture and butter. Bake 20 minutes or until golden brown. Serve with Mustard Sauce. *Makes 8 servings*

Mustard Sauce: In saucepan, combine 1/2 cup sour cream, 1/2 cup mayonnaise or salad dressing, 2 tablespoons dry mustard and 1/2 teaspoon sugar. Heat over low heat, stirring occasionally, until warm.

Grilled Muffuletta

>   4 round hard rolls, split
>   2 tablespoons vinaigrette salad dressing
> 1/3 cup olive salad or tapenade
>   6 ounces *each* thinly sliced Genoa salami, ham
>   and provolone cheese
>   Olive oil

Brush cut sides of rolls with salad dressing. Layer half of olive salad, salami, ham, cheese and remaining olive salad on roll bottoms; close sandwiches with roll tops. Brush outsides of rolls lightly with olive oil. Heat large grill pan over medium heat. Add sandwiches; press down lightly with spatula. Cook 4 to 5 minutes per side or until cheese melts and sandwiches are golden brown. *Makes 4 sandwiches*

Chicken & Spinach Muffuletta

Grilled Cobb Salad Sandwiches

(pictured at right)

    1/2 medium avocado
      1 green onion, chopped
    1/2 teaspoon lemon juice
      2 Kaiser rolls, split
      4 ounces thinly sliced deli chicken or turkey
      4 slices cooked bacon
      1 hard-cooked egg, sliced
      2 slices (1 ounce each) Cheddar cheese
      2 ounces blue cheese
        Tomato slices (optional)
        Olive oil

1. Mash avocado in small bowl; stir in green onion and lemon juice. Season to taste with salt and pepper. Spread avocado mixture on cut sides of roll tops. Layer roll bottoms with remaining ingredients except olive oil; close sandwiches with roll tops. Brush outsides of sandwiches lightly with olive oil.

2. Heat large nonstick skillet over medium heat. Add sandwiches; cook 4 to 5 minutes per side or until cheese melts and sandwiches are golden brown.
Makes 2 sandwiches

Cheeseburgers with Spicy Ranch Sauce

      2 pounds ground beef
      8 slices American cheese
      8 hamburger buns split
        Romaine lettuce leaves
        Tomato slices

SPICY RANCH SAUCE:
    1/2 cup prepared ranch salad dressing
      2 tablespoons fresh chopped cilantro
      2 tablespoons canned, chopped green chilies
      1 tablespoon green jalapeño hot pepper sauce

1. Combine Spicy Ranch Sauce ingredients in medium bowl; cover and refrigerate until ready to use.

2. Lightly shape ground beef into eight 1/2-inch thick patties. Place patties on grid over medium, ash-covered coals. Grill, uncovered, 11 to 13 minutes to medium (160°F) doneness, until no longer pink in center and juices show no pink color, turning occasionally. About 1 minute before burgers are done, top with cheese slices.

3. Line bottom of each bun with lettuce and tomato, as desired; top with burger. Spoon sauce evenly over burgers. Close sandwiches.
Makes 4 servings

Favorite recipe from **National Cattlemen's Beef Association on behalf of The Beef Checkoff**

Grilled Turkey and Brie Cheese Sandwiches

      3 tablespoons *French's®* Spicy Brown Mustard
      1 tablespoon pancake syrup
      1 teaspoon prepared horseradish
      8 (7×6-inch) slices sourdough bread, cut
          1/2 inch thick
    1/2 pound sliced smoked turkey breast
      5 ounces Brie cheese, rind removed and sliced
      1 to 2 tablespoons butter or margarine

1. Combine mustard, syrup and horseradish. Spread evenly onto 4 slices of bread. Layer turkey and cheese on top. Cover with remaining bread slices.

2. Melt butter in large nonstick skillet or griddle. Cook sandwiches, two at a time, about 3 minutes on each side or until golden brown. Cut in half to serve.
Makes 4 sandwiches

Monterey Ranch Ham Sandwiches

      4 (1/2-inch-thick) slices HORMEL®
          CURE 81® ham
    1/4 cup ranch salad dressing
      4 Kaiser rolls, split
      4 (1-ounce) slices Monterey Jack cheese
      8 slices HORMEL® BLACK LABEL® bacon, cooked
    1/2 cup shredded lettuce
      1 tomato, thinly sliced

Broil ham slices 6 inches from heat source 5 to 6 minutes, turning once until golden brown. Spread dressing on cut sides of rolls. Layer ham, cheese, 2 bacon strips, lettuce and tomato slices on roll bottom. Cover with roll top.
Makes 4 servings

Grilled Cobb Salad Sandwich

Turkey and Sharp Cheddar Panini with Cranberry Mayo

(pictured at right)

1/3 cup mayonnaise
1/4 cup dried cranberries
2 tablespoons Dijon mustard
2 tablespoons milk
1/4 to 1/2 teaspoon ground cumin
1 loaf (10 inches) Italian bread
6 ounces smoked deli sliced turkey
2 ounces sharp Cheddar cheese, thinly sliced
1 tablespoon butter

1. Place mayonnaise, cranberries, mustard, milk and cumin in food processor. Cover and process until almost smooth, scraping sides frequently. Cut bread in half horizontally. Spread mayonnaise mixture evenly over cut sides of bread. Layer turkey and cheese on bottom of bread; close sandwich with top of bread.

2. Melt butter in large nonstick skillet over medium heat. Add sandwich; press down lightly with spatula. Cook sandwich 4 to 5 minutes per side or until cheese melts and sandwich is golden brown.

Makes 2 to 4 servings

Stromboli Sticks

(pictured on page 90)

1 package (13.8 ounces) refrigerated pizza crust dough
10 mozzarella cheese sticks
30 thin slices pepperoni
1 jar (1 pound 10 ounces) RAGÚ® Old World Style® Pasta Sauce, heated

1. Preheat oven to 425°F. Grease baking sheet; set aside.

2. Roll pizza dough into 13×10-inch rectangle. Cut in half crosswise, then cut each half into 5 strips.

3. Arrange 1 cheese stick on each strip of pizza dough, then top with 3 slices pepperoni. Fold edges over, sealing tightly.

4. Arrange stromboli sticks on prepared baking sheet, seam side down. Bake 15 minutes or until golden. Serve with Pasta Sauce, heated, for dipping.

Makes 10 sticks

New Orleans Po'Boy Fish Sandwiches

1 cup LAWRY'S® Lemon Pepper Marinade with Lemon Juice
1-1/2 pounds flounder or tilapia fillets
1/4 cup HELLMANN'S® or BEST FOODS® Real Mayonnaise
1/2 cup plain dry bread crumbs
Vegetable oil for frying
4 hoagie or hot dog rolls, split

1. Pour 3/4 cup Lawry's Lemon Pepper Marinade with Lemon Juice over fillets in a large nonaluminum baking dish or plastic bag and turn to coat. Cover, or close bag, and marinate in refrigerator about 30 minutes. Combine remaining 1/4 cup marinade with mayonnaise; set aside.

2. Place bread crumbs in a shallow pie plate. Remove fillets from marinade, discarding marinade. Dip fish in crumbs to coat both sides evenly. Heat 1/4-inch oil in a large skillet over medium-high heat and cook fillets, in batches, until golden brown and fish flakes with a fork, turning once. Drain on paper towels.

3. Evenly spread reserved mayonnaise mixture on both cut-sides of rolls. Top with fillets, thinly sliced tomatoes, shredded lettuce, then tops of rolls.

Makes 4 servings

Bacon & Tomato Melts

4 slices crisp-cooked bacon
4 slices (1 ounce each) Cheddar cheese
1 tomato, sliced
4 slices whole wheat bread
Butter, melted

1. Layer 2 slices bacon, 2 slices cheese and sliced tomato each on 2 bread slices; top with remaining bread slices. Brush outsides of sandwiches with butter.

2. Heat large grill pan or skillet over medium heat. Add sandwiches; press down lightly with spatula. Cook sandwiches 4 to 5 minutes per side or until cheese melts and sandwiches are golden brown.

Makes 2 sandwiches

Turkey and Sharp Cheddar Panini with Cranberry Mayo

Mexican-Style Shredded Beef

3. Let cooking liquid stand 5 minutes to allow fat to rise. Skim off fat. Blend cornstarch and water until smooth. Whisk into liquid in slow cooker. Cook, uncovered, 15 minutes on HIGH until thickened. Return beef to slow cooker. Cover and cook 15 minutes or until heated through. Adjust seasonings. Serve in taco shells. Leftover beef may be refrigerated up to 3 days or frozen up to 3 months. *Makes 5 cups filling*

Classic Italian Burgers

  1-1/2 pounds lean ground beef
    1/4 cup WISH-BONE® Italian Dressing
    1/4 cup finely chopped green onions
      2 tablespoons grated Parmesan cheese
      2 large cloves garlic, finely chopped
      4 hamburger buns
      4 slices mozzarella or provolone cheese
        (optional)
        Lettuce (optional)
        Tomato slices (optional)

In medium bowl, combine ground beef, Wish-Bone Italian Dressing, green onions, Parmesan cheese and garlic; shape into four 3/4-inch-thick patties. Grill 13 minutes or until desired doneness, turning once. Serve on buns with mozzarella cheese, lettuce and tomato. *Makes 4 servings*

Mexican-Style Shredded Beef

(pictured above)

    1 boneless beef chuck shoulder roast (about
      3 pounds)
    1 tablespoon ground cumin
    1 tablespoon ground coriander
    1 tablespoon chili powder
    1 teaspoon salt
  1/2 teaspoon cayenne pepper
    1 cup salsa or picante sauce
    1 tablespoon cornstarch
    2 tablespoons water
      Taco shells, flour or corn tortillas

SLOW COOKER DIRECTIONS
1. Cut roast in half. Combine cumin, coriander, chili powder, salt and cayenne in small bowl. Rub over roast. Place 1/4 cup salsa in 4-quart slow cooker; top with one piece roast. Layer 1/4 cup salsa, remaining beef and 1/2 cup salsa in slow cooker. Cover; cook on LOW 8 to 10 hours.

2. Remove roast from cooking liquid; cool slightly. Trim and discard excess fat from beef. Shred meat with two forks.

Grilled 3-Cheese Sandwiches

    2 slices (1 ounce each) Muenster cheese
    2 slices (1 ounce each) Swiss cheese
    2 slices (1 ounce each) Cheddar cheese
    2 teaspoons Dijon mustard or Dijon mustard
      mayonnaise
    4 slices sourdough bread
      Butter, melted

1. Place 1 slice of each cheese on 2 bread slices. Spread mustard over cheese; top with remaining bread slices. Brush outsides of sandwiches with butter.

2. Heat large nonstick skillet over medium heat. Add sandwiches; press down lightly with spatula. Cook sandwiches 4 to 5 minutes per side or until cheese melts and sandwiches are golden brown.
Makes 2 sandwiches

Mozzarella, Pesto and Fresh Tomato Panini

(pictured below)

8 slices country Italian, sourdough or other
    firm-textured bread
8 slices SARGENTO® Deli Style Sliced
    Mozzarella Cheese
1/3 cup prepared pesto
4 slices ripe tomato
2 tablespoons olive oil

1. Top each of 4 slices of bread with 1 slice of cheese. Spread pesto over cheese. Top with tomatoes and remaining slices of cheese. Close sandwiches with remaining 4 slices of bread.

2. Brush olive oil lightly over both sides of sandwiches. Cook sandwiches over medium-low coals or in preheated ridged grill pan over medium heat 3 to 4 minutes per side or until bread is toasted and cheese is melted.   *Makes 4 servings*

Tuna Bruschetta

4 cloves garlic
1/4 cup extra-virgin olive oil
8 slices (1/2 to 3/4 inch thick *each*) toasted
    French bread, about 3-1/2×5-1/2 inches
2 cups chopped plum tomatoes
1 cup shredded mozzarella cheese or chopped
    fresh mozzarella, drained
1 (3-ounce) STARKIST Flavor Fresh Pouch® Tuna
    (Albacore or Chunk Light)
2 tablespoons minced fresh parsley
1/2 teaspoon salt (optional)
    Coarsely ground black pepper
    Bibb lettuce

In blender or food processor bowl with metal blade, blend garlic and oil. Brush oil mixture on one side of each piece of toast; reserve remaining oil mixture. In medium bowl, lightly combine tomatoes, cheese, tuna, parsley and reserved oil. Add salt, if desired and pepper. Mound about 1/2 cup tuna mixture over each piece of toast. Place 2 pieces of toast on each lettuce-lined salad plate.   *Makes 4 servings*

*Mozzarella, Pesto and
Fresh Tomato Panini*

Grilled Cheese, Ham & Onion Melts

(pictured at right)

   1 tablespoon butter or margarine
   2 medium onions, thinly sliced
   1 teaspoon sugar
 1/3 cup *French's®* Honey Dijon Mustard or
     French's® Sweet 'n Zesty Mustard
  16 slices Muenster cheese
  12 slices deli ham
   8 slices rye bread

1. Melt butter in medium nonstick skillet. Add onions. Cook over medium-high heat until tender, stirring often. Reduce heat to medium-low. Stir in sugar; cook 15 to 20 minutes or until onions are caramelized. Stir in mustard and remove from heat.

2. Place 2 slices cheese and 3 slices ham on each of 4 slices of bread. Spoon 1/4 cup onion mixture over ham. Top with 2 more slices cheese and cover with remaining bread slices.

3. Coat an electric grill pan with nonstick cooking spray. Grill sandwiches about 5 minutes until golden and cheese melts. *Makes 4 servings*

Tip: Sandwiches may be cooked in a nonstick skillet or on an outdoor grill.

Variation: Substitute deli roast beef for ham.

Open-Faced Oven Reubens

   2 slices rye bread
   2 sheets (18×12 inches) heavy-duty foil
1-1/2 cups sauerkraut, divided
   2 fully cooked smoked Polish sausages, cut in
     half lengthwise
   2 sandwich-style dill pickle slices
   2 slices Swiss cheese
 1/4 cup Thousand Island salad dressing, divided

1. Preheat toaster oven or oven to 450°F.

2. Place one bread slice on each sheet of foil. Top with sauerkraut, sausage, pickle and cheese.

3. Double fold sides and ends of foil to seal packets, leaving head space for heat circulation. Place packets on toaster oven tray or baking sheet.

4. Bake 30 to 35 minutes or until sandwiches are heated through.

5. Carefully open one end of packet to allow steam to escape. Open packets and transfer contents top serving plates. Serve with dressing.
Makes 2 servings

Tip: Make Thousand Island salad dressing by mixing together 1/4 cup mayonnaise, 2 tablespoons ketchup and 1 tablespoon chopped dill pickle. Add pickle juice or lemon juice to taste.

Portobello & Fontina Sandwiches

   Olive oil
   2 large portobello mushrooms, stems removed
   Salt and pepper
   2 to 3 tablespoons sun-dried tomato pesto
   4 slices crusty Italian bread
   4 ounces fontina cheese, sliced
 1/2 cup fresh basil leaves

1. Preheat broiler. Line baking sheet with foil.

2. Drizzle 2 teaspoons oil over both sides of mushrooms; season with salt and pepper. Place mushrooms, gill sides up, on prepared baking sheet. Broil mushrooms 4 minutes per side or until tender. Cut into 1/4-inch-thick slices.

3. Spread pesto evenly on 2 bread slices; layer with mushrooms, cheese and basil. Top with remaining bread slices. Brush outsides of sandwiches lightly with oil.

4. Heat large grill pan or skillet over medium heat. Add sandwiches; press down lightly with spatula. Cook sandwiches 4 to 5 minutes per side or until cheese melts and sandwiches are golden brown.
Makes 2 sandwiches

Helpful Hint

Portobellos are large dark brown mushrooms with thick tough stems that should be removed and discarded before cooking. Because of their large size and sturdiness, they are a good choice for broiling and grilling.

Grilled Cheese, Ham & Onion Melt

Breads

Fudgey Peanut Butter Chip Muffins

(pictured at left)

1/2 cup applesauce
1/2 cup quick-cooking rolled oats
1/4 cup (1/2 stick) butter or margarine, softened
1/2 cup granulated sugar
1/2 cup packed light brown sugar
 1 egg
1/2 teaspoon vanilla extract
3/4 cup all-purpose flour
1/4 cup HERSHEY'S SPECIAL DARK™ Cocoa or HERSHEY'S
   Cocoa
1/2 teaspoon baking soda
1/4 teaspoon ground cinnamon (optional)
 1 cup REESE'S® Peanut Butter Chips
   Powdered sugar (optional)

1. Heat oven to 350°F. Line muffin cups (2-1/2 inches in diameter) with paper bake cups.

2. Stir together applesauce and oats in small bowl; set aside. Beat butter, granulated sugar, brown sugar, egg and vanilla in large bowl until well blended. Add applesauce mixture; blend well. Stir together flour, cocoa, baking soda and cinnamon, if desired. Add to butter mixture, blending well. Stir in peanut butter chips. Fill muffin cups 3/4 full with batter.

3. Bake 22 to 26 minutes or until wooden pick inserted in center comes out almost clean. Cool slightly in pan on wire rack. Sprinkle muffin tops with powdered sugar, if desired. Serve warm.   *Makes 12 to 15 muffins*

Fudgey Chocolate Chip Muffins: Omit Peanut Butter Chips. Add 1 cup HERSHEY'S Semi-Sweet Chocolate Chips.

Clockwise from top left: *Pumpkin Bread (p. 110), Easy Chip and Nut Gift Bread (p. 122), Fudgey Peanut Butter Chip Muffins, Cheddary Pull Apart Bread (p. 120)*

Orange-Raisin Bran Muffins

(pictured at right)

MAZOLA NO STICK® Cooking Spray
1/3 cup boiling water
1 cup natural high-fiber bran cereal shreds
1/2 cup raisins
1/2 cup orange juice
1/2 cup KARO® Light or Dark Corn Syrup
1/4 cup sugar
1/4 cup MAZOLA® Oil
1 egg
1 cup flour
1 teaspoon baking soda
1/4 teaspoon salt

1. Preheat oven to 400°F. Spray 12 (2-1/2-inch) muffin pan cups with cooking spray. In large bowl, pour boiling water over cereal; let stand 2 minutes. Stir in raisins, orange juice, corn syrup, sugar, oil and egg.

2. In medium bowl, combine flour, baking soda and salt. Stir flour mixture into cereal mixture until well blended. Spoon into prepared muffin pan cups.

3. Bake 15 to 20 minutes or until lightly browned and firm to touch. Cool in pan on wire rack 5 minutes; remove from pan. *Makes 12 muffins*

Pumpkin Bread

(pictured on page 108)

1 package (about 18 ounces) yellow cake mix
1 can (16 ounces) solid-pack pumpkin
4 eggs
1/3 cup GRANDMA'S® Molasses
1 teaspoon ground cinnamon
1 teaspoon ground nutmeg
1/3 cup chopped nuts (optional)
1/3 cup raisins (optional)

Preheat oven to 350°F. Grease two 9×5-inch loaf pans.

Combine all ingredients in large bowl and mix well. Beat at medium speed 2 minutes. Pour into prepared pans. Bake 60 minutes or until toothpick inserted into centers comes out clean.
Makes 2 loaves

Serving Suggestion: Serve with cream cheese or preserves, or top with cream cheese frosting or ice cream.

Banana-Nana Pecan Bread

1 cup QUAKER® Oats (quick or old fashioned, uncooked)
1/2 cup chopped pecans
3 tablespoons margarine or butter, melted
2 tablespoons firmly packed brown sugar
1 (14-ounce) package banana bread quick bread mix
1 cup water
1/2 cup mashed ripe banana
2 eggs, lightly beaten
3 tablespoons vegetable oil

Heat oven to 375°F. Grease and flour bottom only of 9×5-inch loaf pan. Combine oats, pecans, margarine and sugar; mix well. Reserve 1/2 cup oat mixture for topping; set aside. In bowl, combine remaining oat mixture, quick bread mix, water, banana, eggs and oil. Mix just until dry ingredients are moistened. Pour into prepared pan. Sprinkle top of loaf with reserved oat mixture. Bake 50 to 55 minutes or until wooden pick inserted in center comes out clean. Cool 10 minutes in pan; remove to wire rack. Cool.
Makes 12 servings

Golden Oatmeal Muffins

1 package DUNCAN HINES® Moist Deluxe® Butter Recipe Golden Cake Mix
1 cup uncooked quick-cooking oats (not instant or old-fashioned)
1/4 teaspoon salt
3/4 cup milk
2 eggs, lightly beaten
2 tablespoons butter or margarine, melted

1. Preheat oven to 400°F. Grease 24 (2-1/2-inch) muffin cups (or use paper liners).

2. Combine cake mix, oats and salt in large bowl. Add milk, eggs and melted butter; stir until moistened. Fill muffin cups two-thirds full. Bake at 400°F for 13 minutes or until golden brown. Cool in pan 5 to 10 minutes. Loosen carefully before removing from pan. Serve with honey or your favorite jam. *Makes 24 muffins*

Homemade Cinnamon Rolls

(pictured below)

4-1/4 to 4-3/4 cups all-purpose flour, divided
1 package quick-rising active dry yeast
1-1/4 cups plus 4 to 5 teaspoons milk, divided
1/4 cup granulated sugar
1/4 cup (1/2 stick) plus 6 tablespoons butter, softened, divided
5 teaspoons WATKINS® Ground Cinnamon, divided
2 teaspoons WATKINS® Vanilla, divided
1 teaspoon salt
2 eggs
1/2 cup packed brown sugar
1 cup powdered sugar

Combine 1-1/2 cups flour and yeast in large bowl. Heat 1-1/4 cups milk, granulated sugar, 1/4 cup butter, 1 teaspoon cinnamon, 1 teaspoon vanilla and salt just until mixture is warm (120° to 130°F), stirring constantly. Add to flour mixture with eggs; beat with electric mixer at low speed for 30 seconds, scraping side of bowl frequently. Beat at high speed for 3 minutes.

Stir in as much remaining flour as possible with spoon (dough will be soft). Knead in enough remaining flour to form moderately soft dough, 3 to 5 minutes total. Shape dough into a ball; place in lightly greased bowl, turning once. Cover and let rise in warm place for about 1 to 1-1/2 hours until doubled in size. (Dough is ready to shape when you can lightly press two fingers 1/2 inch into dough and indentation remains.) Punch down dough and divide in half. Place each half on lightly floured surface and smooth into a ball. Cover and let rest 10 minutes.

Preheat oven to 350°F. Grease 13×9-inch baking pan. Roll half of dough into 12×8-inch rectangle on lightly floured surface. Spread with 3 tablespoons butter. Combine brown sugar and remaining 4 teaspoons cinnamon; sprinkle half of mixture over rectangle. Roll up dough from short side; seal edges by brushing with water. Repeat with remaining dough. Slice one roll into 8 pieces and other into 7 pieces. Arrange slices cut sides up in prepared pan. Cover and let rise for about 30 minutes or until nearly doubled.

Bake for 25 to 40 minutes or until light brown. Immediately invert rolls onto wire rack, then invert again. Cool slightly on wire rack. Combine powdered sugar, remaining 4 teaspoons milk and 1 teaspoon vanilla in small bowl until smooth; drizzle glaze over rolls. *Makes 15 rolls*

Homemade Cinnamon Rolls

Garlic Onion Bread

(pictured on front cover)

1/2 cup butter or margarine, softened
2 tablespoons minced garlic
1 tablespoon chopped fresh parsley
1 loaf (14 inches) Italian bread, split lengthwise in half
1-1/3 cups *French's®* French Fried Onions
1/4 cup grated Parmesan cheese

1. Preheat oven to 350°F. Mix butter, garlic and parsley. Spread half the butter mixture onto each cut side of bread. Sprinkle each with *2/3 cup* French Fried Onions and 2 tablespoons cheese.

2. Place bread on baking sheet. Bake 5 minutes or until hot and onions are golden brown. Cut each half into 8 slices. *Makes 8 servings*

Tip: You can substitute 2/3 cup prepared pesto sauce for the butter mixture.

Jumbo Streusel-Topped Raspberry Muffins

Jumbo Streusel-Topped Raspberry Muffins

(pictured above)

2-1/4 cups all-purpose flour, divided
1/4 cup packed brown sugar
2 tablespoons butter
3/4 cup granulated sugar
2 teaspoons baking powder
1/2 teaspoon baking soda
1/2 teaspoon salt
1/2 teaspoon grated lemon peel
3/4 cup plus 2 tablespoons milk
1/3 cup butter, melted
1 egg, beaten
2 cups fresh or frozen raspberries (do not thaw)

1. Preheat oven to 350°F. Grease 6 jumbo (3-1/2-inch) muffin cups.

2. For topping, combine 1/4 cup flour and brown sugar in small bowl. Cut in 2 tablespoons butter with pastry blender or two knives until mixture forms coarse crumbs.

3. Set aside 1/4 cup flour. Combine remaining 1-3/4 cups flour, granulated sugar, baking powder, baking soda, salt and lemon peel in medium bowl. Combine milk, melted butter and egg in small bowl.

4. Add milk mixture to flour mixture; stir until almost blended. Toss frozen raspberries with reserved flour in medium bowl just until coated; gently fold raspberries into muffin batter. Spoon batter into prepared muffin cups, filling three-fourths full. Sprinkle with topping.

5. Bake 25 to 30 minutes or until toothpick inserted into centers comes out clean. Cool in pan 2 minutes; remove to wire rack. Serve warm or at room temperature. *Makes 6 jumbo muffins*

Variation: For regular-size muffins, spoon batter into 12 standard (2-1/2-inch) greased or paper-lined muffin cups. Bake in preheated 350°F oven 21 to 24 minutes or until toothpick inserted into centers comes out clean. Makes 12 muffins.

Jalapeño Corn Muffins

(pictured at right)

MAZOLA NO STICK® Cooking Spray
1 cup flour
1 cup yellow cornmeal
2 teaspoons baking powder
1/4 teaspoon salt
2 eggs
1/2 cup KARO® Light Corn Syrup
1/4 cup MAZOLA® Oil
1 cup cream-style corn
1 cup (4 ounces) shredded Monterey Jack cheese
2 tablespoons chopped, seeded jalapeño peppers, fresh or pickled*

*Jalapeño peppers can sting and irritate the skin, so wear rubber gloves when handling peppers and do not touch your eyes. Wash hands after handling.

1. Preheat oven to 400°F. Spray 12 (2-1/2-inch) muffin pan cups with cooking spray.

2. In medium bowl, combine flour, cornmeal, baking powder and salt.

3. In large bowl, combine eggs, corn syrup and oil. Stir in flour mixture until well blended. Stir in corn, cheese and peppers. Spoon into prepared muffin pan cups.

4. Bake 15 to 20 minutes or until lightly browned and firm to touch. Cool in pan on wire rack 5 minutes; remove from pan. *Makes 12 muffins*

Libby's® Pumpkin Cranberry Bread

3 cups all-purpose flour
1 tablespoon plus 2 teaspoons pumpkin pie spice
2 teaspoons baking soda
1-1/2 teaspoons salt
3 cups granulated sugar
1 can (15 ounces) LIBBY'S® 100% Pure Pumpkin
4 large eggs
1 cup vegetable oil
1/2 cup orange juice or water
1 cup sweetened dried, fresh or frozen cranberries

PREHEAT oven to 350°F. Grease and flour two 9×5-inch loaf pans.

COMBINE flour, pumpkin pie spice, baking soda and salt in large bowl. Combine sugar, pumpkin, eggs, vegetable oil and orange juice in large mixer

bowl; beat until just blended. Add pumpkin mixture to flour mixture; stir just until moistened. Fold in cranberries. Spoon batter into prepared loaf pans.

BAKE for 60 to 65 minutes or until wooden pick inserted in center comes out clean. Cool in pans on wire racks for 10 minutes; remove to wire racks to cool completely. *Makes 2 loaves*

8×4-inch loaf pans:
PREPARE three 8×4-inch loaf pans as directed above. Bake for 55 to 60 minutes.

5×3-inch miniature loaf pans:
PREPARE five or six 5×3-inch miniature-loaf pans as directed above. Bake for 50 to 55 minutes.

Chocolate Chip Scones

2 cups all-purpose flour
1 cup miniature chocolate chips
3/4 cup golden raisins
1/2 cup sugar
2 teaspoons baking powder
1/4 teaspoon baking soda
1/4 teaspoon salt
1/4 teaspoon ground cinnamon
1/2 cup (1 stick) butter, cut into small pieces
1/2 cup buttermilk
2 eggs
1/2 teaspoon vanilla extract
1 tablespoon milk

1. Preheat oven to 350°F. Lightly grease two cookie sheets. Combine flour, chocolate chips, raisins, sugar, baking powder, baking soda, salt and cinnamon in large bowl.

2. Cut in butter with pastry blender or two knives until mixture resembles coarse crumbs. Beat buttermilk, 1 egg and vanilla in small bowl. Add to flour mixture; mix just until sticky dough is formed.

3. Using 2 tablespoons dough for each scone, drop dough onto prepared cookie sheets. Blend remaining egg and milk in small bowl; brush mixture over tops of scones.

4. Bake 12 to 14 minutes or until toothpick inserted into centers comes out clean. Cool 5 minutes on wire rack. Serve warm. *Makes 12 scones*

Jalapeño Corn Muffins

Apple-Cheddar Muffins

(pictured at right)

1 cup whole-wheat flour
1 cup all-purpose white flour
2 tablespoons sugar
1 tablespoon baking powder
1/2 teaspoon salt
1 cup peeled, chopped apple
1 cup grated CABOT® Mild or Sharp Cheddar
2 large eggs
1 cup milk
4 tablespoons CABOT® Salted Butter, melted

1. Preheat oven to 400°F. Butter 12 muffin cups or coat with nonstick cooking spray.

2. In mixing bowl, stir together whole-wheat and white flours, sugar, baking powder and salt. Add apples and cheese and toss to combine.

3. In another bowl, whisk eggs lightly. Whisk in milk and butter. Make well in center of dry ingredients; add milk mixture and gently stir in dry ingredients from side until just combined.

4. Divide batter among prepared muffin cups. Bake for 20 minutes, or until muffins feel firm when lightly pressed on top. *Makes 12 muffins*

Orange Zucchini Loaves

LOAVES

1 package DUNCAN HINES® Moist Deluxe® Orange Supreme Cake Mix
3 egg whites
3/4 cup water
1/3 cup vegetable oil
1 teaspoon ground cinnamon
1 cup grated zucchini
2 teaspoons grated orange peel (see Tip)

SYRUP

1/4 cup granulated sugar
2 tablespoons orange juice
Confectioners' sugar for garnish
Orange slices for garnish (optional)

1. Preheat oven to 350°F. Grease and flour two 8-1/2×4-1/2×2-1/2-inch loaf pans.

2. For loaves, combine cake mix, egg whites, water, oil and cinnamon in large bowl. Beat at low speed with electric mixer until moistened. Beat at medium speed for 2 minutes. Fold in zucchini and orange

peel. Divide evenly into prepared pans. Bake at 350°F for 50 to 55 minutes or until toothpick inserted in center comes out clean. Cool in pans 15 minutes. Loosen loaves from pans. Invert onto cooling racks. Turn right-side up. Poke holes in tops of warm loaves with toothpick or long-tined fork.

3. For syrup, combine granulated sugar and orange juice in small saucepan. Cook on medium heat, stirring constantly, until sugar dissolves. Spoon hot syrup evenly over each loaf. Cool completely. Garnish with confectioners' sugar and orange slices, if desired. *Makes 2 loaves (24 slices)*

Tip: When grating orange peel, avoid the bitter white portion known as the pith.

Apricot Miniature Muffins

1-1/2 cups all-purpose flour
1/2 cup sugar
1/2 cup finely chopped dried apricots
1/4 teaspoon baking powder
1/4 teaspoon baking soda
1/8 teaspoon salt
Pinch ground nutmeg
1/2 cup (1 stick) butter, melted and cooled to room temperature
2 eggs
2 tablespoons milk
1 teaspoon vanilla extract

1. Preheat oven to 350°F. Spray 24 miniature (1-3/4-inch) muffin cups with nonstick cooking spray.

2. Combine flour, sugar, apricots, baking powder, baking soda, salt and nutmeg in large bowl; mix well. Whisk butter, eggs, milk and vanilla in medium bowl. Add butter mixture to flour mixture; mix just until blended. Spoon about 1 tablespoon batter into each prepared muffin cup.

3. Bake 12 to 15 minutes or until toothpick inserted into centers comes out clean.

Makes 24 miniature muffins

Apple-Cheddar Muffins

Cranberry Pecan Wreath

tightly, pinching seam to seal. Form into ring; join ends, pinching to seal. Transfer to greased large baking sheet. Cover; let rise in warm, draft-free place until doubled in size, about 45 to 60 minutes.

Bake at 350°F for 40 to 45 minutes or until done. Remove from pan; cool on wire rack. Drizzle with Orange Glaze. Decorate with additional cranberries, orange slices and pecan halves, if desired.

Makes 1 (10-inch) coffeecake

Cranberry-Pecan Filling: In medium saucepan, combine 1-1/2 cups fresh or frozen cranberries, finely chopped; 1 cup firmly packed brown sugar; and 1/3 cup butter or margarine. Bring to a boil over medium-high heat. Reduce heat; simmer 5 to 7 minutes or until very thick, stirring frequently. Remove mixture from heat; stir in 3/4 cup chopped pecans, toasted.

Orange Glaze: In small bowl, combine 1-1/4 cups sifted powdered sugar; 2 tablespoons butter or margarine, softened; 1 to 2 tablespoons milk; and 2 teaspoons freshly grated orange peel. Stir until smooth.

Pumpkin Corn Muffins

1-1/4 cups all-purpose flour
    1 cup ALBERS® Yellow Corn Meal
  1/3 cup granulated sugar
    4 teaspoons baking powder
  1/2 teaspoon salt
1-1/4 cups LIBBY'S® 100% Pure Pumpkin
    2 large eggs
  1/3 cup milk
  1/4 cup vegetable oil
    1 can (11 ounces) whole-kernel corn, drained
      (optional)

PREHEAT oven to 375°F. Grease or paper-line 18 muffin cups.

COMBINE flour, cornmeal, sugar, baking powder and salt in large bowl. Beat pumpkin, eggs, milk, oil and corn in medium bowl until combined. Add to flour mixture; mix thoroughly. Spoon batter into prepared muffin cups.

BAKE for 25 to 30 minutes or until wooden pick inserted in center comes out clean. Serve warm.

Makes 18 muffins

Cranberry Pecan Wreath

(pictured above)

3-1/2 to 4 cups all-purpose flour
  1/3 cup sugar
    1 envelope FLEISCHMANN'S® RapidRise™ Yeast
  3/4 teaspoon salt
  1/2 cup milk
  1/3 cup butter or margarine
  1/4 cup water
    2 large eggs
    Cranberry-Pecan Filling (recipe follows)
    Orange Glaze (recipe follows)

In large bowl, combine 1-1/2 cups flour, sugar, undissolved yeast, and salt. Heat milk, butter and water until very warm (120° to 130°F); stir into dry ingredients. Stir in eggs and enough remaining flour to make soft dough. Knead on lightly floured surface until smooth and elastic, about 8 to 10 minutes. Cover; let rest 10 minutes.

Roll dough to 30×6-inch rectangle; spread Cranberry-Pecan Filling over dough to within 1/2 inch of edges. Beginning at long end, roll up

Peanut Butter & Chocolate Pull-Apart Rolls

(pictured below)

DOUGH
- 1/2 cup milk
- 1/3 cup water (70° to 80°F)
- 1/4 cup creamy peanut butter, at room temperature
- 1/2 teaspoon salt
- 2-1/4 cups bread flour
- 1/4 cup granulated sugar
- 1-1/2 teaspoons FLEISCHMANN'S® Bread Machine Yeast

FILLING
- 1/2 cup (3 ounces) semisweet chocolate pieces
- 2 tablespoons creamy peanut butter

ICING
- 1/2 cup sifted powdered sugar
- 1 tablespoon creamy peanut butter or cocoa powder
- 2 to 4 teaspoons milk

BREAD MACHINE DIRECTIONS

To make dough, add dough ingredients to bread machine pan in the order suggested by manufacturer. Select dough/manual cycle.

To make filling, combine filling ingredients in small bowl; blend well. To shape and fill, when cycle is complete, remove dough to floured surface. If necessary, knead in additional flour to make dough easy to handle.

Roll dough into 14-inch circle. Cut into 6 wedges; place filling, dividing evenly, at wide end of each wedge. Beginning at wide end, roll up tightly; curve to form crescent. Arrange crescents, seam side down, in spoke fashion on greased large baking sheet. Pinch ends at center to seal. Cover and let rise in warm, draft-free place until doubled in size, about 30 to 45 minutes. Bake at 375°F for 15 to 20 minutes or until done. Remove from pan; cool on wire rack.

To make icing, combine icing ingredients in small bowl; stir until smooth. Drizzle on rolls.

Makes 6 rolls

Note: Dough can be prepared in all size bread machines.

Peanut Butter & Chocolate Pull-Apart Rolls

Aloha Bread

(pictured at right)

1 (10-ounce) jar maraschino cherries
1-3/4 cups all-purpose flour
2 teaspoons baking powder
1/2 teaspoon salt
2/3 cup firmly packed brown sugar
2 eggs
1/3 cup butter or margarine, softened
1 cup mashed ripe bananas
1/2 cup chopped walnuts or macadamia nuts

Drain maraschino cherries, reserving 2 tablespoons juice. Cut cherries into quarters; set aside.

Combine flour, baking powder and salt in small bowl; set aside.

In medium bowl, combine brown sugar, eggs, butter and reserved cherry juice; mix at medium speed of electric mixer until ingredients are thoroughly combined. Add flour mixture alternately with mashed bananas, beginning and ending with flour mixture. Stir in cherries and nuts. Lightly spray 9×5×3-inch loaf pan with nonstick cooking spray. Spread batter evenly in pan.

Bake in preheated 350°F oven 1 hour or until loaf is golden brown and wooden pick inserted near center comes out clean. Remove from pan and cool on wire rack. Store in tightly covered container or wrapped in foil. *Makes 1 loaf*

Favorite recipe from **Cherry Marketing Institute**

Cheddary Pull Apart Bread

(pictured on page 108)

1 round loaf corn or sourdough bread
     (1 pound)*
1/2 cup (1 stick) butter or margarine, melted
1/4 cup French's® Classic Yellow® Mustard
1/2 teaspoon chili powder
1/2 teaspoon seasoned salt
1/4 teaspoon garlic powder
1 cup (4 ounces) shredded Cheddar cheese

You can substitute one 12-inch loaf Italian bread for the corn bread.

Cut bread into 1-inch slices, cutting about 2/3 of the way down through loaf. (Do not cut through bottom crust.) Turn bread 1/4 turn and cut across slices in similar fashion. Combine butter, mustard and seasonings in small bowl until blended. Brush cut

surfaces of bread with butter mixture. Spread bread "sticks" apart and sprinkle cheese inside. Wrap loaf in foil.

Place packet on grid. Cook over medium coals about 30 minutes or until bread is toasted and cheese melts. Pull bread "sticks" apart to serve.
Makes about 8 servings

Banana Peanut Butter Chip Muffins

2 cups all-purpose flour
3/4 cup sugar
2 teaspoons baking powder
1/2 teaspoon baking soda
1/4 teaspoon salt
1 cup mashed ripe bananas (about 2 large)
1/2 cup (1 stick) butter, melted
2 eggs, beaten
1/3 cup buttermilk
1-1/2 teaspoons vanilla extract
1 cup peanut butter chips
1/2 cup chopped peanuts

1. Preheat oven to 375°F. Grease 15 standard (2-1/2-inch) muffins cups or line with paper baking cups.

2. Combine flour, sugar, baking powder, baking soda and salt in medium bowl. Beat bananas, butter, eggs, buttermilk and vanilla in small bowl until well blended.

3. Add banana mixture to flour mixture; stir just until blended. Gently fold in peanut butter chips. Spoon into prepared muffin cups, filling three-fourths full. Sprinkle with chopped peanuts.

4. Bake 20 minutes or until toothpick inserted into centers comes out clean. Cool in pan 2 minutes. Remove from pan; cool completely on wire racks. Serve warm or room temperature.
Makes 15 muffins

Tip: Substitute a mixture of chocolate and peanut butter chips for the peanut butter chips for a combination of three great flavors in one muffin.

Aloha Bread

Hearty Banana Carrot Muffins

(pictured at right)

2 ripe, medium DOLE® Bananas
1 package (14 ounces) oat bran muffin mix
3/4 teaspoon ground ginger
1 medium DOLE® Carrot, shredded (1/2 cup)
1/3 cup light molasses
1/3 cup DOLE® Seedless or Golden Raisins
1/4 cup chopped almonds

• Mash bananas with fork (1 cup).

• Combine muffin mix and ginger in large bowl. Add carrot, molasses, raisins and bananas. Stir just until moistened.

• Spoon batter into paper-lined muffin cups. Sprinkle tops with almonds.

• Bake at 425°F 12 to 14 minutes until browned.

Makes 12 muffins

Easy Chip and Nut Gift Bread

(pictured on page 108)

2 cups all-purpose flour
1 cup sugar
1 teaspoon baking powder
1 teaspoon salt
1/2 teaspoon baking soda
1 cup applesauce
1/2 cup shortening
2 eggs
1 cup HERSHEY'S Cinnamon Chips, HERSHEY'S SPECIAL DARK™ Chocolate Chips or HERSHEY'S Semi-Sweet Chocolate Chips
1/2 cup chopped walnuts
Powdered sugar (optional)

1. Grease three 5-3/4×3-1/4×2-inch miniature loaf pans. Heat oven to 350°F.

2. Combine flour, sugar, baking powder, salt, baking soda, applesauce, shortening and eggs in large bowl. Beat on medium speed of mixer until well blended. Stir in cinnamon chips and walnuts. Divide batter evenly into prepared pans.

3. Bake 45 minutes or until wooden pick inserted in center comes out clean. Cool 10 minutes; remove from pans to wire rack. Cool completely. Sprinkle with powdered sugar, if desired.

Makes 3 small loaves

Savory Cheddar Quickbread

1-1/2 cups unsifted all-purpose flour
3/4 cup yellow cornmeal
2-1/2 teaspoons baking powder
1 teaspoon paprika
1/2 teaspoon baking soda
1/2 teaspoon salt
2 cups (8 ounces) finely shredded Cheddar cheese, divided
1/4 cup chopped chives or green onions
2 eggs
1/2 cup milk
1/4 cup (1/2 stick) unsalted butter, melted
1/4 cup packed light brown sugar
3 tablespoons *French's*® Spicy Brown Mustard

1. Preheat oven to 375°F. Coat 9-inch square baking pan with nonstick cooking spray.

2. Combine flour, cornmeal, baking powder, paprika, baking soda and salt in large bowl. Stir in 1-1/2 cups cheese and chives. Whisk eggs, milk, butter, sugar and mustard in medium bowl; mix until well blended. Stir egg mixture into flour mixture just until moistened. *Do not overmix.* Spread evenly in prepared pan. Sprinkle with 1/2 cup remaining cheese.

3. Bake 30 minutes or until toothpick inserted in center comes out clean. Cool 5 minutes in pan on rack. Carefully loosen sides of bread from pan. Invert bread onto wire rack. Cool 10 minutes. Cut into 2-inch squares. Serve warm or cool.

Makes 16 servings

Helpful Hint

The secret to making tender muffins and quick breads is to lightly mix the dough. When combining the wet ingredients with the dry ingredients, stir just until moist. It is ok for the mixture to be slightly lumpy.

Ooey-Gooey Pineapple Buns

(pictured at right)

2/3 cup packed brown sugar
1/4 cup maple syrup
  2 tablespoons butter, melted
  1 teaspoon vanilla extract
  1 can (8 ounces) pineapple tidbits, drained
1/2 cup chopped pecans
1/2 cup flaked coconut
  1 package (12 ounces) refrigerated flaky biscuits
     (10 biscuits)

1. Preheat oven to 350°F.

2. Combine brown sugar, maple syrup, butter and vanilla in 11×7-inch baking dish. Sprinkle with pineapple tidbits, pecans and coconut.

3. Cut biscuits into quarters; arrange over coconut. Bake 25 to 30 minutes or until deep golden brown. Invert onto serving plate; serve warm.

Makes 10 servings

Bacon Cheddar Muffins

  2 cups all-purpose flour
3/4 cup sugar
  2 teaspoons baking powder
1/2 teaspoon baking soda
1/2 teaspoon salt
3/4 cup plus 2 tablespoons milk
1/3 cup butter, melted
  1 egg, lightly beaten
  1 cup (4 ounces) shredded Cheddar cheese
1/2 cup crumbled crisp-cooked bacon (about
    6 slices)

1. Preheat oven to 350°F. Grease 12 standard (2-1/2-inch) muffin cups or line with paper baking cups.

2. Combine flour, sugar, baking powder, baking soda and salt in medium bowl. Combine milk, butter and egg in small bowl; mix well. Add milk mixture to flour mixture; stir just until blended. Gently stir in cheese and bacon. Spoon batter into prepared muffin cups, filling three-fourths full.

3. Bake 15 to 20 minutes or until toothpick inserted into centers comes out clean. Cool in pan 2 minutes; remove to wire rack. Serve warm or at room temperature.

Makes 12 muffins

Chocolate Streusel Pecan Muffins

TOPPING
  1/4 cup all-purpose flour
  1/4 cup packed brown sugar
  1/4 teaspoon ground cinnamon
    2 tablespoons butter, melted
  1/4 cup chopped pecans

MUFFINS
1-3/4 cups (11.5-ounce package) NESTLÉ® TOLL
    HOUSE® Milk Chocolate Morsels, *divided*
  1/3 cup milk
    3 tablespoons butter
    1 cup all-purpose flour
    2 tablespoons granulated sugar
    2 teaspoons baking powder
  1/4 teaspoon ground cinnamon
  3/4 cup chopped pecans
    1 large egg
  1/2 teaspoon vanilla extract

FOR TOPPING
COMBINE flour, brown sugar, cinnamon and butter in small bowl with fork until mixture resembles coarse crumbs. Stir in nuts.

FOR MUFFINS
PREHEAT oven to 375°F. Grease or paper-line 12 muffin cups.

COMBINE *1 cup* morsels, milk and butter over hot (not boiling) water. Stir until morsels are melted and mixture is smooth.

COMBINE flour, granulated sugar, baking powder, cinnamon, pecans and *remaining* morsels in large bowl.

COMBINE egg, vanilla extract and melted morsel mixture in small bowl; stir into flour mixture just until moistened. Spoon into prepared muffin cups, filling 2/3 full. Sprinkle with topping.

BAKE for 20 to 25 minutes. Cool in pan for 5 minutes; remove to wire rack to cool completely.

Makes 12 muffins

Main Dishes

Tamale Pie

(pictured at left)

1 tablespoon vegetable oil
1/2 cup chopped onion
1/3 cup chopped sweet red pepper
1 garlic clove, minced
3/4 pound ground turkey
3/4 teaspoon chili powder
1/2 teaspoon dried oregano
1 can (14-1/2 ounces) Mexican-style stewed tomatoes
1 can (15 ounces) chili beans in mild chili sauce
1 cup corn
1/4 teaspoon pepper
1 package (8-1/2 ounces) corn muffin mix plus ingredients to prepare mix
2 cups taco-flavored shredded cheese, divided

1. Heat oil in large skillet over medium heat. Add onion and sweet pepper; cook until crisp-tender. Stir in garlic. Add turkey; cook until turkey is no longer pink, stirring occasionally. Stir in chili powder and oregano. Add tomatoes; cook and stir 2 minutes. Stir in beans, corn and pepper; simmer 10 minutes or until liquid is reduced by about half.

2. Preheat oven to 375°F. Lightly grease 1-1/2- to 2-quart baking dish. Prepare corn muffin mix according to package directions; stir in 1/2 cup cheese.

3. Spread half of turkey mixture in prepared baking dish; sprinkle with 3/4 cup cheese. Top with remaining turkey mixture and 3/4 cup cheese. Top with corn muffin batter. Bake 20 to 22 minutes or until light golden brown.

Makes 4 to 6 servings

Clockwise from top left: *Herbed Pork Roast & Creamy Mushroom Gravy (p. 142), Cocoa Spiced Beef Stir-Fry (p. 136), Cheesy Stuffed Meatballs & Spaghetti (p. 167), Tamale Pie*

Spicy Chicken
Tortilla Casserole

(pictured at right)

1 tablespoon vegetable oil
1 cup chopped green bell pepper
1 small onion, chopped
2 cloves garlic, finely chopped
1 pound (about 4) boneless, skinless chicken
    breast halves, cut into bite-size pieces
1 jar (16 ounces) ORTEGA® Salsa, any variety
1 can (2.25 ounces) sliced ripe olives
6 corn tortillas, cut into halves
2 cups (8 ounces) shredded Monterey Jack or
    cheddar cheese
    Sour cream (optional)

PREHEAT oven to 350°F.

HEAT oil in large skillet over medium-high heat.
Add bell pepper, onion and garlic; cook for 2 to
3 minutes or until vegetables are tender.

ADD chicken; cook, stirring frequently, for 3 to
5 minutes or until chicken is no longer pink in
center. Stir in salsa and olives; remove from heat.

PLACE 6 tortilla halves onto bottom of ungreased
8-inch square baking pan. Top with half of chicken
mixture and 1 cup cheese; repeat.

BAKE for 15 to 20 minutes or until bubbly. Serve
with sour cream.   *Makes 8 servings*

Pork Chops O'Brien

1 tablespoon vegetable oil
6 pork chops, 1/2 to 3/4 inch thick
1/2 teaspoon seasoned salt
1 can (10-3/4 ounces) condensed cream
    of celery soup
1/2 cup milk
1/2 cup sour cream
1/4 teaspoon pepper
1 bag (24 ounces) frozen O'Brien or
    hash brown potatoes, thawed
1 cup (4 ounces) shredded Cheddar cheese,
    divided
1-1/3 cups *French's*® French Fried Onions, divided

Preheat oven to 350°F. In large skillet, heat oil.
Brown pork chops on both sides; drain. Sprinkle
chops with seasoned salt; set aside. In large bowl,
combine soup, milk, sour cream, pepper and

1/2 teaspoon seasoned salt. Stir in potatoes, 1/2 cup
cheese and *2/3 cup* French Fried Onions. Spoon
mixture into 13×9-inch baking dish; arrange pork
chops on top. Bake, covered, at 350°F for 35 to
40 minutes or until pork chops are done. Top chops
with remaining 1/2 cup cheese and *2/3 cup* onions;
bake, uncovered, 5 minutes or until onions are
golden brown.   *Makes 6 servings*

Speedy Brunswick Stew

8 boneless skinless chicken thighs, cut into
    bite-size pieces
1 teaspoon salt, divided
1/4 teaspoon pepper
2 tablespoons vegetable oil
1 onion, cut lengthwise into 1/4-inch slices
1 can (28 ounces) diced tomatoes
2-1/4 cups water, divided
1 package (10 ounces) frozen lima beans
1 package (10 ounces) frozen whole kernel corn
1 tablespoon Worcestershire sauce
2 teaspoons chicken bouillon granules
1 teaspoon sugar
2 tablespoons all-purpose flour
2 tablespoons chopped fresh parsley

Sprinkle chicken with 1/4 teaspoon salt and pepper.
Heat oil in Dutch oven over medium-high heat. Add
chicken and onion; cook and stir about 5 minutes.

Add tomatoes, 2 cups water, beans, corn,
Worcestershire, bouillon granules, sugar and
remaining 3/4 teaspoon salt. Bring to a boil over
high heat. Reduce heat to low. Cover and simmer
20 minutes or until chicken and vegetables are
fork-tender.

Mix flour and remaining 1/4 cup water in small bowl.
Stir flour mixture into stew. Cook, stirring, until
slightly thickened. Sprinkle with chopped parsley.
            Makes 6 to 8 servings

Favorite recipe from **Delmarva Poultry Industry,
Inc.**

Spicy Chicken Tortilla Casserole

Mojo Pork
with Orange-Apple Salsa

(pictured at right)

1 tablespoon minced garlic
2 tablespoons olive oil
1/2 cup *Frank's® RedHot® Chile 'n Lime™* Hot Sauce
1/2 cup orange juice
2 tablespoons grated orange zest
1/4 cup minced fresh cilantro
2 tablespoons chili powder
1 teaspoon dried oregano
2 boneless pork tenderloins (2 pounds)
1/2 cup sour cream
    Orange-Apple Salsa (recipe follows)

1. Sauté garlic in oil; cool. Slowly stir in *Chile 'n Lime™* Hot Sauce, orange juice, zest, cilantro, chili powder and oregano. Reserve 1/4 cup marinade.

2. Place pork into resealable plastic food storage bags. Pour remaining marinade over pork. Seal bags; marinate in refrigerator 1 to 3 hours. Combine remaining marinade with sour cream; set aside in refrigerator.

3. Grill pork over medium-high direct heat for 30 minutes or until center is no longer pink. Slice pork and drizzle with spicy sour cream. Serve with Orange-Apple Salsa.   *Makes 6 to 8 servings*

Orange-Apple Salsa

3 navel oranges, peeled, sectioned and
    cut into small pieces
2 large apples, cored and diced
2 tablespoons chopped red onion
2 tablespoons chopped fresh cilantro
2 tablespoons *Frank's® RedHot® Chile 'n Lime™*
    Hot Sauce

Combine ingredients in bowl; chill until ready to serve.   *Makes about 3 cups*

Green Beans and Ham

2 cups cubed cooked ham
1 can (10-3/4 ounces) condensed cream of
    mushroom soup, undiluted
1/2 cup milk
1 bag (16 ounces) BIRDS EYE® frozen Cut Green
    Beans
1 can (2.8 ounces) French fried onions

• In microwave-safe casserole dish, mix ham, soup, milk and green beans.

• Cover and microwave on HIGH 10 to 12 minutes or until well heated, stirring halfway through cook time. Uncover; sprinkle with fried onions.

• Microwave, uncovered, 3 to 5 minutes. Serve hot.
    Makes 6 servings

Roast Turkey Breast with
Sausage and Apple Stuffing

8 ounces bulk pork sausage
1 medium apple, cored, peeled and finely
    chopped
1 shallot or small onion, finely chopped
1 stalk celery, finely chopped
1/4 cup chopped hazelnuts
1/2 teaspoon rubbed sage, divided
1/2 teaspoon salt, divided
1/2 teaspoon pepper, divided
1 tablespoon butter
1 whole boneless turkey breast
    (4-1/2 to 5 pounds), thawed if frozen
4 to 6 fresh sage leaves (optional)
1 cup chicken broth

1. Preheat oven to 325°F. Crumble pork sausage into large skillet. Add apple, shallot and celery. Cook and stir until sausage is cooked through and apple and vegetables are tender. Stir in hazelnuts, and 1/4 teaspoon *each* sage, salt and pepper.

2. Mash butter with remaining 1/4 teaspoon *each* sage, salt and pepper. Spread over turkey breast skin. (If desired, loosen skin over turkey breast. Arrange sage leaves under skin.) Spoon sausage stuffing into turkey cavity. Close cavity with metal skewers. Place turkey, breast side down, on rack in shallow roasting pan. Pour broth into pan.

3. Roast turkey 45 minutes. Remove turkey from oven; turn breast side up. Baste with broth. Return to oven and roast 1 hour, or until meat thermometer registers 180°F in the thigh. Remove from oven. Let turkey rest 10 minutes before slicing.
    Makes 6 servings

Mojo Pork with Orange-Apple Salsa

Chicken Dijon with Noodles

(pictured at right)

2 tablespoons butter
4 skinless, boneless chicken breast halves
1 medium onion, chopped (about 1/2 cup)
1 can (10-3/4 ounces) Campbell's® Condensed
    Cream of Mushroom Soup (Regular,
    98% Fat Free or 25% Less Sodium)
1/4 cup apple juice or milk
1 tablespoon Dijon-style mustard
1 tablespoon chopped fresh parsley or
    1 teaspoon dried parsley flakes
Hot cooked noodles

1. Heat the butter in a 10-inch skillet over medium-high heat. Add the chicken and cook for 10 minutes or until it's well browned on both sides. Remove the chicken and set aside.

2. Reduce the heat to medium. Add the onion and cook until tender.

3. Stir the soup, apple juice, mustard and parsley into the skillet. Heat to a boil. Return the chicken to the skillet and reduce the heat to low. Cover and cook for 5 minutes or until the chicken is cooked through. Serve with the noodles.

Makes 6 servings

Ranch-Style Beef Stew

2 pounds beef cubes, cut into 1/2-inch pieces
1 tablespoon olive oil
1 jar (1 pound 10 ounces) RAGÚ® Chunky Pasta
    Sauce
1 can (14-1/2 ounces) beef broth
1/2 cup pimento-stuffed green olives, halved
1 can (4 ounces) chopped green chilies,
    undrained
1 tablespoon dried oregano leaves, crushed

1. Season beef, if desired, with salt and pepper. In 6-quart saucepan or Dutch oven, heat olive oil over medium-high heat and brown meat in two batches.

2. Stir in Pasta Sauce, broth, olives, chilies and oregano. Bring to a boil over high heat. Reduce heat to low and simmer covered, stirring occasionally, 1 hour or until beef is tender.

3. Serve, if desired, over hot cooked egg noodles or rice. Garnish, if desired, with chopped fresh cilantro.
Makes 6 servings

Mexican Stuffed Shells

1 pound ground beef
1 jar (12 ounces) mild or medium picante sauce
1 can (8 ounces) tomato sauce
1/2 cup water
1 can (4 ounces) chopped green chilies, drained
1 cup (4 ounces) shredded Monterey Jack
    cheese, divided
1-1/3 cups *French's*® French Fried Onions
12 pasta stuffing shells, cooked in unsalted water
    and drained

Preheat oven to 350°F. In large skillet, brown ground beef; drain. In small bowl, combine picante sauce, tomato sauce and water. Stir 1/2 cup sauce mixture into beef along with chilies, 1/2 cup cheese and *2/3 cup* French Fried Onions; mix well. Spread half of remaining sauce mixture in bottom of 10-inch round baking dish. Stuff cooked shells with beef mixture. Arrange shells in baking dish; top with remaining sauce. Bake, covered, at 350°F for 30 minutes or until heated through. Top with remaining *2/3 cup* onions and cheese; bake, uncovered, 5 minutes or until cheese is melted.

Makes 6 servings

Bays® Welsh Rarebit

4 BAYS® English Muffins, split
2 packages (10 ounces each) frozen Welsh
    rarebit (Cheddar cheese sauce)
2 teaspoons prepared honey mustard
8 slices ripe tomato
8 slices cut bacon, preferably applewood
    smoked, halved crosswise, cooked crisp
3 tablespoons chopped chives

Lightly toast muffin halves; place open-faced on four serving plates. Cook rarebit according to package directions; stir in mustard. Top muffin halves with sliced tomatoes. Arrange bacon over tomatoes in a crisscross fashion. Spoon rarebit evenly over muffin halves and sprinkle with chives.
Makes 4 servings

Variation: For a heartier rarebit, place sliced deli smoked turkey breast on muffin halves before topping with cheese, tomato and chives.

Chicken Dijon with Noodles

Quick Taco Macaroni & Cheese

(pictured below)

1 pound lean ground beef or turkey
1 package (1 ounce) LAWRY'S® Taco Spices
   & Seasonings
1 package (1 pound) large elbow macaroni,
   cooked and drained
4 cups (16 ounces) shredded cheddar cheese
2 cups milk
3 eggs, beaten

Spray 13×9×2-inch baking dish with nonstick
cooking spray. In medium skillet, brown ground
meat; drain fat. Stir in Taco Spices & Seasonings.
Layer half of macaroni in bottom of dish. Top with
half of cheese. Spread taco meat over top. Repeat
layers of macaroni and cheese. In medium bowl,
beat together milk and eggs. Pour egg mixture over
macaroni. Bake in preheated 350°F oven for 30 to
35 minutes or until golden.   *Makes 6 to 8 servings*

Variation: For spicier flavor, try using LAWRY'S®
Chili Spices & Seasonings OR Lawry's® Hot Taco
Spices & Seasonings instead of Taco Spices &
Seasonings.

Quick Taco Macaroni & Cheese

Country-Style Lasagna

9 lasagna noodles (2 inches wide)
2 cans (14-1/2 ounces each) DEL MONTE®
   Stewed Tomatoes - Italian Recipe
 Milk
2 tablespoons butter or margarine
3 tablespoons all-purpose flour
1 teaspoon dried basil, crushed
1 cup diced cooked ham
2 cups (8 ounces) shredded mozzarella cheese

1. Cook noodles according to package directions;
rinse, drain and separate noodles.

2. Meanwhile, drain tomatoes, reserving liquid;
pour liquid into measuring cup. Add milk to
measure 2 cups.

3. Melt butter in large saucepan; stir in flour and
basil. Cook over medium heat 3 minutes, stirring
constantly. Stir in reserved liquid; cook until
thickened, stirring constantly. Season to taste with
salt and pepper, if desired. Stir in tomatoes.

4. Spread thin layer of sauce in of 11×7-inch or
2-quart baking dish. Top with 3 noodles and
1/3 each of sauce, ham and cheese; repeat layers
twice, ending with cheese.

5. Bake, uncovered, at 375°F 25 minutes. Serve with
grated Parmesan cheese and garnish, if desired.
Makes 6 servings

Ham Pot Pie

1 (10-3/4-ounce) can condensed cream of
   broccoli soup, undiluted
1/3 cup milk
1/8 teaspoon dried thyme leaves
1/4 teaspoon coarsely ground pepper
2 (5-ounce) cans HORMEL® chunk ham, drained
   and flaked*
1 (10-ounce) package frozen mixed vegetables,
   thawed and drained.
1 (4-1/2-ounce) can refrigerated buttermilk
   biscuits (6 count)

*HORMEL® chunk breast of chicken may be substituted here.

Heat oven to 400°F. In 1-1/2-quart round baking dish,
combine soup, milk, thyme and pepper. Stir in ham
and vegetables. Bake 20 to 25 minutes. Separate
biscuits; cut each biscuit into quarters. Arrange
biscuits over ham mixture. Bake 12 to 15 minutes
longer or until biscuits are golden brown.
Makes 6 servings

Autumn Pork Chop

Autumn Pork Chops

(pictured above)

1 tablespoon vegetable oil
4 bone-in pork chops, 1/2-inch thick
1 can (10-3/4 ounces) Campbell's®
    Condensed Cream of Celery Soup
    (Regular or 98% Fat Free)
1/2 cup apple juice or water
2 tablespoons spicy-brown mustard
1 tablespoon honey
    Generous dash ground black pepper
    Hot cooked medium egg noodles

1. Heat the oil in a 10-inch skillet over medium-high heat. Add the pork chops and cook until the chops are well browned on both sides. Remove the pork chops and set aside.

2. Stir the soup, apple juice, mustard, honey and black pepper into the skillet. Heat to a boil. Return the pork chops to the skillet and reduce the heat to low. Cover and cook for 5 minutes or until the chops are cooked through. Serve with the noodles.

Makes 4 servings

Citrus Balsamic Salmon

8 fresh salmon fillets, 3/4-inch thick (about
    1-1/2 pounds)
    Freshly ground black pepper
3 tablespoons olive oil
4-1/2 teaspoons cornstarch
1-3/4 cups Swanson® Chicken Broth (Regular,
    Natural Goodness™ or Certified Organic)
3 tablespoons balsamic vinegar
1 tablespoon orange juice
1 tablespoon brown sugar
1 teaspoon grated orange peel

1. Place the salmon in a 12×8×2-inch shallow baking dish. Sprinkle with the black pepper and drizzle with the oil. Bake at 350°F. for 15 minutes or until the fish flakes easily when tested with a fork.

2. Stir the cornstarch, broth, vinegar, orange juice, brown sugar and orange peel in a 2-quart saucepan over high heat. Cook and stir until the mixture boils and thickens.

3. Place the salmon on a serving platter and serve with the sauce.

Makes 8 servings

Zesty Chicken Succotash

(pictured at right)

    1 (3- to 4-pound) chicken, cut up and skinned,
       if desired
    1 onion, chopped
    1 rib celery, sliced
    1/4 cup *Frank's® RedHot®* Original Cayenne Pepper
       Sauce
  1-1/2 cups frozen lima beans
    1 package (10 ounces) frozen whole kernel corn
    2 tomatoes, coarsely chopped

1. Heat *1 tablespoon oil* in large skillet until hot. Add chicken; cook 10 minutes or until browned on all sides. Drain off all but 1 tablespoon fat. Add onion and celery; cook and stir 3 minutes or until tender.

2. Stir in *3/4 cup water,* **Frank's RedHot** Sauce and remaining ingredients. Heat to boiling. Reduce heat to medium-low. Cook, covered, 20 to 25 minutes or until chicken is no longer pink near bone. Sprinkle with chopped fresh parsley, if desired.

Makes 6 servings

Cocoa Spiced Beef Stir-Fry

(pictured on page 126)

    2 cups beef broth
    3 tablespoons soy sauce
    2 tablespoons cornstarch
    2 tablespoons HERSHEY'S Cocoa
    2 teaspoons minced garlic (about 4 cloves)
  1-1/2 teaspoons ground ginger
    1 teaspoon crushed red pepper flakes
    1 pound boneless top round or flank beef steak
    3 tablespoons vegetable oil, divided
  1-1/2 cups large onion pieces
    1 cup carrot slices
    3 cups fresh broccoli florets and pieces
  1-1/2 cups sweet red pepper slices
      Hot cooked rice
      Additional soy sauce
      Cashew or peanut pieces (optional)

1. Stir together beef broth, soy sauce, cornstarch, cocoa, garlic, ginger and red pepper flakes; set aside. Cut beef steak into 1/4-inch-wide strips.

2. Heat large skillet or wok over high heat about 1 minute or until hot. Drizzle about 1 tablespoon oil into pan; heat about 30 seconds. Add beef strips; stir-fry until well browned. Remove from heat; set aside.

3. Drizzle remaining 2 tablespoons oil into pan; add onion pieces and carrots. Stir-fry until onion is crisp, but tender. Add broccoli and red pepper strips; cook until crisp-tender.

4. Return beef to pan; add broth mixture. Cook and stir until mixture comes to a boil and thickens. Serve over hot rice with additional soy sauce and cashew pieces, if desired. *Makes 4 to 6 servings*

Spaghetti Squash Primavera

    1 medium spaghetti squash (about 3 pounds)
    1 can (28 ounces) diced tomatoes
    2 cups sliced mushrooms
    1 cup grated carrot
  1/4 cup diced sweet red pepper
  1/2 cup frozen green peas
    1 tablespoon balsamic vinegar
    1 teaspoon Italian seasoning or oregano
    1 teaspoon minced garlic
  1/4 cup shredded Parmesan cheese

MICROWAVE DIRECTIONS

1. Pierce spaghetti squash to center in several places. Place on microwavable plate; microwave on HIGH 12 to 14 minutes. (If oven doesn't have a turntable, turn squash three times during cooking.) Remove from microwave; cut in half lengthwise. When cool enough to handle, scrape out seeds. Set aside.

2. Place tomatoes in 2-1/2-quart heavy saucepan; bring to a boil over medium-high heat. Add mushrooms, carrot, sweet pepper, peas, vinegar, Italian seasoning and garlic. Reduce heat; cover and simmer 15 minutes or until sauce is thick.

3. To serve, shred spaghetti squash with fork. Equally divide between four pasta bowls. Top with 1 cup sauce. Garnish with cheese.

Makes 4 servings

Zesty Chicken Succotash

Confetti Capellini

(pictured at right)

Non-stick cooking spray
2 cups frozen whole kernel corn, thawed
1 red bell pepper, chopped
1 yellow bell pepper, chopped
3/4 cup chopped red onion
1-1/2 cups heavy cream
1 to 2 tablespoons chili powder
2 cups (12 ounces) chopped HORMEL®
     CURE 81® ham
1/4 teaspoon black pepper
12 ounces capellini or angel hair pasta, cooked
     and drained
2 tomatoes, peeled, seeded and chopped
1/4 cup minced fresh cilantro

In skillet coated with cooking spray, sauté corn,
bell peppers and onion over medium heat 5 minutes
or until tender. Add cream and chili powder. Bring
to a boil; boil 5 minutes or until cream has slightly
thickened, stirring occasionally. Stir in ham and
black pepper. Pour over capellini and toss well. To
serve, sprinkle with chopped tomatoes and cilantro.
Makes 6 servings

Tag-Along Tuna Bake

3 to 4 tablespoons butter or margarine, softened
12 slices bread
1 can (12-1/2 ounces) water-packed tuna,
     drained and flaked
1 cup chopped celery
1-1/3 cups *French's*® French Fried Onions, divided
2 cups milk
1 can (10-3/4 ounces) condensed cream of
     mushroom soup, undiluted
1 cup mayonnaise
4 eggs, lightly beaten
3 slices (3/4 ounce each) processed American
     cheese, cut diagonally into halves

Butter 1 side of each bread slice; arrange 6 slices,
buttered-side down in 13×9-inch baking dish.
Layer tuna, celery and *2/3 cup* French Fried Onions
evenly over bread. Top with remaining bread slices,
buttered side down. In medium bowl, combine
milk, soup, mayonnaise and eggs; mix well. Pour
evenly over layers in baking dish; cover and
refrigerate overnight. Remove from refrigerator 30
minutes before baking. Bake, covered, at 350°F for
30 minutes. Uncover and bake 15 minutes or until

center is set. Arrange cheese slices down center
of casserole, overlapping slightly, points all in one
direction. Top with remaining *2/3 cup* onions; bake,
uncovered, 5 minutes or until onions are golden
brown.   *Makes 8 servings*

Hearty Sausage Meatball Stew

1 pound BOB EVANS® Italian Roll Sausage
2 eggs
1/2 cup dried bread crumbs
1 teaspoon Italian seasoning, divided
3/4 teaspoon dried basil leaves, divided
1/2 teaspoon black pepper, divided
1/2 teaspoon seasoned salt
1/4 cup olive oil
1 large onion, chopped
4 ribs celery, chopped
2 large carrots, cut into 1/2-inch-thick slices
     with crinkle cutter
2 medium zucchini, cut into 1/2-inch-thick
     circles with crinkle cutter
2 quarts (8 cups) chicken broth
2 (14-1/2-ounce) cans diced tomatoes
8 ounces rotini, fusilli, gemelli or other pasta,
     cooked according to package directions
1/2 cup grated Romano cheese

To prepare meatballs, preheat oven to 400°F.
Combine sausage, eggs, bread crumbs, 1/2 teaspoon
Italian seasoning, 1/4 teaspoon basil, 1/4 teaspoon
pepper and seasoned salt in medium bowl; mix
well. Shape into 1-inch balls and place on ungreased
baking sheet. Bake 25 minutes; let cool.

Heat oil in heavy-bottomed saucepan or Dutch
oven. Add onion, celery and carrots; cook over
medium heat until soft. Add zucchini; cover and
cook 5 minutes. Add chicken broth and tomatoes;
simmer 30 minutes. Add meatballs, rotini, remaining
1/2 teaspoon Italian seasoning, 1/2 teaspoon basil
and 1/4 teaspoon pepper; simmer 30 minutes
more. Ladle into bowls; sprinkle each serving with
1 tablespoon Romano cheese. Refrigerate leftovers.
Makes 6 to 8 servings

Confetti Capellini

Classic Veg•All®
Chicken Pot Pie

(pictured at right)

　2 cans (15 ounces each) VEG•ALL® Original
　　Mixed Vegetables, drained
　1 can (10 ounces) cooked chicken, drained
　1 can (10-3/4 ounces) cream of chicken soup
　1/4 teaspoon dried thyme
　1/4 teaspoon black pepper
　2 (9-inch) frozen ready-to-bake pie crust, thawed

1. Preheat oven to 375°F. In medium bowl, combine Veg•All, chicken, soup, and thyme; mix well. Fit one pie crust into 9-inch pie pan; pour vegetable mixture into pie crust. Top with remaining crust; crimp edges to seal and prick top with fork.

2. Bake for 30 to 45 minutes (on lower rack) or until crust is golden brown and filling is hot. Allow pie to cool slightly before cutting into wedges to serve.

Makes 4 servings

Roasted Pork Tenderloins
with Maple-Mustard Sauce

　2 pork tenderloins (about 2 pounds)
　1 tablespoon BERTOLLI® Extra Virgin Olive Oil
　1 small sweet onion, finely chopped
　1 clove garlic, finely chopped
　1/3 cup pure maple syrup or 1/4 cup pancake
　　syrup
　1 tablespoon prepared whole grain mustard
　1/8 teaspoon salt
　1/2 cup HELLMANN'S® or BEST FOODS® Real
　　Mayonnaise

1. Preheat oven to 425°F.

2. In roasting pan, arrange pork and season with salt and pepper. Roast pork 25 minutes or until desired doneness.

3. Meanwhile, in medium saucepan, heat Olive Oil over medium-high heat and cook onion, stirring occasionally, 5 minutes or until starting to brown. Add garlic and cook 30 seconds. Stir in syrup, mustard and salt. With wire whisk, beat in Hellmann's or Best Foods Real Mayonnaise until blended. Simmer 1 minute. Serve sauce with thinly sliced pork. *Makes 6 servings*

Taco Topped Potatoes

　1 pound ground beef or turkey
　1 cup salsa
　2 to 3 tablespoons *Frank's® RedHot®* Original
　　Cayenne Pepper Sauce
　2 teaspoons ground chili powder
　4 medium hot baked potatoes, split
　1 cup shredded Cheddar cheese
1-1/2 cups *French's®* French Fried Onions

1. Cook meat in large skillet over medium-high heat until browned and no longer pink; drain. Stir in salsa, **Frank's RedHot** Sauce and chili powder. Bring to boiling. Reduce heat to medium-low. Cook 5 minutes, stirring often.

2. To serve, spoon meat mixture over potatoes. Top with cheese and French Fried Onions. Splash on more **Frank's RedHot** Sauce to taste. Garnish as desired. *Makes 4 servings*

Tip: To cook potatoes quick, scrub and prick. Microwave on HIGH 20 minutes or until tender.

Meatball Stroganoff

　1 can (10-3/4 ounces) condensed cream of
　　mushroom soup, undiluted
　1 container (8 ounces) sour cream
　1 cup milk
　1 package (about 15 ounces) frozen prepared
　　meatballs, thawed and cut in half if large
　4 cups cooked egg noodles (5 ounces uncooked)
　1 cup (4 ounces) shredded Swiss cheese
　2 cups *French's®* French Fried Onions, divided
1/4 cup minced fresh parsley
　1 tablespoon *French's®* Worcestershire Sauce
　1 teaspoon paprika

1. Preheat oven to 350°F. Coat 3-quart shallow baking dish with vegetable cooking spray.

2. Combine soup, sour cream and milk in large bowl. Stir in meatballs, noodles, cheese, *1 cup* French Fried Onions, parsley, Worcestershire and paprika. Spoon into prepared baking dish.

3. Bake 25 minutes or until heated through. Stir. Sprinkle with remaining *1 cup* onions; bake 5 minutes or until onions are golden brown.

Makes 4 servings

Classic Veg•All® Chicken Pot Pie

Turkey Roulade

Turkey Roulade

(pictured above)

1 pound (10 slices) uncooked, boneless turkey
    breast
1 container (15 ounces) ricotta cheese
1-1/2 cups (6 ounces) shredded mozzarella cheese,
    divided
1 package (10 ounces) frozen chopped spinach,
    thawed, squeezed dry
1 teaspoon garlic salt
1 tablespoon olive or vegetable oil
1 cup chopped onion
2 cloves garlic, minced
1 can (14-1/2 ounces) CONTADINA® Recipe
    Ready Diced Tomatoes, undrained
1 cup chicken broth
1 can (6 ounces) CONTADINA Tomato Paste
1 teaspoon Italian herb seasoning
1 teaspoon salt
1 teaspoon black pepper

1. Pound turkey slices between 2 pieces of plastic
wrap to 1/8-inch thickness.

2. Combine ricotta cheese, 1 cup mozzarella cheese,
spinach and garlic salt in medium bowl. Spread
1/3 cup cheese mixture onto each turkey slice; roll
up. Secure with toothpick. Place rolls in 13×9-inch
baking dish.

3. Heat oil in large skillet. Add onion and garlic;
sauté for 2 minutes. Add undrained tomatoes, broth,
tomato paste, Italian seasoning, salt and pepper.
Bring to a boil.

4. Reduce heat to low; simmer for 10 minutes. Spoon
sauce over rolls; cover.

5. Bake in preheated 425°F oven for 20 to 25 minutes
or until turkey is no longer pink in center. Sprinkle
with remaining 1/2 cup mozzarella cheese. Bake for
additional 5 minutes or until cheese is melted.

Makes 10 servings

Herbed Pork Roast
& Creamy Mushroom Gravy

(pictured on page 126)

1 teaspoon each minced fresh rosemary, parsley
    and thyme or 1/4 teaspoon each dried
    rosemary, parsley flakes and thyme leaves,
    crushed
1 clove garlic, minced
2-1/2- to 3-pound boneless pork loin roast
1 can (10-3/4 ounces) Campbell's®
    Condensed Cream of Mushroom Soup
    (Regular, 98% Fat Free or 25% Less Sodium)
1/2 cup water

1. Stir together the rosemary, parsley, thyme and
garlic in small bowl. Cut small slits into the surface
of the roast with a knife. Stuff the herb mixture into
the slits. Place the roast in a roasting pan.

2. Bake at 325°F. for 1 hour 30 minutes or until pork
is cooked through. Remove the roast from the pan
to a cutting board and let it stand for 10 minutes.

3. Stir the soup into the pan drippings in the
roasting pan. Gradually stir in the water. Cook and
stir over medium heat until the mixture is hot and
bubbling. Thinly slice the pork. Pour the gravy into
a gravy boat and serve it with the pork.

Makes 8 servings

Baked Penne & Ham

(pictured below)

1 package (1.8 ounces) white sauce mix
2 cups milk
1-1/2 cups (6 ounces) shredded fontina cheese,
  divided
3 cups cooked penne pasta (2 cups uncooked)
2 cups *French's*® French Fried Onions, divided
1 cup diced boiled ham
1/2 cup frozen peas
1/3 cup chopped oil-packed sun-dried tomatoes,
  drained

1. Prepare white sauce mix according to package directions using 2 cups milk. Stir in 1 cup cheese. Cook over low heat, stirring constantly, until cheese melts.

2. Combine pasta, *1 cup* French Fried Onions, ham, peas and tomatoes in large bowl. Add cheese sauce and toss to coat. Transfer to shallow 2-quart microwave-safe dish.

3. Microwave, covered, on HIGH 5 minutes. Stir. Sprinkle with remaining onions and cheese. Microwave on HIGH 3 minutes or cheese is melted and onions are golden. *Makes 4 servings*

French Country Chicken Stew

1/4 pound sliced bacon, diced
4 boneless, skinless chicken breast halves, cut
  into 1-inch pieces
1 medium onion, chopped
2 cloves garlic, minced
1 teaspoon dried thyme leaves, crushed
1 can (14-1/2 ounces) DEL MONTE® Cut Green
  Beans, drained
1 can (15 ounces) kidney beans, drained
1 can (14-1/2 ounces) DEL MONTE Stewed
  Tomatoes - Original Recipe
Salt and pepper to taste

1. Cook bacon in large skillet over medium-high heat until almost crisp. Add chicken, onion, garlic and thyme.

2. Cook and stir until onion and garlic are soft, about 5 minutes. Pour off drippings.

3. Add remaining ingredients; bring to a boil over high heat. Reduce heat to low. Simmer, uncovered, 10 minutes. *Makes 4 servings*

Baked Penne & Ham

Savory Chicken & Biscuits

(pictured on right)

2 tablespoons BERTOLLI® Olive Oil
1 pound boneless, skinless chicken breasts or thighs, cut into 1-inch pieces (about 2 cups)
1 medium onion, chopped
1 cup thinly sliced carrots
1 cup thinly sliced celery
1 envelope LIPTON® RECIPE SECRETS® Savory Herb with Garlic Soup Mix*
1 cup milk
1 package (10 ounces) refrigerated flaky buttermilk biscuits

*Also terrific with LIPTON® RECIPE SECRETS® Golden Onion Soup Mix.

1. Preheat oven to 375°F.

2. In 12-inch skillet, heat olive oil over medium-high heat and cook chicken, stirring occasionally, 5 minutes or until almost done. Stir in onion, carrots and celery; cook, stirring occasionally, 3 minutes. Stir in soup mix blended with milk. Bring to a boil over medium-high heat, stirring occasionally; cook 1 minute.

3. Turn into lightly greased 2-quart casserole; arrange biscuits on top of chicken mixture, with edges touching. Bake 10 minutes or until biscuits are golden brown. *Makes 4 servings*

Chipotle Turkey Strata

6 to 8 (1/2-inch-thick) Italian bread slices
2 tablespoons chipotle sauce*
2 cups chopped cooked dark turkey meat
1-1/2 cups shredded Cheddar cheese,** divided
5 large eggs
2-1/2 cups milk
1/2 teaspoon salt
1/4 teaspoon pepper

*If you can't find chipotle sauce, substitute 1 tablespoon tomato sauce mixed with 1 tablespoon adobo sauce with chipotles.

**For a spicier dish, substitute Monterey Jack cheese with jalapeño peppers.

1. Preheat oven to 325°F. Grease 9-inch square baking pan. Arrange 3 to 4 bread slices to cover bottom of pan. Cut bread to fit, if necessary. Spread chipotle sauce over bread. Spread turkey over sauce. Sprinkle 1 cup cheese over turkey. Cover with remaining 3 to 4 bread slices.

2. Beat together eggs, milk, salt and pepper. Pour over bread; press down firmly so bread absorbs liquid. Top with remaining 1/2 cup cheese. Bake, uncovered, 60 to 70 minutes or until set and golden brown. Remove from oven. Let stand 10 to 15 minutes before cutting. *Makes 6 servings*

Tip: This dish can be assembled up to 8 hours in advance. Cover with foil and chilled. Bake a few minutes longer, if necessary.

Sausage-Stuffed Green Peppers

4 medium green peppers
1 tablespoon vegetable oil
1 pound sweet Italian pork sausage, casing removed
1 teaspoon dried oregano leaves, crushed
1 medium onion, chopped (about 1/2 cup)
1 cup shredded part-skim mozzarella cheese (4 ounces)
2 cups Prego® Traditional Italian Sauce

1. Cut a thin slice from the top of each pepper, cut in half lengthwise and discard the seeds and white membranes.

2. Place the pepper shells in a 13×9×2-inch shallow baking dish or roasting pan and set them aside.

3. Heat the oil in a 10-inch skillet over medium-high heat. Add the sausage and cook until it's well browned, stirring to break up the meat. Add the oregano and onion and cook until the onion is tender. Pour off any fat. Stir in the cheese.

4. Spoon the sausage mixture into the pepper shells. Pour the pasta sauce over the peppers. **Cover.**

5. Bake at 400°F. for 40 minutes or until the sausage is cooked through and the peppers are tender. *Makes 8 servings*

Pizza Pie Meatloaf

(pictured at right)

2 pounds ground beef
1-1/2 cups shredded mozzarella cheese, divided
1/2 cup unseasoned dry bread crumbs
1 cup tomato sauce, divided
1/4 cup grated Parmesan cheese
1/4 cup *French's*® Worcestershire Sauce
1 tablespoon dried oregano leaves
1 plum tomato, thinly sliced
1/2 cup sliced green bell pepper
1-1/3 cups *French's*® French Fried Onions

1. Preheat oven to 350°F. Combine beef, *1/2 cup* mozzarella cheese, bread crumbs, *1/2 cup* tomato sauce, Parmesan cheese, Worcestershire and oregano in large bowl; stir with fork until well blended.

2. Place meat mixture into round pizza pan with edge or pie plate and shape into 9×1-inch round. Bake 35 minutes or until no longer pink in center and internal temperature reads 160°F. Drain fat.

3. Top with remaining *1/2 cup* tomato sauce, sliced tomato, green bell pepper strips, mozzarella cheese and French Fried Onions. Bake 5 minutes or until cheese is melted and onions are golden. Cut into wedges to serve. *Makes 6 to 8 servings*

Quick Turkey Tetrazzini

1/2 cup chopped onion
2 tablespoons butter or margarine
1 (10-3/4-ounce) can condensed cream of mushroom soup, undiluted
3/4 cup water
1/2 cup shredded Cheddar cheese
2 (5-ounce) cans HORMEL® chunk turkey, drained and flaked
2 tablespoons chopped fresh parsley
2 tablespoons chopped pimiento
1/4 teaspoon black pepper
4 cups cooked spaghetti
1/4 cup grated Parmesan cheese
Salt and black pepper

In large saucepan or Dutch oven, cook onion in butter until tender. Stir in soup; gradually stir in water. Add Cheddar cheese; heat, stirring frequently, until cheese melts. Remove from heat. Stir in turkey, parsley, pimiento, and pepper. Toss mixture with spaghetti; mix well. Pour into 2-quart casserole. Sprinkle Parmesan cheese over top. Bake in preheated 350°F oven 30 minutes or until hot and bubbly. Season to taste with salt and pepper.
Makes 6 to 8 servings

Empanadas

1 loaf (1 pound) frozen bread dough, thawed
1/4 cup raisins
1 tablespoon apple cider vinegar
1 pound ground beef or turkey
1 medium onion, chopped
2 cloves garlic, finely chopped
1 jar (16 ounces) ORTEGA® Salsa (any flavor), divided
1/4 cup slivered almonds
2 tablespoons brown sugar
1/2 teaspoon ground cinnamon
1/4 teaspoon salt
1/2 cup (2 ounces) shredded Monterey Jack cheese
1 egg, lightly beaten

COMBINE raisins and vinegar in small bowl; soak for 15 to 20 minutes or until raisins are plump.

PREHEAT oven to 375°F. Grease baking sheet.

COMBINE beef, onion and garlic in large skillet; cook over medium-high heat for 4 to 5 minutes or until no longer pink; drain. Add 1/2 cup salsa, almonds, raisin mixture, sugar, cinnamon and salt. Bring to a boil. Cook for 3 to 4 minutes or until flavors are blended.

DIVIDE dough into 6 pieces; roll into balls. On well-floured board, roll each ball into a 6-inch circle. Place 1/2 cup beef filling on bottom half of circle; sprinkle with cheese. Fold top half of dough over filling; crimp edges with tines of fork. Pierce top with fork. Place on prepared baking sheet; brush with egg.

BAKE for 20 to 25 minutes or until golden. Serve with remaining salsa. *Makes 6 servings*

Tip: ORTEGA salsas make a great accompaniment for these authentic beef-filled pies. Prepare smaller empanadas and serve as appetizers to a Mexican meal.

Pizza Pie Meatloaf

Salsa Pork Braise

(pictured at right)

2 tablespoons olive oil
4 pounds boneless pork shoulder butt
2 large carrots, chopped (about 1 cup)
3 cloves garlic, chopped
1 jar (24 ounces) chunky salsa
2 cups Swanson® Chicken Broth (Regular,
 Natural Goodness™ or Certified Organic)
2 tablespoons tomato paste
1 tablespoon chili powder
 Cooked rice

1. Heat **1 tablespoon** of the oil in an oven-safe 6-quart saucepot over medium-high heat. Add the pork and cook until it's well browned on all sides. Remove the pork and set aside.

2. Add remaining oil to the saucepot. Reduce the heat to medium. Add the carrots and garlic and cook until tender.

3. Stir the salsa, broth, tomato paste and chili powder into the saucepot. Heat to a boil. Return the pork to the saucepot and reduce the heat to low.

4. Cover the saucepot and bake at 350°F for 2 hours or until the meat is fork-tender.

5. Remove the roast from the saucepot to a cutting board and let it stand for 10 minutes. Thinly slice the pork and return meat to the saucepot. Serve over rice. *Makes 12 servings*

Make Ahead: Pork can be made 1 day ahead. Cool and refrigerate. Reheat over medium heat before serving.

Shredded Pork Sandwiches: Using 2 forks, shred the pork. Return the shredded pork to the saucepot. Divide the pork and sauce mixture among round sandwich rolls.

Cheddary Sausage Frittata

4 eggs
1/4 cup milk
1 package (12 ounces) bulk pork breakfast
 sausage
1 poblano pepper, seeded and chopped
1 cup (4 ounces) shredded Cheddar cheese

1. Preheat broiler. Combine eggs and milk in medium bowl; whisk until well blended. Set aside.

2. Heat 12-inch ovenproof nonstick skillet over medium-high heat. Add sausage; cook until no longer pink, stirring to break up meat. Transfer sausage to paper towels with slotted spoon. Drain fat; set aside.

3. Add pepper to same skillet; cook and stir 2 minutes or until crisp-tender. Return sausage to skillet. Add egg mixture; stir until blended. Cover; cook over medium-low heat 10 minutes or until eggs are almost set.

4. Sprinkle cheese over frittata; broil 2 minutes or until cheese is melted. Cut into 4 wedges. Serve immediately. *Makes 4 servings*

Tip: If skillet is not ovenproof, wrap handle in heavy-duty aluminum foil.

Ranchero Oven-Fried Chicken

3 cups Pepperidge Farm® Herb Seasoned or
 Cornbread Stuffing, crushed
1/2 cup all-purpose flour
1 can (10-3/4 ounces) Campbell's® Condensed
 Tomato Soup
1/2 cup mayonnaise
1 tablespoon water
1 teaspoon chili powder
4 pounds chicken parts (breasts, thighs, or
 drumsticks)*

Remove skin if desired.

1. Put the crushed stuffing and flour on 2 separate plates.

2. Stir the soup, mayonnaise, water, chili powder and cumin in a shallow dish. Lightly coat the chicken with the flour. Dip the chicken into the soup mixture, then coat with the stuffing crumbs. Put the chicken on a baking sheet.

3. Bake at 400°F. for 50 minutes or until the chicken is cooked through. Serve the chicken warm or at room temperature. *Makes 8 servings*

Cooking for a Crowd: Recipe may be doubled.

Cuban-Style Marinated Skirt Steak

(pictured at right)

2 pounds beef skirt steak, cut into 6-inch pieces
2 cups orange juice, divided
1/2 cup lemon juice
1/2 cup lime juice
1/4 cup olive oil
5 garlic cloves, minced
1 teaspoon dried oregano
1 large onion, halved and thinly sliced
2 teaspoons grated orange peel, plus more for garnish
3 cups cooked white rice
3 cups cooked black beans

1. Place steak in glass dish. Mix 1 cup orange juice, lemon juice, lime juice, oil, garlic and oregano in small bowl; set aside 1/2 cup. Pour remaining juice mixture over steak. Marinate, covered, in refrigerator 30 minutes.

2. Combine remaining 1 cup orange juice, onion and 2 teaspoons orange peel in separate bowl; set aside.

3. Prepare grill for direct cooking. Remove steak from marinade; discard marinade. Place steak on grid over high heat. Grill steak, covered, 6 to 10 minutes or until desired doneness, turning once. Let stand, covered with tented foil, 5 minutes before slicing.

4. Slice meat across the grain into thin slices. Remove onions from orange juice; arrange on top of meat. Sprinkle each serving with about 1 tablespoon reserved juice mixture and additional orange peel. Serve with rice and black beans.

Makes 6 servings

Porcupine Meatballs

2 bags SUCCESS® Rice, divided
1 pound ground turkey
1 can (10-3/4 ounces) condensed tomato soup
1/3 cup water
1 tablespoon onion powder
1/2 teaspoon salt
1/2 teaspoon pepper

Prepare one bag of rice according to package directions. Cool.

Place cooked rice in large bowl. Add ground turkey; mix well. Shape into 1-inch balls; set aside.

Combine tomato soup, water, onion powder, salt and pepper in medium saucepan; mix well. Cook, stirring occasionally, over medium heat until hot, about 10 minutes.

Carefully add meatballs to soup mixture; cover. Reduce heat to medium-low; simmer until meatballs are no longer pink in center, stirring occasionally, about 15 minutes. Meanwhile, prepare remaining bag of rice according to package directions. Serve meatball mixture over hot rice.

Makes 6 servings

Chicken with Grilled Pineapple Salsa

1-1/4 cups WISH-BONE® Italian Dressing or Robusto Italian Dressing
1/4 cup firmly packed dark brown sugar
1/4 cup PLUS 2 tablespoons chopped fresh cilantro
2 pounds boneless chicken thighs
2 tablespoons orange juice
1/4 teaspoon salt
1/8 teaspoon ground red pepper
1 medium pineapple, peeled and cut into 3/4-inch-thick slices
1 large red onion, cut into 1/2-inch thick slices

1. For marinade, blend Wish-Bone Italian Dressing, sugar and 1/4 cup cilantro. In large, shallow nonaluminum baking dish or plastic bag, pour 3/4 cup marinade over chicken; turn to coat. Cover, or close bag, and marinate in refrigerator, turning occasionally, 3 to 24 hours. Refrigerate remaining marinade.

2. Meanwhile, for salsa, in medium bowl, combine 2 tablespoons refrigerated marinade, remaining 2 tablespoons cilantro, orange juice, salt and pepper; set aside.

3. Remove chicken from marinade, discarding marinade. Grill or broil chicken, pineapple and onion, turning once and brushing frequently with remaining refrigerated marinade. Grill until pineapple and onion are tender and chicken is thoroughly cooked. Chop pineapple and onion and toss with salsa mixture. Serve salsa with chicken.

Makes 4 servings

Cuban-Style Marinated Skirt Steak

Vegetable Lasagna

(pictured below)

2 cans (10-3/4 ounces each) Campbell's®
    Condensed Cream of Broccoli Soup
    (Regular or 98% Fat Free)
1-1/2 cups milk
    Vegetable cooking spray
1 tablespoon butter
3-3/4 cups sliced mushrooms (about 10 ounces)
2 medium red or orange peppers, cut into
    2-inch-long thin strips (about 3 cups)
2 medium zucchini, thinly sliced (about 3 cups)
1 medium onion, thinly sliced (about 1/2 cup)
12 uncooked no-boil lasagna noodles
2 cups shredded Monterey Jack cheese
    (8 ounces)

1. Stir the soup and milk in a small bowl and set
aside. Spray a 13×9×2-inch shallow baking dish
with cooking spray.

2. Heat the butter in a 12-inch skillet over medium
heat. Add the mushrooms, peppers, zucchini and
onion and cook until tender.

Vegetable Lasagna

3. Spread **1 cup** soup mixture in the bottom of the
prepared dish. Arrange **3** of the noodles and top
with **one-third** of the vegetable mixture, **1 cup** of
the soup mixture and **1/2 cup** of the cheese. Repeat
layers twice. Top with remaining **3** noodles. Pour
remaining soup mixture over noodles. **Cover.**

4. Bake at 375°F. for 40 minutes. Uncover and
sprinkle with remaining cheese. Bake 10 minutes
more or until hot. Let the lasagna stand for
10 minutes.   *Makes 8 servings*

Ham & Macaroni Twists

2 cups elbow macaroni or rotini, cooked in
    unsalted water and drained
1-1/2 cups (8 ounces) cubed cooked ham
1-1/3 cups *French's*® French Fried Onions, divided
1 package (8 ounces) frozen broccoli spears,*
    thawed and drained
1 cup milk
1 can (10-3/4 ounces) condensed cream of
    celery soup, undiluted
1 cup (4 ounces) shredded Cheddar cheese,
    divided
1/4 teaspoon garlic powder
1/4 teaspoon pepper

**1 small head fresh broccoli (about 1/2 pound) can be substituted
for frozen spears. Divide into spears and cook 3 to 4 minutes before
using.*

Preheat oven to 350°F. In 12×8-inch baking dish,
combine hot macaroni, ham and *2/3 cup* French
Fried Onions. Divide broccoli spears into 6 small
bunches. Arrange bunches of spears down center
of dish, alternating direction of flowerets. In small
bowl, combine milk, soup, 1/2 cup cheese and
seasonings; pour over casserole. Bake, covered,
at 350°F for 30 minutes or until heated through.
Top with remaining 1/2 cup cheese and sprinkle
remaining *2/3 cup* onions down center; bake,
uncovered, 5 minutes or until onions are golden
brown.   *Makes 4 to 6 servings*

Microwave Directions: In 12×8-inch microwave-
safe dish, prepare macaroni mixture and arrange
broccoli spears as above. Prepare soup mixture as
above; pour over casserole. Cook, covered, on HIGH
8 minutes or until broccoli is done. Rotate dish
halfway through cooking time. Top with remaining
cheese and onions as above; cook, uncovered,
1 minute or until cheese melts. Let stand 5 minutes.

Grilled T-Bone Steaks With BBQ Rub

Grilled T-Bone Steaks with BBQ Rub

(pictured above)

2 to 4 well-trimmed beef T-Bone or Porterhouse steaks, cut 1 inch thick (about 2 to 4 pounds)

BBQ RUB:
    2 tablespoons chili powder
    2 tablespoons packed brown sugar
    1 tablespoon ground cumin
    2 teaspoons minced garlic
    2 teaspoons cider vinegar
    1 teaspoon Worcestershire sauce
    1/4 teaspoon ground red pepper

Combine rub ingredients; press evenly onto beef steaks. Place steaks on grid over medium, ash-covered coals. Grill, uncovered, 14 to 16 minutes for medium rare to medium doneness, turning occasionally. Remove bones and carve steaks into slices, if desired. *Makes 4 servings*

Tip: To broil, place steaks on rack in broiler pan so surface of beef is 3 to 4 inches from heat. Broil 15 to 20 minutes for medium rare to medium doneness, turning once.

Favorite recipe from **National Cattlemen's Beef Association on behalf of The Beef Checkoff**

Veg•All® Beef & Cheddar Bake

    2 cans (15 ounces each) VEG•ALL® Original Mixed Vegetables, drained
    3 cups shredded Cheddar cheese
    2 cups cooked elbow macaroni
    1 pound extra-lean ground beef, cooked and drained
    1/2 cup chopped onion
    1/4 teaspoon black pepper

1. Preheat oven to 350°F.

2. In large mixing bowl, combine Veg•All, cheese, macaroni, ground beef, onion and pepper; mix well. Pour mixture into large casserole.

3. Bake for 30 to 35 minutes. Serve hot.
Makes 4 to 6 servings

Italian Chicken Breasts

(pictured at right)

   1 **pound BOB EVANS® Italian Roll Sausage**
   1 **cup sliced fresh mushrooms**
   1 **clove garlic, minced**
   3 **(8-ounce) cans tomato sauce**
   1 **(6-ounce) can tomato paste**
1-1/2 **teaspoons Italian seasoning**
   4 **boneless, skinless chicken breast halves**
   1 **cup (4 ounces) shredded mozzarella cheese**
     Hot cooked pasta

Preheat oven to 350°F. Crumble sausage into large skillet. Cook over medium heat until browned, stirring occasionally. Remove sausage; set aside. Add mushrooms and garlic to drippings; cook and stir until tender. Stir in reserved sausage, tomato sauce, tomato paste and seasoning. Bring to a boil. Reduce heat to low; simmer 15 minutes to blend flavors. Meanwhile, arrange chicken in greased 11×7-inch baking dish. Pour tomato sauce mixture over chicken; cover with foil. Bake 40 minutes; uncover. Sprinkle with cheese; bake 5 minutes more. Serve over pasta. Refrigerate leftovers.

Makes 4 servings

Cornish Hens with Andouille Stuffing

   4 **Cornish game hens (1-1/4 pounds each), thawed if frozen**
   6 **tablespoons butter, divided**
   2 **links (8 ounces) fully cooked andouille or chicken andouille sausage, chopped**
   1 **cup chopped onion**
1/2 **cup thinly sliced celery**
1-1/4 to 1-1/2 **cups water**
   1 **bag (8 ounces) herb stuffing mix**
   1 **teaspoon dried thyme**
   1 **teaspoon paprika or smoked paprika**
   1 **teaspoon garlic salt**
1/4 **teaspoon pepper**
   1 **cup cranberry chutney or whole-berry cranberry sauce**

1. Preheat oven to 375°F. Butter 3-quart baking dish; set aside. Pat hens dry with paper towels.

2. Melt 2 tablespoons butter in large saucepan over medium heat. Add sausage, onion and celery; cook 8 to 10 minutes or until vegetables are tender and sausage is browned, stirring occasionally. Add water (use 1-1/2 cups water for a moister stuffing); bring to a boil. Remove from heat. Add stuffing mix; toss well to combine.

3. Spoon 1/2 cup stuffing into each hen cavity. Place hens on rack in shallow roasting pan. Tie legs together, if desired. Place remaining stuffing in prepared baking dish.

4. Melt remaining 4 tablespoons butter. Add thyme, paprika, garlic salt and pepper; mix well. Spoon half of butter mixture over hens. Roast hens 30 minutes. Bake remaining stuffing with hens 25 minutes. Brush remaining butter mixture over hens. Roast 20 to 25 minutes more or until internal temperature reaches 180°F in thigh. Serve hens and stuffing with cranberry chutney.

Makes 4 servings

Ortega® Fiesta Bake

   2 **pounds ground beef**
1/2 **cup chopped onion**
3/4 **cup ORTEGA® Salsa, any variety**
   1 **package (1.25 ounces) ORTEGA Taco Seasoning Mix**
1/4 **cup water**
   1 **cup whole kernel corn**
   1 **can (2-1/4 ounces) sliced olives, drained**
   1 **package (8-1/2 ounces) corn muffin mix**
   1 **large egg**
1/3 **cup milk**
   1 **cup (4 ounces) shredded Cheddar cheese**
   1 **can (4 ounces) ORTEGA Diced Green Chiles**

PREHEAT oven to 350°F.

COOK beef and onion in large skillet until beef is browned; drain. Stir in salsa, seasoning mix and water. Cook over low heat for 5 to 6 minutes or until mixture thickens; stir in corn and olives. Spoon into 8-inch square baking dish.

COMBINE muffin mix, egg and milk until smooth; stir in cheese and chiles. Spread over meat mixture.

BAKE for 30 to 35 minutes or until corn topping is golden brown. *Makes 6 servings*

Italian Chicken Breast

Thyme-Roasted Salmon with Horseradish-Dijon Sour Cream

(pictured at right)

2 (6-ounce) salmon fillets, patted dry
1 tablespoon olive oil
1/2 teaspoon dried thyme
1/2 teaspoon lemon-pepper
1/3 cup sour cream
2 tablespoons mayonnaise
2 teaspoons prepared horseradish
1/2 teaspoon Worcestershire sauce
1/2 teaspoon Dijon mustard
1/4 teaspoon salt

1. Preheat oven to 400°F.

2. Line a baking sheet with foil. Arrange fillets on foil, then sprinkle evenly with oil, thyme and lemon pepper. Bake 12 to 14 minutes or until opaque in center.

3. Meanwhile, combine remaining ingredients in a small bowl; stir to blend well. Serve sauce with salmon.
Makes 2 servings

Spanish-Style Chicken & Rice

2 tablespoons BERTOLLI® Olive Oil
1 clove garlic, finely chopped
1 cup uncooked regular rice
1 envelope LIPTON® RECIPE SECRETS® Onion Soup Mix
2-1/2 cups hot water
1 cup frozen peas, partially thawed
1/2 cup chopped red or green bell pepper
8 green olives, sliced
1 (2-1/2- to 3-pound) chicken, cut into serving pieces

1. Preheat oven to 400°F.

2. In 13×9-inch baking or roasting pan, combine olive oil with garlic; heat in oven 5 minutes. Stir in uncooked rice until coated with oil. Add soup mix blended with hot water; stir in peas, bell pepper and olives. Press chicken pieces into rice mixture. Bake 35 minutes or until chicken is thoroughly cooked and rice is tender. Cover and let stand 10 minutes before serving.
Makes about 4 servings

Serving Suggestion: Serve this tasty dish with cooked green beans and fresh fruit for dessert.

Sausage 'n' Apples

1 pound BOB EVANS® Original Recipe Roll Sausage
2 tablespoons chopped onion
1 clove garlic, minced *or* 1/8 teaspoon garlic powder
8 medium Granny Smith apples
1 cup apple juice
1/4 cup packed brown sugar

Preheat oven to 350°F. Crumble sausage into large skillet. Add onion and garlic. Cook over medium-high heat until sausage is browned, stirring occasionally. Drain off any drippings. Core apples and stuff with sausage mixture. Place in 13×9-inch baking dish. Pour juice over apples; sprinkle tops with brown sugar. Bake 40 minutes or until apples are soft. Serve warm. Refrigerate leftovers.
Makes 4 servings

Southwest Ham 'n' Cheese Quiche

4 (8-inch) flour tortillas
2 tablespoons butter or margarine, melted
2 cups pizza 4-cheese blend
1-1/2 cups (8 ounces) diced HORMEL® CURE 81® ham
1/2 cup sour cream
1/4 cup salsa
3 eggs, beaten
Salsa
Sour cream

Heat oven to 350°F. Cut 3 tortillas in half. Place remaining whole tortilla in bottom of greased 10-inch quiche dish or tart pan; brush with melted butter. Arrange tortilla halves around edge of dish, rounded sides up, overlapping to form pastry shell. Brush with remaining butter. Place 9-inch round cake pan inside quiche dish. Bake 5 minutes. Cool; remove cake pan. In large bowl, combine cheese and ham. Stir in sour cream, salsa and eggs. Pour into tortilla shell. Bake 55 to 60 minutes or until knife inserted in center comes out clean. Let stand 5 minutes. Serve with additional salsa and sour cream.
Makes 6 servings

Thyme-Roasted Salmon with Horseradish-Dijon Sour Cream

Succulent Roast Turkey

(pictured at right)

1 (12-pound) fresh or thawed frozen turkey
1/4 cup (1/2 stick) butter, melted, divided
Salt and pepper
1-1/2 cups apple cider or apple juice
2 cups chicken broth, divided
Cider Pan Gravy (recipe follows)

1. Preheat oven to 325°F. Pat turkey dry. Stuff turkey, if desired. Place on rack in large shallow roasting pan.

2. Brush turkey with 2 tablespoons butter. Season with salt and pepper. Pour cider and 1 cup broth into bottom of roasting pan. Roast turkey 1 hour 30 minutes. Brush remaining 2 tablespoons butter over turkey; add remaining 1 cup broth and continue roasting 1 hour. Baste turkey with pan juices; add additional broth if pan is dry to prevent drippings from burning. Continue baking until internal temperature of thigh meat registers 180°F and legs move easily in sockets, 30 minutes to 1 hour longer.

3. Transfer turkey to carving board or serving platter; tent with foil and let stand 20 to 30 minutes before carving. Reserve drippings for gravy (drippings will be dark). Make Cider Pan Gravy. Serve with warm turkey.   *Makes 10 to 12 servings*

Cider Pan Gravy

Reserved drippings from roasting pan
3 tablespoons all-purpose flour
2 cups chicken broth or turkey stock
1/4 cup whipping cream
Salt and pepper

Pour drippings into measuring cup; spoon off 3 tablespoons fat and transfer to medium saucepan. Discard remaining fat. Add flour; cook over medium heat 1 minute, stirring constantly. Gradually stir in chicken broth, then defatted reserved drippings. Cook over medium heat 10 minutes, stirring occasionally. Stir in cream; season with salt and pepper.   *Makes 8 to 10 servings*

Helpful Hint

Make extra gravy for meals later in the week such as a turkey potpie. Combine frozen mixed vegetables and shredded cooked turkey with the leftover gravy. Top with biscuit or pie dough for a hearty delicious dinner.

Italian-Style Meat Loaf

1 egg
1-1/2 pounds lean ground beef or turkey
8 ounces hot or mild Italian sausage, casings removed
1 cup CONTADINA® Seasoned Bread Crumbs
1 can (8 ounces) CONTADINA Tomato Sauce, divided
1 cup finely chopped onion
1/2 cup finely chopped green bell pepper

1. Beat egg lightly in large bowl. Add beef, sausage, bread crumbs, 3/4 cup tomato sauce, onion and bell pepper; mix well.

2. Press into ungreased 9×5-inch loaf pan. Bake, uncovered, in preheated 350°F oven for 60 minutes.

3. Spoon remaining tomato sauce over meat loaf. Bake 15 minutes longer or until no longer pink in center; drain. Let stand for 10 minutes before serving.   *Makes 8 servings*

Sloppy Joe Casserole

1 pound ground beef
1 can (10-3/4 ounces) Campbell's® Condensed Tomato Soup
1/4 cup water
1 teaspoon Worcestershire sauce
1/8 teaspoon ground black pepper
1 package (7.5 ounces) refrigerated biscuits (10)
1/2 cup shredded Cheddar Cheese

1. Heat the oven to 400°F.

2. Cook the beef in a 10-inch skillet over medium-high heat until the beef is well browned, stirring frequently to break up meat. Pour off any fat.

3. Stir the soup, water, Worcestershire and black pepper into skillet. Heat to a boil. Spoon the beef mixture into a 1-1/2-quart casserole. Arrange the biscuits over the beef mixture around the edge of the casserole.

4. Bake for 15 minutes or until the biscuits are golden brown. Sprinkle the cheese over the beef mixture.   *Makes 5 servings*

Succulent Roast Turkey

*Charred Steak Taco
with Citrus Chipotle Sauce*

Charred Steak Taco
with Citrus Chipotle Sauce

(pictured above)

1/2 cup *French's® Gourmayo™* Chipotle Chili
    Mayonnaise
1/2 cup sour cream
  2 tablespoons lime juice
  2 tablespoons orange juice concentrate
    Steak Rub (recipe follows)
  2 pounds flank steak
  8 (8-inch) flour tortillas, heated
1/2 cup salsa
  2 cups shredded lettuce

1. Combine mayonnaise, sour cream, lime juice and orange juice concentrate in small bowl; set aside.

2. Sprinkle about 2 tablespoons Steak Rub onto each side of steak, rubbing spice mixture into meat. Grill steak over medium heat 15 minutes until medium rare or to desired doneness. Let stand 10 minutes.

3. To assemble tacos, thinly slice steak. Arrange steak on half of each tortilla, dividing evenly. Fold tortillas over. Top with salsa, lettuce and Citrus Chipotle Sauce. *Makes 8 servings*

Steak Rub: Combine 3 tablespoons brown sugar, 1 tablespoon chili powder, 1-1/2 teaspoons coarse salt and 1/2 teaspoon ground black pepper in small bowl.

Note: For a main-dish salad, serve steak and Citrus Chipotle Sauce over salad greens.

Italian Chicken
with Sausage and Peppers

  2 tablespoons olive oil
2-1/2 pounds bone-in chicken pieces
1/2 to 3/4 pound sweet Italian sausage
  2 sweet green peppers, chopped
  1 onion, chopped
  1 carrot, finely chopped
  2 garlic cloves, minced
  1 can (15 ounces) tomato sauce
  1 can (10-3/4 ounces) condensed tomato soup,
    undiluted
1/4 teaspoon dried oregano
1/4 teaspoon dried basil
  1 bay leaf
    Salt and pepper

SLOW COOKER DIRECTIONS
1. Heat oil in large skillet over medium-high heat. Cook chicken, skin side down, about 10 minutes, turning to brown both sides. Remove from skillet; set aside.

2. In same skillet, cook sausage 4 to 5 minutes or until browned. Remove sausage from skillet; cut into 1-inch pieces. Set aside. Drain off all but 1 tablespoon fat from skillet.

3. Add sweet peppers, onion, carrot and garlic to skillet. Cook and stir 4 to 5 minutes or until vegetables are tender.

4. Add tomato sauce, tomato soup, oregano, basil and bay leaf; mix well. Season with salt and pepper. Transfer mixture to 4-quart slow cooker.

5. Add chicken and sausage to slow cooker. Cover; cook on LOW 6 to 8 hours or on HIGH 4 to 6 hours. Remove and discard bay leaf before serving.
Makes 6 servings

Glazed Ham and Sweet Potato Kabobs

(pictured below)

1 large sweet potato (12 ounces), peeled
1 boneless ham slice (12 ounces), 1/4 inch thick
1/4 cup (1/2 stick) butter
1/4 cup packed dark brown sugar
2 tablespoons cider vinegar
2 tablespoons molasses
1 tablespoon Worcestershire sauce
1 tablespoon yellow mustard
3/4 teaspoon ground cinnamon
1/2 teaspoon ground allspice
1/8 teaspoon crushed red pepper flakes
16 fresh pineapple chunks (about 1 inch)
1 package (10 ounces) mixed salad greens

1. Cut sweet potato into 16 pieces; place in shallow microwavable dish with 1/4 cup water. Cover; microwave on HIGH 4 minutes or until fork-tender. Drain; cool about 5 minutes.

2. Cut ham slice into 20 (1-inch) pieces; set aside.

3. For glaze, combine butter, brown sugar, vinegar, molasses, Worcestershire, mustard, cinnamon, allspice and pepper flakes in large saucepan. Bring to a boil over high heat. Reduce heat to medium high. Cook 2 minutes or until sauce reduces to 1/2 cup. Remove from heat; cool.

4. Prepare grill for direct cooking. Thread ham, potato and pineapple, starting and ending with ham, onto 4 (12-inch) skewers.*

5. Arrange skewers on grid over medium heat. Grill 6 to 8 minutes, turning every 2 minutes and brushing with sauce until potatoes are brown and ham is heated through. Let stand, covered with tented foil, 5 minutes before serving.

6. To serve, place mixed greens on platter. Remove ham, sweet potato and pineapple from skewers; arrange on top of greens. Serve immediately.

Makes 4 servings

Soak wooden skewers in water 20 minutes before using to prevent burning.

Just for fun: Toast 6 to 8 large marshmallows on skewers alongside the kabobs. Separate the sweet potatoes and top with warm marshmallows. Yum!

Glazed Ham and Sweet Potato Kabobs

Rigatoni

(pictured at right)

2 pounds BOB EVANS® Italian Dinner
    Link Sausage
2 medium onions, sliced
3 green bell peppers, sliced
3 red bell peppers, sliced
3 cloves garlic, minced
1 tablespoon sugar
1 teaspoon dried oregano leaves
1 teaspoon dried basil leaves
1 teaspoon dried thyme leaves
    Salt and black pepper to taste
1 (1-quart) can crushed Italian plum tomatoes,
    undrained
1 pound rigatoni pasta, cooked according to
    package directions and drained
    Chopped fresh parsley (optional)

Cut sausage into 1-inch pieces. Cook in large saucepan over medium-high heat until well browned. Remove sausage to paper towels; set aside. Drain off all but 1/4 cup drippings. Add all remaining ingredients except tomatoes, pasta and parsley to drippings. Cook and stir until vegetables are tender. Stir in reserved sausage and tomatoes with juice. Bring to a boil. Reduce heat to low; simmer 15 minutes. Serve over hot pasta. Garnish with chopped parsley, if desired. Refrigerate leftovers.   *Makes 8 to 10 servings*

Seared Pork Roast
with Currant Cherry Salsa

1-1/2 teaspoons chili powder
3/4 teaspoon salt
1/2 teaspoon garlic powder
1/2 teaspoon paprika
1/4 teaspoon ground allspice
1 tablespoon vegetable oil
1 boneless pork loin roast (about 2 pounds)
    Nonstick cooking spray
1/2 cup water
1 bag (16 ounces) frozen pitted dark cherries,
    thawed, drained and halved
1/4 cup currants or dark raisins
1 teaspoon balsamic vinegar
1 teaspoon grated orange peel
1/8 to 1/4 teaspoon crushed red pepper
    flakes

SLOW COOKER DIRECTIONS

1. Combine chili powder, salt, garlic powder, paprika and allspice in small bowl. Coat roast evenly with spice mixture. Heat oil in large skillet over medium-high heat. Brown roast on all sides; place in 4-quart slow cooker.

2. To deglaze skillet, pour water into pan, stirring to scrape up browned bits. Pour around sides of roast. Cover; cook on LOW 2 to 4 hours or until meat reaches 160°F. (For tenderness, do not cook on HIGH.)

3. Remove pork. Tent with foil; keep warm.

4. Strain juices from slow cooker; discard solids. Pour juices into small saucepan; keep warm over low heat.

5. Add cherries, currants, vinegar, orange peel and pepper flakes to slow cooker. Cover and cook on HIGH 30 minutes.

6. To serve, slice pork and spoon warm juices over meat. Serve with salsa.   *Makes 8 servings*

Note: To thicken salsa, mix 1 teaspoon cornstarch with 1 tablespoon water. Stir into cherry mixture in slow cooker. Cook until thickened.

Hearty Beef Stew

1 pound ground beef
1 tablespoon minced garlic
1 jar (14 ounces) marinara sauce
1 can (10-1/2 ounces) condensed beef broth
1 package (16 ounces) Italian-style frozen
    vegetables
2 cups southern-style hash brown potatoes
2 tablespoons *French's*® Worcestershire Sauce
2 cups *French's*® French Fried Onions

1. Brown beef with garlic in large saucepan until no longer pink; drain. Add sauce, broth, vegetables, potatoes and Worcestershire. Bring to boiling; cover. Reduce heat to medium-low. Cook 10 minutes or until vegetables are crisp-tender.

2. Spoon stew into bowls. Sprinkle with French Fried Onions. Serve with garlic bread, if desired.   *Makes 6 servings*

Rigatoni

Italian Sausage Supper

(pictured at right)

1 pound mild Italian sausage, casing removed
1 cup chopped onion
3 medium zucchini, sliced (about 1-1/2 cups)
1 can (6 ounces) CONTADINA® Tomato Paste
1 cup water
1 teaspoon dried basil leaves, crushed
1/2 teaspoon salt
3 cups cooked rice
1 cup (4 ounces) shredded mozzarella cheese
1/4 cup (1 ounce) grated Romano cheese

1. Brown sausage with onion in large skillet, stirring to break up sausage; drain, reserving 1 tablespoon drippings.

2. Spoon sausage mixture into greased 2-quart casserole dish. Add zucchini to skillet; sauté for 5 minutes or until crisp-tender.

3. Combine tomato paste, water, basil and salt in medium bowl. Stir in rice. Spoon over sausage mixture. Arrange zucchini slices on top; sprinkle with mozzarella and Romano cheeses.

4. Cover. Bake in preheated 350°F oven for 20 minutes.   *Makes 6 servings*

Turkey Paella

1 tablespoon olive oil
1 small onion, chopped
1 garlic clove, minced
8 ounces uncooked bulk chorizo sausage*
2 cups chicken broth
1/4 teaspoon crushed saffron threads *or*
        ground turmeric
2 cups diced cooked turkey (preferably
        dark meat)
1 cup uncooked rice
1 medium tomato, diced
    Salt and pepper
1/2 pound large raw shrimp, peeled and
        deveined
1 cup frozen peas, thawed
1/4 cup diced pimiento

Chorizo, a spicy Mexican pork sausage, is flavored with garlic and chiles. It's available in most supermarkets, but if you can't find it, substitute 8 ounces bulk pork sausage plus 1/4 teaspoon cayenne pepper.

1. Heat oil in 12-inch skillet over medium-high heat. Add onion; cook and stir 3 to 5 minutes or until

onion is translucent. Add garlic and chorizo, stirring to break up meat. Brown chorizo. Pour off fat.

2. Add broth and saffron. Bring to a boil. Reduce heat; add turkey, rice and tomato. Season with salt and pepper. Bring to a boil; scrape up browned bits. Cover and reduce heat. Simmer 20 minutes or until liquid is absorbed and rice is tender (mixture may be slightly soupy).

3. Stir in shrimp, peas and pimientos. Cook 5 minutes or until shrimp are pink and opaque.
          Makes 4 to 6 servings

Szechuan Grilled Flank Steak

1 beef flank steak (1-1/4 to 1-1/2 pounds)
1/4 cup seasoned rice wine vinegar
1/4 cup soy sauce
2 tablespoons dark sesame oil
4 garlic cloves, minced
2 teaspoons minced fresh ginger
1/2 teaspoon crushed red pepper flakes
1/4 cup water
1/2 cup thinly sliced green onions
2 to 3 teaspoons sesame seeds, toasted
    Hot cooked rice

1. Place steak in large resealable food storage bag. Combine vinegar, soy sauce, oil, garlic, ginger and pepper flakes in small bowl; pour over steak. Seal bag; turn to coat. Marinate in refrigerator 3 hours, turning once.

2. Prepare grill for direct cooking. Remove steak from bag, reserving marinade. Place steak on grid over medium heat. Grill, uncovered, 17 to 21 minutes for medium rare to medium or until desired doneness, turning once.

3. Combine water and reserved marinade in small saucepan. Bring to a rolling boil over high heat. Boil 1 minute.

4. Slice steak across grain into thin slices. Drizzle slices with boiled marinade. Sprinkle with green onions and sesame seeds. Serve with rice.
          Makes 4 to 6 servings

Dijon Pork Roast with Cranberries

Dijon Pork Roast with Cranberries

(pictured above)

1/4 teaspoon ground allspice
1/4 teaspoon salt
1/4 teaspoon ground black pepper
  1 boneless pork loin roast (2 to 2-1/2 pounds), trimmed of excess fat
  2 tablespoons *French's®* Honey Dijon Mustard
  2 tablespoons honey
  2 teaspoons grated orange peel
1-1/3 cups *French's®* French Fried Onions, divided
  1 cup dried cranberries

SLOW COOKER DIRECTIONS

1. Combine allspice, salt and pepper; sprinkle over roast. Place meat in 4-quart slow cooker. Blend mustard, honey and orange peel; pour over roast. Sprinkle with *2/3 cup* French Fried Onions and cranberries.

2. Cover and cook on LOW setting for 4 to 6 hours (or on HIGH for 2 to 3 hours) until meat is fork-tender.

3. Remove pork to serving platter. Skim fat from sauce in slow cooker; transfer sauce to serving bowl. Slice meat and serve with fruit sauce; sprinkle with remaining onions. *Makes 6 servings*

Note: Cook times vary depending on type of slow cooker used. Check manufacturer's recommendations for cooking pork roast.

Southwestern Ham and Rice

  1 (10-ounce) package frozen mixed vegetables
1-1/2 cups sliced fresh mushrooms
  1/2 cup chopped onion
  1 tablespoon butter or margarine
  1 (11-ounce) can nacho cheese soup
  1/2 cup milk
  2 cups (12 ounces) chopped HORMEL® CURE 81® ham
  4 cups hot cooked rice

Prepare mixed vegetables according to package directions; drain well. In large skillet over medium-high heat, sauté mushrooms and onion in butter until tender. Stir in soup and milk. Add ham and cooked vegetables. Simmer until thoroughly heated. Serve over rice. *Makes 4 servings*

Veal Stew with Horseradish

1-1/4 pounds veal for stew, trimmed and cut into 1-inch cubes
  2 medium sweet potatoes, peeled and cut into 1-inch pieces
  1 can (14-1/2 ounces) diced tomatoes
  1 package (10 ounces) frozen corn
1-1/2 cups frozen lima beans
  1 large onion, chopped
  1 cup vegetable broth
  1 tablespoon chili powder
  1 tablespoon prepared horseradish
  1 tablespoon honey

SLOW COOKER DIRECTIONS

1. Combine all ingredients in 4-quart slow cooker.

2. Cover and cook on LOW 7 to 8 hours or until veal is tender. *Makes 6 servings*

Lemony Olive Chicken

(pictured below)

1 tablespoon vegetable oil
4 skinless, boneless chicken breast halves
1 can (10-3/4 ounces) Campbell's®
    Condensed Cream of Chicken Soup
    (Regular or 98% Fat Free)
1/4 cup milk
1 tablespoon lemon juice
1/8 teaspoon black pepper
1/2 cup sliced pimento-stuffed Spanish olives
4 lemon slices
    Hot cooked rice

1. Heat the oil in a 10-inch skillet over medium-high heat. Add the chicken and cook for 10 minutes or until it's well browned on both sides. Remove the chicken and set aside.

2. Stir the soup, milk, lemon juice, black pepper and olives into skillet. Top with the lemon slices. Heat to a boil. Return the chicken to the skillet and reduce the heat to low. Cover and cook for 5 minutes or until the chicken is cooked through. Serve with the rice.   *Makes 4 servings*

Cheesy Stuffed Meatballs & Spaghetti

(pictured on front cover and page 126)

1 pound ground beef
1/2 cup Italian seasoned dry bread crumbs
1 egg
2 ounces mozzarella cheese, cut into
    12 (1/2-inch) cubes
1 jar (1 pound 10 ounces) RAGÚ® Old World
    Style® Pasta Sauce
8 ounces spaghetti, cooked and drained

1. In medium bowl, combine ground beef, bread crumbs and egg; shape into 12 meatballs. Press 1 cheese cube into each meatball, enclosing completely.

2. In 3-quart saucepan, bring Pasta Sauce to a boil over medium-high heat. Gently stir in uncooked meatballs.

3. Reduce heat to low and simmer covered, stirring occasionally, 20 minutes or until meatballs are done. Serve over hot spaghetti. Sprinkle, if desired, with grated Parmesan cheese.   *Makes 4 servings*

Lemony Olive Chicken

Creamy Blush Sauce with Turkey and Penne

(pictured at right)

4 turkey thighs, skin removed (about 3 pounds)
1 jar (1 pound 9.75 ounces) Prego® Chunky Garden Mushroom & Green Pepper Italian Sauce
1/2 teaspoon crushed red pepper
1/2 cup half-and-half
    Tube-shaped pasta (penne), cooked and drained
    Grated Parmesan cheese

1. Put the turkey in a 3 1/2- to 5-quart slow cooker. Pour the Italian sauce over the turkey and sprinkle with the red pepper.

2. Cover and cook on LOW for 7 to 8 hours* or until turkey is fork-tender and cooked through. Remove the turkey from the cooker. Remove the turkey meat from the bones.

3. Stir the turkey meat and the half-and-half into the cooker. Cover and cook for 10 minutes or until hot. Spoon the sauce over the turkey and pasta. Sprinkle with cheese.   *Makes 8 servings*

*Or on HIGH for 4 to 5 hours

Easy Substitution Tip: Substitute 8 bone-in chicken thighs (about 2 pounds) for the turkey thighs. Serves 4.

Grilled Sausage with Summer Vegetables and Mostaccioli

1 package BOB EVANS® Italian Grillin' Sausage or Italian Dinner Links (approximately 5 links)
2 medium green or yellow bell peppers, seeded and coarsely sliced
2 medium onions, thinly sliced
2 medium zucchini, unpeeled and sliced
4 cloves garlic, minced
1/4 cup olive oil
8 Italian plum tomatoes, cut into quarters
16 ounces mostaccioli or ziti, cooked according to package directions
1/2 cup grated Parmesan cheese
2 tablespoons chopped fresh basil

Precook sausage 10 minutes in gently boiling water. Remove from water and grill over medium coals until lightly browned and no longer pink. Cut into 3/4-inch slices.

Cook and stir bell peppers, onions, zucchini and garlic in olive oil in large skillet over medium heat about 10 minutes or until onions are translucent. Add tomatoes; cook and stir 5 minutes more. Transfer to large bowl; toss with grilled sausage and hot cooked mostaccioli. Sprinkle with cheese and basil. Refrigerate leftovers.   *Makes 6 servings*

Cajun Chicken and Rice

4 chicken drumsticks, skin removed
4 chicken thighs, skin removed
2 teaspoons Cajun seasoning
3/4 teaspoon salt, divided
2 tablespoons vegetable oil
1 can (14-1/2 ounces) chicken broth
1 cup uncooked rice
1 medium sweet green pepper, coarsely chopped
1 medium sweet red pepper, coarsely chopped
1/2 cup finely chopped green onions
2 garlic cloves, minced
1/2 teaspoon dried thyme
1/4 teaspoon ground turmeric

1. Preheat oven to 350°F. Lightly coat 3-quart baking dish with nonstick cooking spray; set aside.

2. Pat chicken dry. Sprinkle both sides with Cajun seasoning and 1/4 teaspoon salt. Heat oil in large skillet over medium-high heat. Add chicken; cook 8 to 10 minutes or until browned on all sides. Transfer to plate; set aside.

3. Add broth to skillet. Bring to a boil, scraping bottom and sides of pan. Add remaining ingredients. Stir well. Pour into prepared baking dish. Place browned chicken on top. Cover tightly with foil. Bake 1 hour or until chicken is done (180°F).
                    Makes 6 servings

Variation: For a one-skillet meal, use an ovenproof skillet. Place browned chicken on mixture in skillet, cover, and bake as directed.

*Creamy Blush Sauce
with Turkey and Penne*

Greek Chicken

(pictured at right)

12 garlic cloves, unpeeled
3 pounds chicken leg and thigh pieces
4 tablespoons lemon juice, divided
3 tablespoons olive oil
2 tablespoons chopped fresh rosemary leaves
  or 2 teaspoons dried rosemary
3/4 teaspoon salt
1/2 teaspoon pepper
  Additional sprigs fresh rosemary and lemon
  wedges

1. Preheat oven to 375°F. Arrange garlic in shallow roasting pan. Place chicken over garlic. Combine 2 tablespoons lemon juice, oil and rosemary in small bowl; spoon evenly over chicken. Sprinkle chicken with salt and pepper. Bake 50 to 55 minutes or until cooked through (180°F). Transfer chicken to serving platter; keep warm.

2. Squeeze garlic pulp from skins; discard skins. Place garlic pulp in roasting pan; add remaining 2 tablespoons lemon juice. Cook over medium heat, mashing garlic and stirring to scrape up browned bits. Pour sauce over chicken; garnish with rosemary sprigs and lemon wedges.

Makes 4 servings

Hint: To add more lemon flavor, tuck a few lemon wedges or slices among the chicken pieces before roasting.

Tip: Unpeeled cloves of garlic usually burst open while roasting, making it a cinch to squeeze out the softened, creamy roasted garlic with your thumb and forefinger. If the cloves have not burst open, simply slice off the end with a knife and squeeze out the garlic.

Garlic Beef Stir-Fry

1 cup red or yellow bell pepper strips
3 cloves garlic, minced
1 tablespoon oil
12 ounces boneless beef sirloin steak, cut into
  thin bite-size strips
1 can (14-1/2 ounces) DEL MONTE® Cut Green
  Beans, drained
1/4 cup stir-fry sauce
  Hot cooked rice (optional)

1. Cook and stir bell pepper strips and garlic in hot oil in large skillet 2 to 3 minutes or until tender. Remove from skillet.

2. Add beef; cook and stir 2 to 3 minutes or until desired doneness. Stir in pepper mixture, beans and stir-fry sauce; heat through. Serve over hot cooked rice, if desired.

Makes 4 servings

Tip: Let your kids choose the vegetable for dinner one night a week.

Jerk Turkey Stew

1 tablespoon vegetable oil
1 small red onion, chopped
1 garlic clove, minced
1/2 teaspoon ground ginger
1/4 teaspoon salt
1/4 teaspoon pepper
1/8 to 1/4 teaspoon cayenne pepper*
1/8 teaspoon ground allspice
1 can (28 ounces) diced tomatoes
3 cups diced cooked turkey
2 cups cooked sweet potato, cut into
  1/2-inch pieces
1/2 cup turkey broth or gravy
1 tablespoon lime juice
1 tablespoon minced fresh chives

*1/8 teaspoon makes a mildly hot dish; 1/4 teaspoon is very hot.

1. Heat oil in Dutch oven over medium heat. Add onion and garlic; cook and stir 5 minutes. Add ginger, salt, pepper, cayenne and allspice. Cook 20 seconds to blend spices. Stir in tomatoes, turkey, sweet potato and broth. Reduce heat to low; simmer 15 minutes.

2. Stir in lime juice; cover and let dish stand 10 to 15 minutes to allow flavors to blend. Sprinkle with chives just before serving.

Makes 4 servings

Greek Chicken

Rigatoni with Sausage & Beans

(pictured at right)

  1 pound sweet Italian sausage links, cut in
    1/2-inch pieces
  1 jar (1 pound 10 ounces) RAGÚ® Chunky
    Gardenstyle Pasta Sauce
  1 can (19 ounces) cannellini or white kidney
    beans, rinsed and drained
1/8 to 1/4 teaspoon dried rosemary leaves,
    crushed (optional)
  1 box (16 ounces) rigatoni or ziti pasta, cooked
    and drained

1. In 12-inch skillet, brown sausage over medium-high heat; drain. Stir in Pasta Sauce, beans and rosemary.

2. Bring to a boil over high heat. Reduce heat to low and simmer uncovered, stirring occasionally, 10 minutes or until sausage is done. Serve over hot pasta. *Makes 4 servings*

Baked Pork Chops
with Garden Stuffing

      Vegetable cooking spray
  1 can (10-3/4 ounces) Campbell's® Condensed
    Golden Mushroom Soup
3/4 cup water
  1 bag (16 ounces) frozen vegetable combination
    (broccoli, cauliflower, carrots)
  1 tablespoon butter
  4 cups Pepperidge Farm® Herbed Seasoned
    Stuffing
  6 boneless pork chops, 3/4-inch thick

1. Spray a 13×9×2-inch shallow baking dish with cooking spray.

2. Stir **1/3 cup** of the soup and **1/2 cup** of the water, vegetables and butter in a 2-quart saucepan. Heat to a boil. Remove from heat. Add the stuffing and mix lightly to coat.

3. Spoon the stuffing mixture into the prepared dish. Arrange chops over the stuffing mixture.

4. Stir the remaining soup and remaining water. Spoon over the chops. Bake at 400°F. for 40 minutes or until the chops are cooked through.
Makes 6 servings

Tuna-Swiss Pie

  2 cups cooked white rice (2/3 cup uncooked)
  1 tablespoon butter or margarine
1/4 teaspoon garlic powder
  3 eggs, divided
1-1/3 cups *French's®* French Fried Onions, divided
  1 cup (4 ounces) shredded Swiss cheese, divided
  2 cans (6 ounces each) water-packed tuna,
    drained and flaked
  1 cup milk
1/4 teaspoon salt
1/4 teaspoon black pepper

Preheat oven to 400°F. To hot rice in saucepan, add butter, garlic powder and 1 slightly beaten egg; mix thoroughly. Spoon rice mixture into ungreased 9-inch pie plate. Press rice mixture firmly across bottom and up side of pie plate to form a crust. Layer *2/3 cup* French Fried Onions, 1/2 cup cheese and the tuna evenly over rice crust. In small bowl, combine milk, remaining 2 eggs and the seasonings; pour over tuna filling. Bake, uncovered, at 400°F for 30 to 35 minutes or until center is set. Top with remaining 1/2 cup cheese and *2/3 cup* onions; bake, uncovered, 1 to 3 minutes or until onions are golden brown *Makes 4 to 6 servings*

Taco Cups

  1 pound lean ground beef, turkey or pork
  1 package (1 ounce) LAWRY'S® Taco Spices
    & Seasonings
1/2 cup water
1/4 cup salsa
  2 packages (8 ounces each) refrigerator biscuits
1/2 cup (2 ounces) shredded cheddar cheese

In medium skillet, brown ground beef until crumbly; drain fat. Stir in Taco Spices & Seasonings and water. Bring to a boil; reduce heat to low and cook, uncovered, 10 minutes. Stir in salsa. Separate biscuits and press each biscuit into an ungreased muffin cup. Spoon equal amounts of meat mixture into each muffin cup; sprinkle each with cheese. Bake, uncovered, in 350°F oven for 12 minutes.
Makes about 16 taco cups

Turkey and Stuffing Casserole

(pictured at right)

Vegetable cooking spray
1 can (10-3/4 ounces) Campbell's®
   Condensed Cream of Mushroom Soup
   (Regular, 98% Fat Free or 25% Less Sodium)
1 cup milk or water
1 bag (16 ounces) frozen vegetable combination
   (broccoli, cauliflower, carrots), thawed
2 cups cubed cooked turkey or chicken
4 cups Pepperidge Farm® Cubed Herb Seasoned
   Stuffing
1 cup shredded Swiss or Cheddar cheese
   (4 ounces)

1. Spray a 12×8×2-inch shallow baking dish with cooking spray and set aside.

2. Mix the soup and milk in a large bowl. Stir in the vegetables, turkey and stuffing. Spoon the mixture into the prepared dish.

3. Bake at 400°F. for 20 minutes or until hot and bubbly. Stir.

4. Sprinkle the cheese over the turkey mixture. Bake for 5 minutes more or until the cheese melts.
Makes 6 servings

Campbell's Kitchen Tip: Substitute 1 can (9.75 ounces) Swanson® Premium White Chunk Chicken Breast, drained, for the cubed cooked turkey.

Mexican Steak Tacos

1 (3.5-ounce) boil-in-bag long-grain rice
1 tablespoon ORTEGA® Salsa, any variety
2 teaspoons ground cumin
1 teaspoon garlic powder
1 teaspoon ORTEGA Taco Sauce (any variety)
1/4 teaspoon salt
1 pound boneless beef sirloin steak
   Nonstick cooking spray
1 can (about 14 ounces) diced tomatoes, drained
1 can (4 ounces) ORTEGA Diced Green Chiles
1 package (12) ORTEGA Taco Shells
12 lime wedges
   Sour cream (optional)

COOK rice. Combine salsa, cumin, garlic powder, taco sauce and salt. Rub mixture over both sides of steak.

SPRAY a broiler pan with cooking spray. Place steak on pan. Broil steak for 4 minutes on each side or until desired degree of doneness. Cut steak into thin slices.

COMBINE rice, tomatoes and chiles. Place mixture in shells.

TOP rice mixture with beef slices. Squeeze juice from limes over beef. Top with sour cream, if desired. *Makes 12 servings*

Thyme-Scented Roast Brisket Dinner

1 beef brisket (4 to 5 pounds)
4 garlic cloves, minced
2 teaspoons dried thyme
1 teaspoon salt
1/2 teaspoon pepper
2 large onions, thinly sliced
1 can (14-1/2 ounces) beef broth
2 pounds red potatoes, halved or quartered
1 pound baby carrots
2 tablespoons butter
2 tablespoons all-purpose flour

1. Preheat oven to 350°F.

2. Place brisket, fat side up, in large roasting pan; sprinkle with garlic, thyme, salt and pepper. Separate onion slices into rings; scatter over brisket. Pour broth over onions. Cover; roast 2-1/2 hours. Uncover; stir onions into sauce. Arrange potatoes and carrots around brisket. Cover; roast 45 minutes more or until brisket and vegetables are fork-tender.

3. Turn off oven. Transfer brisket to carving board; tent with foil and let stand 10 minutes. Transfer vegetables with slotted spoon to ovenproof serving bowl; keep warm in oven.

4. Melt butter in medium saucepan over medium heat. Add flour; cook and stir 1 minute. Stir in juices; cook 3 to 4 minutes or until sauce thickens, stirring constantly.

5. Carve brisket across the grain into thin slices. Serve with warm vegetables and sauce.
Makes 8 servings

Turkey and Stuffing Casserole

*Classic Beef Ribeye Roast
with Herb Shallot Sauce*

Classic Beef Ribeye Roast with Herb Shallot Sauce

(pictured above)

1 beef ribeye roast, small end (4 to 6 pounds)
2 tablespoons chopped fresh thyme
2 tablespoons garlic-pepper seasoning
2 tablespoons minced shallot
2 teaspoons chopped fresh thyme
1 cup dry red wine
2 teaspoons country Dijon-style mustard
1 tablespoon butter, softened
   Salt and pepper

1. Heat oven to 350°F. Combine 2 tablespoons thyme and garlic-pepper seasoning; press evenly onto all surfaces of beef roast.

2. Place roast, fat side up, on rack in shallow roasting pan. Insert ovenproof meat thermometer so tip is centered in thickest part of beef, not resting in fat. Do not add water or cover. Roast in 350°F oven 1-3/4 to 2 hours for medium rare; 2 to 2-1/2 hours for medium doneness.

3. Remove roast when meat thermometer registers 135°F for medium rare; 150°F for medium. Transfer roast to carving board; tent loosely with aluminum foil. Let stand 15 to 20 minutes. (Temperature will continue to rise about 10°F to reach 145°F for medium rare; 160°F for medium.)

4. Meanwhile skim fat from drippings. Combine drippings, shallot and 2 teaspoons thyme in medium saucepan. Cook and stir over medium heat 2 to 3 minutes or until shallots are crisp-tender. Stir in wine and mustard; bring to a boil. Reduce heat; simmer 8 to 10 minutes or until sauce is reduced to 3/4 cup. Stir in butter. Season with salt and pepper as desired.

5. Carve roast into slices. Serve with sauce.
Makes 6 to 8 servings

Favorite recipe from **National Cattlemen's Beef Association on behalf of The Beef Checkoff**

Cheese Enchiladas with Green Chiles

1 **can (10 ounces) ORTEGA® Enchilada Sauce**
1 **cup ORTEGA Salsa-Homestyle Recipe**
15 **(6-inch) corn tortillas**
1 **pound Monterey Jack cheese, sliced into 15 strips**
1 **can (7 ounces) ORTEGA Whole Green Chiles, sliced into 3 strips each, 15 strips total**
1 **cup (4 ounces) shredded Monterey Jack cheese**

PREHEAT oven to 350°F.

COMBINE enchilada sauce and salsa in medium bowl; mix well. Pour *1-1/2 cups* sauce mixture onto bottom of ungreased 13×9-inch baking dish.

HEAT tortillas, one at a time, in lightly greased medium skillet over medium heat for 20 seconds on each side or until soft. Place 1 strip cheese and 1 strip chile in center of each tortilla; roll up. Place seam-side down in baking pan. Repeat with remaining tortillas, cheese and chiles. Ladle *remaining* sauce mixture over enchiladas; sprinkle with shredded cheese.

BAKE, covered, for 20 minutes. Remove cover; bake for additional 5 minutes or until heated through and cheese is melted. *Makes 6 to 8 servings*

Broccoli, Turkey and Noodle Skillet

(pictured below)

1 tablespoon butter
1 sweet green pepper, chopped
1 cup frozen chopped broccoli, thawed
1/4 teaspoon pepper
1-1/2 cups chicken broth
1/2 cup milk or half-and-half cream
2 cups diced cooked turkey breast
1 package (about 4 ounces) chicken and
    broccoli pasta mix
1/4 cup sour cream

1. Melt butter in large nonstick skillet over medium heat. Add sweet pepper, broccoli and pepper; cook 5 minutes or until vegetables are crisp-tender. Add broth and milk; bring to a boil. Stir in turkey and pasta mix.

2. Reduce heat to low. Cook 8 to 10 minutes or until noodles are tender. Remove from heat. Stir in sour cream. Let stand, uncovered, 5 minutes or until sauce is thickened.   *Makes 4 servings*

Ham Loaf

1 pound ground pork
1/2 pound ham, ground
3/4 cup milk
1/2 cup fresh bread crumbs
1 egg
1 tablespoon instant tapioca
1/2 teaspoon prepared horseradish
3 to 4 drops red food color (optional)

SAUCE
1/2 cup ketchup
2 tablespoons packed brown sugar
1 tablespoon Worcestershire sauce

In large bowl, mix together pork, ham, milk, crumbs, egg, tapioca, horseradish and food color, if desired, until well blended. Place mixture in loaf pan and bake at 325°F for 1 hour. In small bowl, stir together Sauce ingredients. Pour Sauce over Ham Loaf and bake for another 30 minutes, basting occasionally with Sauce. Remove from oven; let stand 10 minutes before removing from pan. Slice to serve.

Makes 6 servings

Favorite recipe from **National Pork Board**

*Broccoli, Turkey
and Noodle Skillet*

Hearty Sausage & Rice Casserole

(pictured at right)

1 pound bulk pork sausage
1 package (8 ounces) sliced mushrooms
   (about 3 cups)
2 large stalks celery, coarsely chopped
   (about 1 cup)
1 large red pepper, coarsely chopped
   (about 1 cup)
1 large onion, coarsely chopped (about 1 cup)
1 teaspoon dried thyme leaves, crushed
1/2 teaspoon dried marjoram leaves, crushed
1 box (6 ounces) long-grain and wild rice mix
1-3/4 cups Swanson® Chicken Broth (Regular,
   Natural Goodness™ or Certified Organic)
1 can (10-3/4 ounces) Campbell's®
   Condensed Cream of Mushroom Soup
   (Regular, 98% Fat Free or Less Sodium)
1 cup shredded Cheddar cheese (4 ounces)

1. Cook the sausage in a 12-inch skillet over medium-high heat until the sausage is well browned, stirring frequently to break up the meat. Pour off any fat.

2. Add the mushrooms, celery, pepper, onion, thyme, marjoram and seasoning packet from the rice blend and cook until the vegetables are tender-crisp.

3. Stir the broth, soup, rice blend and **1/2 cup** cheese in a 13×9×2-inch shallow baking dish. Stir in the sausage mixture. **Cover.**

4. Bake at 375°F. for 1 hour or until the casserole is hot and bubbly and the rice is tender. Stir the rice mixture. Sprinkle with the remaining cheese.

Makes 6 servings

Easy Substitution: For an extra-special touch, substitute 1 package (8 ounces) baby portobello mushrooms, sliced, for the sliced mushrooms.

Florentine Chicken

2 boxes (10 ounces each) BIRDS EYE® frozen
   Chopped Spinach
1 package (1.25 ounces) hollandaise sauce mix
1/2 teaspoon TABASCO®* Pepper Sauce or to taste
1/3 cup shredded Cheddar cheese, divided
1-1/2 cups cooked cubed chicken

*Tabasco® is a registered trademark of McIlhenny Company.

Preheat oven to 350°F.

Cook spinach according to package directions; drain. Prepare hollandaise sauce according to package directions.

Blend spinach, hollandaise sauce, Tabasco sauce and half of cheese. Pour into 9×9-inch baking dish; top with chicken.

Sprinkle remaining cheese on top. Bake 10 to 12 minutes or until heated through.

Makes 4 servings

Beef Stew with Bacon, Onion and Sweet Potatoes

1 pound beef stew meat (1-inch chunks)
1 can (14-1/2 ounces) beef broth
2 medium sweet potatoes, peeled, cut into
   2-inch chunks
1 large onion, cut into 1-1/2-inch chunks
2 slices thick-cut bacon, diced
1 teaspoon dried thyme
1 teaspoon salt
1/4 teaspoon pepper
2 tablespoons cornstarch
2 tablespoons water

SLOW COOKER DIRECTIONS

1. Coat 4-quart slow cooker with nonstick cooking spray. Combine beef, broth, potatoes, onion, bacon, thyme, salt and pepper in slow cooker. Cover; cook on LOW 7 to 8 hours or on HIGH 4 to 5 hours or until meat and vegetables are tender.

2. Transfer beef and vegetables with slotted spoon to serving bowl. Cover with foil to keep warm.

3. Turn slow cooker to HIGH. Combine cornstarch and water until smooth. Stir into juices. Cook, uncovered, 15 minutes or until thickened, stirring occasionally. Return beef and vegetables to slow cooker. Cover and cook 15 minutes or until warm.

Makes 4 servings

Substitution: Use 1 pound carrots or white potatoes, cut into 2-inch chunks, instead of sweet potatoes.

Hearty Sausage & Rice Casserole

Spicy Barbecued Meat Loaf

(pictured at right)

1 to 2 slices rye bread, torn into pieces
1 large onion, cut into chunks
3 garlic cloves, peeled
1 tablespoon butter
1 pound ground beef chuck
1 pound bulk pork sausage
2 eggs
3/4 cup hickory-flavored barbecue sauce, divided
3/4 teaspoon salt
1/4 teaspoon pepper

1. Preheat oven to 375°F. Line jelly-roll pan or shallow roasting pan with foil.

2. Make fresh bread crumbs by processing torn bread in food processor. Transfer 3/4 cup bread crumbs to large bowl; set aside. (Any remaining crumbs may be frozen up to 3 months.) Add onion and garlic to food processor; process until finely chopped.

3. Melt butter in large skillet over medium heat. Add chopped onion and garlic; cook 6 minutes or until softened, stirring occasionally. Let cool 5 minutes.

4. Add beef, sausage, eggs, 1/4 cup barbecue sauce, salt and pepper to reserved bread crumbs. Add onion mixture; mix well.

5. Transfer meat mixture to prepared pan; form into 9×6-inch oval. Bake 30 minutes. Spread remaining 1/2 cup barbecue sauce over meat loaf; bake 30 minutes more or until internal temperature reaches 160°F. Let stand 5 minutes before slicing.

Makes 8 servings

Cheesy Ham & Broccoli Stuffed Potatoes

4 large baking potatoes
1 (5-ounce) can HORMEL® chunk ham, drained and flaked
1/2 (10-ounce) package frozen chopped broccoli, thawed and drained
1 cup sour cream with chive and onion seasoning
1 cup shredded Sharp Cheddar cheese, divided

Microwave potatoes on HIGH (100% power) 12 to 14 minutes or until fork tender. Wrap in foil and allow to stand 5 minutes. Slice away skin from top of each potato; carefully scoop out pulp, leaving shells intact. Mash pulp. Add chunk ham, broccoli, sour cream and 1/2 cup cheese to the potato pulp; stir well. Stuff shells with potato mixture; sprinkle with remaining cheese. Microwave on HIGH (100% power) 2 to 3 minutes or until cheese is melted.

Makes 4 servings

Cha-Cha-Cha Casserole

Nonstick cooking spray
1 can (about 7 ounces) whole green chiles, drained
1 pound ground turkey or chicken
1 cup chopped onion
3 garlic cloves, minced
1 tablespoon chili powder
1 teaspoon salt
1 teaspoon ground cumin
1 can (14-1/2 ounces) diced tomatoes with green chiles
2 cups corn kernels
1 can (16 ounces) refried beans
2 cups (8 ounces) shredded Mexican cheese blend
2 cups crushed tortilla chips
1 cup diced seeded fresh tomato
1/2 cup sliced green onions

1. Preheat oven to 375°F. Spray 8-inch square baking dish with cooking spray. Cut chiles in half lengthwise; place in single layer in prepared dish.

2. Spray medium nonstick skillet with cooking spray. Cook and stir turkey, onion, garlic, chili powder, salt and cumin over medium heat until turkey is no longer pink. Add canned tomatoes; cook about 10 minutes or until liquid evaporates.

3. Spoon turkey mixture over chiles; top with corn and beans. Sprinkle with cheese and crushed chips. Bake 30 minutes; let stand 5 minutes before serving. Sprinkle with fresh tomato and green onions.

Makes 6 servings

Spicy Barbecued Meat Loaf

Desserts

Spicy Butterscotch Snack Cake

(pictured at left)

- 1 cup (2 sticks) butter or margarine, softened
- 1 cup sugar
- 2 eggs
- 1/2 teaspoon vanilla extract
- 1/2 cup applesauce
- 2-1/2 cups all-purpose flour
- 1-1/2 to 2 teaspoons ground cinnamon
- 1 teaspoon baking soda
- 1/2 teaspoon salt
- 1-3/4 cups (11-ounce package) HERSHEY'S Butterscotch Chips
- 1 cup chopped pecans (optional)
  Powdered sugar or frozen whipped topping, thawed (optional)

1. Heat oven to 350°F. Lightly grease 13×9×2-inch baking pan.

2. Beat butter and sugar in large bowl until fluffy. Add eggs and vanilla; beat well. Mix in applesauce. Stir together flour, cinnamon, baking soda and salt; gradually add to butter mixture, beating until well blended. Stir in butterscotch chips and pecans, if desired. Spread in prepared pan.

3. Bake 35 to 40 minutes or until wooden pick inserted in center comes out clean. Cool completely in pan. Dust with powdered sugar or serve with whipped topping, if desired.

Makes 12 to 16 servings

Clockwise from top left: *Spicy Butterscotch Snack Cake, Lemon Nut White Chip Cookies (p. 190), Double Chip Brownies (p. 188), Pumpkin Pecan Pie (p. 200)*

Double Cherry Crumbles

(pictured at right)

1/2 (18-ounce) package refrigerated oatmeal raisin cookie dough*
1/2 cup uncooked old-fashioned oats
3/4 teaspoon ground cinnamon
1/2 teaspoon ground ginger
2 tablespoons cold butter, cut into small pieces
1 cup chopped pecans, toasted**
1 bag (16 ounces) frozen pitted unsweetened dark sweet cherries, thawed
2 cans (21 ounces each) cherry pie filling

Save remaining 1/2 package of dough for another use.

**To toast pecans, spread in single layer on baking sheet. Bake in preheated 350°F oven 7 to 10 minutes or until golden brown, stirring frequently.*

1. Preheat oven to 350°F. Lightly grease eight 1/2-cup ramekins; place on baking sheet. Let dough stand at room temperature about 15 minutes.

2. For topping, beat dough, oats, cinnamon and ginger in large bowl until well blended. Cut in butter with pastry blender or two knives. Stir in pecans.

3. Combine cherries and pie filling in large bowl. Divide cherry mixture evenly among prepared ramekins; sprinkle with topping. Bake about 25 minutes or until topping is browned. Serve warm.

Makes 8 servings

Take-Me-To-A-Picnic Cake

1 cup water
1 cup (2 sticks) butter or margarine
1/2 cup HERSHEY'S Cocoa
2 cups sugar
1-3/4 cups all-purpose flour
1 teaspoon baking soda
1/2 teaspoon salt
3 eggs
3/4 cup dairy sour cream
Peanut Butter Chip Frosting (recipe follows)
Chocolate Garnish (recipe follows, optional)

1. Grease and flour 15-1/2×10-1/2×1-inch jelly-roll pan. Heat oven to 350°F.

2. Combine water, butter and cocoa in medium saucepan. Cook over medium heat, stirring occasionally, until mixture boils. Boil 1 minute. Remove from heat. Stir together sugar, flour, baking soda and salt in large bowl. Add eggs and sour cream; beat until blended. Add cocoa mixture; beat just until blended. Pour into prepared pan.

3. Bake 25 to 30 minutes or until wooden pick inserted in center comes out clean. Cool on wire rack. Prepare Peanut Butter Chip Frosting. Spread over cake. Prepare Chocolate Garnish; drizzle over top, if desired. *Makes about 20 servings*

Peanut Butter Chip Frosting: Combine 1/3 cup butter or margarine, 1/3 cup milk and 1-2/3 cups (10-ounce package) REESE'S® Peanut Butter Chips in medium saucepan. Cook over low heat, stirring constantly, until chips are melted and mixture is smooth. Remove from heat; stir in 1 teaspoon vanilla extract. Place 1 cup powdered sugar in medium bowl. Gradually add chip mixture; beat well. Cool, stirring occasionally, until of spreading consistency. Makes about 2 cups frosting.

Chocolate Garnish: Place 1/2 cup HERSHEY'S Semi-Sweet Chocolate Chips and 1 teaspoon shortening (not butter, margarine, spread or oil) in small microwave-safe bowl. Microwave at HIGH (100%) 1 minute; stir until chips are melted and mixture is smooth.

Lemon Chiffon Cheesecake

1 package (8 ounces) cream cheese, softened
1/2 cup sugar
1/2 cup HELLMANN'S® or BEST FOODS® Real Mayonnaise
2 eggs
2 teaspoons grated lemon peel
1 teaspoon vanilla extract
1 (9-inch) graham cracker crust
1 cup cherry or blueberry pie filling (optional)

1. Preheat oven 350°F.

2. In mixing bowl with electric mixer, beat cream cheese, sugar and Hellmann's or Best Foods Real Mayonnaise until smooth. Gradually beat in eggs, lemon peel and vanilla until smooth. Pour into prepared crust.

3. Bake 25 minutes or until center is almost set. On wire rack, cool 1 hour. Refrigerate 1 hour or overnight. To serve, top with cherry pie filling.

Makes 8 servings

Grandma's Favorite Sugarcakes

(pictured at right)

2/3 cup butter or margarine, softened
1-1/2 cups packed light brown sugar
1 cup granulated sugar
2 eggs
2 teaspoons vanilla extract
4-1/2 cups all-purpose flour
2 teaspoons baking soda
1 teaspoon baking powder
1 teaspoon salt
1 cup buttermilk or sour milk*
2 cups (12-ounce package) HERSHEY'S Mini Chips Semi-Sweet Chocolate
2 cups chopped walnuts or pecans
Vanilla frosting (optional)
Colored sugar or sprinkles (optional)

To sour milk: Use 1 tablespoon white vinegar plus milk to equal 1 cup.

1. Heat oven to 350°F. Grease cookie sheet.

2. Beat butter, brown sugar and granulated sugar until well blended in large mixing bowl. Add eggs and vanilla; beat until creamy. Stir together flour, baking soda, baking powder and salt; add alternately with buttermilk to butter mixture, beating well after each addition. Stir in small chocolate chips and nuts. Drop by level 1/4 cups or heaping tablespoons 2 inches apart onto prepared cookie sheet.

3. Bake 12 to 14 minutes or until golden brown. Remove to wire rack and cool completely. Frost with favorite vanilla frosting; garnish with colored sugar, if desired.   *Makes 36 cookies*

Gingerbread Upside-Down Cake

1 can (20 ounces) DOLE® Pineapple Slices
1/2 cup margarine, softened, divided
1 cup packed brown sugar, divided
10 maraschino cherries
1 egg
1/2 cup dark molasses
1-1/2 cups all-purpose flour
1 teaspoon baking soda
1 teaspoon ground ginger
1/2 teaspoon ground cinnamon
1/2 teaspoon salt

• Preheat oven to 350°F. Drain pineapple slices; reserve 1/2 cup syrup. In 10-inch cast iron skillet, melt 1/4 cup margarine. Remove from heat. Add 1/2 cup brown sugar and stir until blended. Arrange pineapple slices in skillet. Place 1 cherry in center of each slice.

• In large mixer bowl, beat remaining 1/4 cup margarine and 1/2 cup brown sugar until light and fluffy. Beat in egg and molasses. In small bowl, combine flour, baking soda, ginger, cinnamon and salt.

• In small saucepan, bring reserved pineapple syrup to a boil. Add dry ingredients to creamed mixture alternately with hot syrup. Spread evenly over pineapple slices in skillet. Bake 30 to 40 minutes or until wooden pick inserted in center comes out clean. Let stand in skillet on wire rack 5 minutes. Invert onto serving plate.

Makes 8 to 10 servings

Oatmeal Scotchies

1 cup (2 sticks) margarine or butter, softened
3/4 cup granulated sugar
3/4 cup firmly packed brown sugar
2 eggs
1 teaspoon vanilla or 2 teaspoons grated orange peel (about 1 orange)
1-1/4 cups all-purpose flour
1 teaspoon baking soda
1/2 teaspoon salt (optional)
1/2 teaspoon ground cinnamon
3 cups QUAKER® Oats (quick or old fashioned, uncooked)
2 cups (12 ounces) butterscotch flavored morsels

Heat oven to 375°F. Beat together margarine, sugars, eggs and vanilla until creamy. Gradually add combined flour, baking soda, salt and cinnamon; mix well. Stir in remaining ingredients. Drop by level measuring tablespoonfuls onto ungreased cookie sheets. Bake 7 to 8 minutes for a chewy cookie or 9 to 10 minutes for a crisp cookie. Cool 2 minutes on cookie sheets; remove to wire racks. Cool completely. Store tightly covered.

Makes about 48 cookies

Pumpkin Pie Crunch

(pictured at right)

 1 can (16 ounces) solid pack pumpkin
 1 can (12 ounces) evaporated milk
 3 eggs
1-1/2 cups sugar
 4 teaspoons pumpkin pie spice
 1/2 teaspoon salt
 1 package DUNCAN HINES® Moist Deluxe®
  Classic Yellow Cake Mix
 1 cup chopped pecans
 1 cup butter or margarine, melted
  Whipped topping

1. Preheat oven to 350°F. Grease bottom only of 13×9×2-inch baking pan.

2. Combine pumpkin, evaporated milk, eggs, sugar, pumpkin pie spice and salt in large bowl. Pour into prepared pan. Sprinkle dry cake mix evenly over pumpkin mixture. Top with pecans. Drizzle with melted butter. Bake at 350°F for 50 to 55 minutes or until golden. Cool completely. Serve with whipped topping. Refrigerate leftovers.

Makes 16 to 20 servings

Tip: For a richer flavor, try using DUNCAN HINES® Moist Deluxe® Butter Recipe Golden Cake Mix.

Double Chip Brownies

(pictured on page 182)

 3/4 cup HERSHEY'S Cocoa
 1/2 teaspoon baking soda
 2/3 cup butter or margarine, melted and divided
 1/2 cup boiling water
 2 cups sugar
 2 eggs
1-1/3 cups all-purpose flour
 1 teaspoon vanilla extract
 1/4 teaspoon salt
 1 cup HERSHEY'S Milk Chocolate Chips
 1 cup REESE'S® Peanut Butter Chips

1. Heat oven to 350°F. Grease 13×9×2-inch baking pan.

2. Stir together cocoa and baking soda in large bowl; stir in 1/3 cup melted butter. Add boiling water; stir until mixture thickens. Stir in sugar, eggs and remaining 1/3 cup melted butter; stir until smooth. Add flour, vanilla and salt; blend

thoroughly. Stir in milk chocolate chips and peanut butter chips. Spread in prepared pan.

3. Bake 35 to 40 minutes or until brownies begin to pull away from sides of pan. Cool completely in pan on wire rack. Cut into squares.

Makes about 36 brownies

Very Cherry Pie

 4 cups frozen unsweetened tart cherries
 1 cup dried tart cherries
 1 cup granulated sugar
 2 tablespoons quick-cooking tapioca
 1/2 teaspoon almond extract
  Pastry for double-crust 9-inch pie
 1/4 teaspoon ground nutmeg
 1 tablespoon butter

Combine frozen cherries, dried cherries, sugar, tapioca and almond extract in large mixing bowl; mix well. (It is not necessary to thaw cherries before using.) Let cherry mixture stand 15 minutes.

Line 9-inch pie plate with pastry; fill with cherry mixture. Sprinkle with nutmeg. Dot with butter. Cover with top crust, cutting slits for steam to escape. Or, cut top crust into strips for lattice top.

Bake in preheated 375°F oven about 1 hour or until crust is golden brown and filling is bubbly. If necessary, cover edge of crust with foil to prevent overbrowning.

Makes 8 servings

Note: Two (14.5-ounce) cans unsweetened tart cherries, well drained, can be substituted for frozen tart cherries. Dried cherries are available at gourmet and specialty food stores and at selected supermarkets.

Favorite recipe from **Cherry Marketing Institute**

Almond Cake

(pictured at right)

 1 can (8 ounces) almond paste
 3 eggs
 1 package (about 18 ounces) white cake mix
 1-1/4 cups water
 1/3 cup vegetable oil
 1 cup seedless raspberry preserves
 1 carton (16 ounces) whipped vanilla frosting
   Candy-coated almonds

1. Preheat oven to 350°F. Grease two 9-inch round cake pans.

2. Combine almond paste and eggs in large bowl; stir until smooth. Add cake mix, water and oil to almond paste mixture. Beat 1 minute with electric mixer on low speed. Increase to medium-low speed; beat 2 minutes or until well blended. Divide batter evenly in prepared pans.

3. Bake 35 minutes or until toothpick inserted into centers comes out clean. Cool cakes completely in pans on wire racks.

4. Remove from pans. Place one layer on serving plate. Spread with preserves to within 1/4 inch of edge. Top with remaining layer. Frost sides and top of cake with frosting. Garnish with almonds.

Makes 12 servings

Lemon Nut
White Chip Cookies

(pictured on page 182)

 1-1/2 cups all-purpose flour
  3/4 teaspoon baking soda
  1/2 teaspoon salt
  3/4 cup (1-1/2 sticks) butter or margarine, softened
  1/2 cup packed brown sugar
  1/4 cup granulated sugar
   1 large egg
   1 tablespoon lemon juice
   2 cups (12-ounce package) NESTLÉ® TOLL HOUSE® Premier White Morsels
   1 cup coarsely chopped walnuts or cashew nuts
   1 teaspoon grated lemon peel

PREHEAT oven to 375°F.

COMBINE flour, baking soda and salt in small bowl. Beat butter, brown sugar and granulated sugar

in large mixer bowl until creamy. Beat in egg and lemon juice; gradually beat in flour mixture. Stir in morsels, nuts and lemon peel. Drop by rounded tablespoon onto ungreased baking sheets.

BAKE for 7 to 10 minutes or until edges are lightly browned. Cool on baking sheets for 3 minutes; remove to wire racks to cool completely.

Makes about 3 dozen cookies

Simple and Delicious
Peach Cobbler

COBBLER
   2 cans (21 ounces each) peach pie filling
  1/2 cup granulated sugar
  3/4 teaspoon WATKINS® Ground Cinnamon
  1/4 teaspoon WATKINS® Nutmeg
   1 can (10 ounces) refrigerated flaky biscuit dough
  1/4 cup (1/2 stick) butter, melted

VANILLA WHIPPED CREAM
   1 cup heavy whipping cream
   2 to 4 tablespoons powdered sugar
   1 teaspoon WATKINS® Vanilla

For Cobbler, preheat oven to 400°F. Place peach pie filling in 13×9-inch baking dish. Combine granulated sugar, cinnamon and nutmeg in small bowl. Separate each biscuit into 2 sections. Dip each section into butter; roll in sugar mixture to coat. Arrange on top of peach layer. Bake for 20 to 25 minutes or until golden brown.

Meanwhile, prepare whipped cream. Chill small bowl and beaters of electric mixer. Beat cream in chilled bowl until it begins to thicken. Add powdered sugar and vanilla; beat until stiff peaks form. (Do not overbeat.) Serve cobbler warm with whipped cream. *Makes 10 servings*

Note: Cherry or blueberry pie filling may be substituted for peach.

Almond Cake

Fruit-Filled Chocolate Chip Meringue Nests

Fruit-Filled Chocolate Chip Meringue Nests

(pictured above)

MERINGUES
    4 large egg whites
    1/2 teaspoon salt
    1/2 teaspoon cream of tartar
    1 cup granulated sugar
    2 cups (12-ounce package) NESTLÉ® TOLL
        HOUSE® Semi-Sweet Chocolate Morsels

CHOCOLATE SAUCE
    2/3 cup (5 fluid-ounce can) NESTLÉ®
        CARNATION® Evaporated Milk
    1 cup (6 ounces) NESTLÉ® TOLL HOUSE®
        Semi-Sweet Chocolate Morsels
    1 tablespoon granulated sugar
    1 teaspoon vanilla extract
        Pinch salt
    3 cups fresh fruit or berries (whole blackberries,
        blueberries or raspberries, sliced kiwi,
        peaches or strawberries)

FOR MERINGUES
PREHEAT oven to 300°F. Lightly grease baking sheets.

BEAT egg whites, salt and cream of tartar in large mixer bowl until soft peaks form. Gradually add sugar; beat until sugar is dissolved. Gently fold in morsels. Spread meringue into ten 3-inch nests with deep wells about 2 inches apart on prepared baking sheets.

BAKE for 35 to 45 minutes or until meringues are dry and crisp. Cool on baking sheets for 5 minutes; remove to wire racks to cool completely.

FOR CHOCOLATE SAUCE
HEAT evaporated milk to a boil in small, *heavy-duty* saucepan. Stir in morsels. Cook, stirring constantly, until mixture is slightly thickened and smooth. Remove from heat; stir in sugar, vanilla extract and salt.

FILL meringues with fruit and drizzle with Chocolate Sauce; serve immediately.   *Makes 10 servings*

Blueberry Cobbler

    4 cups fresh or thawed frozen blueberries
    1/2 teaspoon WATKINS® Lemon Extract
    1 cup all-purpose flour
    1/2 cup plus 2 tablespoons sugar, divided
    1 teaspoon WATKINS® Baking Powder
        Dash salt
    2 egg whites, lightly beaten
    1 tablespoon WATKINS® Original Grapeseed Oil
    1 teaspoon WATKINS® Vanilla
    1/4 teaspoon WATKINS® Ground Cinnamon or
        more to taste

Preheat oven to 350°F. Spray 1-1/2 quart baking dish with WATKINS® Cooking Spray. Add blueberries and lemon extract to dish; toss lightly. Combine flour, 1/2 cup sugar, baking powder and salt in medium bowl; mix well. Beat egg whites, oil and vanilla in small bowl until well blended. Make well in center of dry ingredients; add egg white mixture and stir just until moistened.

Drop 8 equal mounds of dough onto blueberries. Combine remaining 2 tablespoons sugar and cinnamon; sprinkle over top. Bake for 35 minutes or until bubbly and browned.   *Makes 8 servings*

Key Lime Angel Food Torte

(pictured below)

> 1 package (16 ounces) angel food cake mix, plus
>   ingredients to prepare mix
> 1 can (14 ounces) sweetened condensed milk
> 2/3 cup bottled key lime juice
> 1 container (8 ounces) whipped topping, thawed
> 1/3 cup flaked sweetened coconut
>   Grated peel of 1 lime

1. Preheat oven to 350°F. Prepare and bake cake mix according to package directions, using an ungreased tube pan. Remove from oven; turn pan upside down on wire rack to cool completely.

2. Combine sweetened condensed milk and lime juice in medium bowl. Whisk until smooth. Fold in whipped topping. Cover and refrigerate.

3. Loosen cake sides; remove from pan. With bottom side up, slice cake in half horizontally with a serrated knife. Then slice each half in half again to create four layers; keep layers together and set aside.

4. To assemble, place bottom cake layer cut side up on serving platter. Spread one quarter of key lime filling (about 1 cup) onto bottom layer. Top with second layer; spread with another one quarter of filling. Repeat once more and top with last section of cake (creating four layers of cake separated by three layers of filling).

5. Ice top of cake with remaining filling, allowing some to run down sides. Sprinkle coconut and lime peel on top; refrigerate about 1 hour or until set.

Makes 12 servings

Helpful Hint

To make the best angel food cake, it's important to not grease the pan so that batter can grip the sides and rise as high as possible. Using a tube pan with a removable bottom also makes releasing the cake much easier.

Key Lime Angel Food Torte

Lemon Bars

(pictured at right)

CRUST
- 2 cups all-purpose flour
- 1/2 cup powdered sugar
- 1 cup (2 sticks) butter or margarine, softened

FILLING
- 1 can (14 ounces) NESTLÉ® CARNATION® Sweetened Condensed Milk
- 4 large eggs
- 2/3 cup lemon juice
- 1 tablespoon all-purpose flour
- 1 teaspoon baking powder
- 1/4 teaspoon salt
- 4 drops yellow food coloring (optional)
- 1 tablespoon grated lemon peel
- Sifted powdered sugar (optional)

PREHEAT oven to 350°F.

FOR CRUST
COMBINE flour and sugar in medium bowl. Cut in butter with pastry blender or two knives until mixture is crumbly. Press lightly onto bottom and halfway up sides of ungreased 13×9-inch baking pan.

BAKE for 20 minutes.

FOR FILLING
BEAT sweetened condensed milk and eggs in large mixer bowl until fluffy. Beat in lemon juice, flour, baking powder, salt and food coloring just until blended. Fold in lemon peel; pour over crust.

BAKE for 20 to 25 minutes or until filling is set and crust is golden brown. Cool in pan on wire rack. Refrigerate for about 2 hours. Cut into bars; sprinkle with powdered sugar. *Makes 48 bars*

S'Morffins

- 6 BAYS® English Muffins, lightly toasted and buttered
- 8 milk chocolate bars (1.55 ounces each) divided
- 3 cups miniature marshmallows, divided
- 3 pints super-premium vanilla ice cream
- 1-1/2 cups coarsely chopped and toasted walnuts, divided
- Hot fudge or caramel sauce, warmed (optional)

Place muffins on foil-lined baking sheet. Break chocolate bars into squares. Top each muffin half with eight chocolate squares. Broil, in preheated broiler, to just lightly melt chocolate. Arrange 1/4 cup marshmallows on each muffin half; press into melted chocolate. Broil muffins about 6 inches from heat source, until the marshmallows are puffed and golden brown and chocolate has melted. Scoop ice cream onto prepared muffin halves; then top with 2 tablespoons walnuts. Spoon heated fudge or caramel sauce over each S'Morffin, if desired. Serve immediately. *Makes 12 servings*

TIP: Rotate pan to toast marshmallows evenly.

Pumpkin Orange Cookies

- 2-1/2 cups all-purpose flour
- 1/2 teaspoon baking soda
- 1/2 teaspoon salt
- 1 cup (2 sticks) butter or margarine, softened
- 1 cup granulated sugar
- 1/2 cup packed brown sugar
- 1 large egg
- 1 can (15 ounces) LIBBY'S® 100% Pure Pumpkin
- 2 tablespoons orange juice
- 1 teaspoon grated orange peel
- 1/2 cup chopped nuts (optional)
- Orange Glaze (recipe follows)

PREHEAT oven to 375°F.

COMBINE flour, baking soda and salt in medium bowl. Combine butter, granulated sugar and brown sugar in large mixer bowl; beat until creamy. Add egg, pumpkin, orange juice and orange peel; beat until combined. Gradually add flour mixture; beat until combined. Stir in nuts. Drop dough by rounded tablespoon onto ungreased baking sheets.

BAKE for 12 to 14 minutes or until edges are set. Remove to wire racks to cool completely. Spread each cookie with about 1/2 teaspoon Orange Glaze. *Makes about 48 cookies*

Orange Glaze: COMBINE 1-1/2 cups sifted powdered sugar, 2 to 3 tablespoons orange juice and 1/2 teaspoon grated orange peel in medium bowl until smooth.

Chocolate Rice Pudding

(pictured at right)

>   2 cups water
>   1 cup uncooked UNCLE BEN'S® ORIGINAL
>   CONVERTED® Brand Rice
>   2 tablespoons butter
>   1/4 cup sugar
>   2 teaspoons cornstarch
>   2 cups milk
>   1/2 teaspoon vanilla
>   2 egg yolks
>   1/2 cup semisweet chocolate chips

1. Bring water to a boil in large saucepan. Stir in rice and butter. Reduce heat; cover and simmer 20 minutes. Remove from heat. Let stand covered until all liquid is absorbed, about 5 minutes.

2. Combine sugar and cornstarch in small bowl; add to hot rice in saucepan. Stir in milk.

3. Bring mixture to a boil, stirring occasionally. Boil 1 minute, stirring constantly. Remove from heat; stir in vanilla.

4. Beat egg yolks in small bowl. Stir about 1 cup of hot rice mixture into beaten egg yolks.

5. Stir egg yolk mixture back into remaining rice mixture in saucepan.

6. Cook rice mixture over medium heat, stirring frequently, just until mixture starts to bubble. Remove from heat; add chocolate chips and stir until melted.

7. Spoon into individual serving dishes. Chill. Garnish, if desired.   *Makes 6 servings*

Irresistible Peanut Butter Chip Brownies

>   1 cup (2 sticks) butter or margarine, softened
>   1 package (3 ounces) cream cheese, softened
>   2 cups sugar
>   3 eggs
>   1 teaspoon vanilla extract
>   1 cup all-purpose flour
>   3/4 cup HERSHEY'S Cocoa
>   1/2 teaspoon salt
>   1/4 teaspoon baking powder
> 1-2/3 cups (10-ounce package) REESE'S® Peanut
>   Butter Chips
>   Brownie Frosting (recipe follows, optional)

1. Grease bottom of 13×9×2-inch baking pan. Heat oven to 325°F.

2. Beat butter, cream cheese and sugar until fluffy. Beat in eggs and vanilla. Combine flour, cocoa, salt and baking powder; gradually add to butter mixture, beating well. Stir in chips. Spread batter in pan.

3. Bake 35 to 40 minutes or until brownies begin to pull away from sides of pan. Cool completely. Frost with Brownie Frosting, if desired. Cut into bars.
          Makes about 36 bars

Brownie Frosting: Beat 3 tablespoons softened butter or margarine and 3 tablespoons HERSHEY'S Cocoa until blended. Gradually add 1-1/3 cups powdered sugar and 3/4 teaspoon vanilla extract alternately with 1 to 2 tablespoons milk, beating to spreading consistency. Makes about 1 cup.

Pecan Pie Bars

>   1 package (18 ounces) refrigerated sugar
>   cookie dough
>   1/2 cup all-purpose flour
>   3 eggs
>   3/4 cup dark corn syrup
>   3/4 cup sugar
>   1 teaspoon vanilla extract
>   1/4 teaspoon salt
>   3 cups chopped pecans

1. Preheat oven to 350°F. Lightly grease 13×9-inch baking pan. Let dough stand at room temperature about 15 minutes.

2. Combine dough and flour in large bowl; beat until well blended. Press dough evenly onto bottom and 1/2-inch up sides of prepared pan. Bake 20 minutes.

3. Meanwhile, beat eggs in large bowl until fluffy and light in color. Add corn syrup, sugar, vanilla and salt; beat until well blended. Pour over partially baked crust; sprinkle evenly with pecans.

4. Bake 25 to 30 minutes or until center is just set. Cool completely in pan on wire rack.
          Makes about 24 bars

Chocolate Rice Pudding

Fudgy Banana Oat Cake

(pictured at right)

TOPPING
1 cup QUAKER® Oats (quick or old fashioned, uncooked)
1/2 cup firmly packed brown sugar
1/4 cup (1/2 stick) margarine or butter, chilled

FILLING
1 cup (6 ounces) semisweet chocolate pieces
2/3 cup sweetened condensed milk (not evaporated milk)
1 tablespoon margarine or butter

CAKE
1 package (18.25 ounces) devil's food cake mix
1-1/4 cups mashed ripe bananas (about 3 large)
1/3 cup vegetable oil
3 eggs
Banana slices (optional)
Sweetened whipped cream (optional)

Heat oven to 350°F. Lightly grease bottom only of 13×9-inch baking pan or spray with no-stick cooking spray. For topping, combine oats and brown sugar. Cut in margarine until mixture is crumbly; set aside.

For filling, in small saucepan, heat chocolate pieces, sweetened condensed milk and margarine over low heat until chocolate is melted, stirring occasionally. Remove from heat; set aside.

For cake, combine cake mix, bananas, oil and eggs in large mixing bowl. Blend at low speed of electric mixer until dry ingredients are moistened. Beat at medium speed 2 minutes. Spread batter evenly into prepared pan. Drop chocolate filling by teaspoonfuls evenly over batter. Sprinkle with reserved oat topping. Bake 40 to 45 minutes or until cake pulls away from sides of pan and topping is golden brown. Cool cake in pan on wire rack. Cut into squares. Garnish with banana slices and sweetened whipped cream, if desired. *Makes 15 servings*

Refreshing Lemon Cake

1 package DUNCAN HINES® Moist Deluxe® Butter Recipe Golden Cake Mix
1 container DUNCAN HINES® Creamy Home-Style Cream Cheese Frosting
3/4 cup purchased lemon curd
Lemon drop candies, crushed for garnish (optional)

1. Preheat oven to 375°F. Grease and flour two 8- or 9-inch round cake pans.

2. Prepare, bake and cool cakes following package directions for basic recipe.

3. To assemble, place one cake layer on serving plate. Place 1/4 cup frosting in small resealable plastic food storage bag. Cut off one corner. Pipe a bead of frosting on top of layer around outer edge. Fill remaining area with lemon curd. Top with second cake layer. Spread remaining frosting on sides and top of cake. Garnish top of cake with crushed lemon candies, if desired. *Makes 12 to 16 servings*

Tip: You can substitute DUNCAN HINES® Buttercream or Classic Vanilla Frosting, if desired.

Chocolate Harvest Nut Pie

1/2 cup packed light brown sugar
1/3 cup HERSHEY'S Cocoa
1/4 teaspoon salt
1 cup light corn syrup
3 eggs
3 tablespoons butter or margarine, melted
1-1/2 teaspoons vanilla extract
1/2 cup coarsely chopped pecans
1/2 cup coarsely chopped walnuts
1/4 cup slivered almonds
1 unbaked (9-inch) pie crust
Whipped topping (optional)

1. Heat oven to 350°F. Stir together brown sugar, cocoa and salt. Add corn syrup, eggs, butter and vanilla; stir until well blended. Stir in pecans, walnuts and almonds. Pour into unbaked pie crust. To prevent overbrowning of crust, cover edge of pie with foil.

2. Bake 30 minutes. Remove foil. Bake additional 25 to 30 minutes or until puffed across top. Remove from oven to wire rack. Cool completely.

3. Garnish with whipped topping and additional nuts, if desired. Cover; store leftover pie in refrigerator. *Makes 8 servings*

Fudgy Banana Oat Cake

Coconut Lemon Torte

(pictured on front cover and at right)

     1 (14-ounce) can EAGLE BRAND® Sweetened
          Condensed Milk (NOT evaporated milk)
     2 egg yolks
   1/2 cup lemon juice
     1 teaspoon grated lemon rind (optional)
          Yellow food coloring (optional)
     1 (18.25- or 18.5-ounce) package white
          cake mix
 1-3/4 cups frozen nondairy whipped topping, thawed
          Flaked coconut

1. In medium saucepan, combine EAGLE BRAND®, egg yolks, lemon juice, lemon rind (optional) and food coloring (optional). Over medium heat, cook and stir until slightly thickened, about 10 minutes. Chill.

2. Preheat oven to 350°F. Prepare cake mix as package directs. Pour batter into greased and floured two 9-inch round layer cake pans.

3. Bake 30 minutes or until toothpick inserted near centers comes out clean. Remove from pans. Cool.

4. With sharp knife, remove crust from top of each cake layer. Split layers. Spread equal portions of lemon mixture between layers and on top to within 1 inch of edge.

5. Frost side and 1-inch rim on top of cake with whipped topping. Coat side of cake with coconut; garnish as desired. Store leftovers covered in refrigerator.   *Makes one (9-inch) cake*

Holiday Bread Pudding

    16 slices bread, cubed
     1 cup dried cranberries or raisins
     2 cans (12 fluid ounces *each*) NESTLÉ®
          CARNATION® Evaporated Milk
     4 large eggs, lightly beaten
     4 tablespoons butter, melted
   3/4 cup packed brown sugar
     1 tablespoon vanilla extract
     1 teaspoon ground cinnamon
   1/2 teaspoon ground nutmeg
          Caramel sauce (optional)

PREHEAT oven to 350°F. Grease 12×8-inch baking dish.

COMBINE bread and cranberries in large bowl.

Combine evaporated milk, eggs, butter, sugar, vanilla extract, cinnamon and nutmeg in medium bowl. Pour egg mixture over bread mixture; mix well. Pour mixture into prepared baking dish. Let stand for 10 minutes.

BAKE for 35 to 45 minutes or until knife inserted in center comes out clean. Top with caramel sauce. Garnish as desired.   *Makes 8 servings*

Pumpkin Pecan Pie

(pictured on page 182)

     1 can (15 ounces) solid-pack pumpkin
     1 can (14 ounces) sweetened condensed milk
   1/4 cup (1/2 stick) butter, softened
     2 eggs
     1 teaspoon ground cinnamon
     1 teaspoon vanilla extract
   1/2 teaspoon ground nutmeg
   1/4 teaspoon salt
     1 (6-ounce) graham cracker pie crust
     2 tablespoons packed brown sugar
     2 tablespoons dark corn syrup
     1 tablespoon butter, melted
   1/2 teaspoon maple flavoring
     1 cup chopped pecans

1. Preheat oven to 400°F.

2. Combine pumpkin, condensed milk, softened butter, 1 egg, cinnamon, vanilla, nutmeg and salt in large bowl; beat until well blended. Pour into pie crust. Bake 20 minutes.

3. Beat remaining egg, brown sugar, corn syrup, melted butter and maple flavoring in medium bowl with electric mixer at medium speed until well blended. Stir in pecans.

4. Remove pie from oven; top with pecan mixture. *Reduce oven temperature to 350°F.* Bake 25 minutes or until knife inserted near center comes out clean.
           Makes 8 to 10 servings

Coconut Lemon Torte

Aunt Ruth's Favorite White Cake

Aunt Ruth's Favorite White Cake

(pictured above)

    1 package (18-1/4 ounces) white cake mix
1-1/4 cups water
    3 eggs
    2 tablespoons vegetable oil
    1 teaspoon vanilla extract
1/2 teaspoon almond extract
    Creamy White Frosting (recipe follows)

1. Preheat oven to 350°F. Grease and flour two 9-inch round cake pans.

2. Beat cake mix, water, eggs and oil in large bowl with electric mixer at medium speed until well blended. Add vanilla and almond extracts; beat until well blended. Divide batter evenly between prepared pans.

3. Bake 30 to 35 minutes or until toothpick inserted near centers comes out clean. Cool on wire racks 10 minutes. Remove cakes from pans to racks; cool completely.

4. Prepare Creamy White Frosting. Fill and frost cake with frosting.   *Makes one 2-layer cake*

Creamy White Frosting

3 tablespoons all-purpose flour
1 cup milk
1 cup (2 sticks) butter, softened
1 cup confectioners' sugar
1 teaspoon vanilla extract

1. Combine flour and milk in medium saucepan. Bring to a boil over medium heat. Cook and stir 1 to 2 minutes or until thickened. Cool.

2. Beat butter in large bowl until creamy. Add confectioners' sugar; beat until fluffy. Blend in vanilla. Add flour mixture; beat until thick and smooth.

Mott's® Magic Apple Roll

    2 cups MOTT'S® Natural Apple Sauce
1/2 teaspoon ground cinnamon
    4 egg whites
3/4 cup granulated sugar
2/3 cup all-purpose flour
3/4 teaspoon baking powder
1/4 teaspoon salt
    1 teaspoon vanilla extract
    1 tablespoon powdered sugar

1. Preheat oven to 400°F. Spray 15×10×1 inch jelly-roll pan with nonstick cooking spray. Line with waxed paper; spray with cooking spray. Pour applesauce into pan, spreading evenly. Sprinkle with cinnamon.

2. In large bowl, beat egg whites with electric mixer at high speed until foamy. Gradually add granulated sugar, beating until mixture is thick and light.

3. In small bowl, sift together flour, baking powder and salt. Fold into egg-white mixture with vanilla. Gently pour batter over applesauce mixture, spreading evenly.

4. Bake 15 to 18 minutes or until lightly browned. Cool on wire rack 5 minutes. Invert cake, apple side up, onto clean, lint-free dish towel sprinkled with powdered sugar; peel off waxed paper. Trim edges of cake. Starting at narrow end, roll up cake. Place, seam side down, on serving plate. Cool completely. Sprinkle top with powdered sugar. Cut into 10 slices.

Makes 10 servings

Banana Cream and Chocolate Pie

(pictured below)

1 bar (7 ounces) milk chocolate, grated
1 (6-ounce) chocolate cookie crumb pie crust
1-1/2 cups cold milk
1 package (4-serving size) instant banana or French vanilla pudding and pie filling mix
1 container (8 ounces) frozen nondairy whipped topping, thawed, divided
2 medium bananas, sliced, divided
Mint leaves for garnish (optional)

1. Sprinkle grated chocolate evenly over pie crust; set aside.

2. Combine milk and pudding mix in large bowl. Whisk until blended. Fold in 1-1/2 cups whipped topping.

3. Pour half of pudding mixture into crust. Layer slices from one banana evenly over pudding. Spread remaining pudding mixture over bananas.

4. Chill 2 hours. Garnish with remaining banana, whipped topping and mint leaves, if desired. Refrigerate leftovers.   *Makes 8 servings*

Chocolate Caramel Brownies

1 package (18.25 ounces) chocolate cake mix
1 cup chopped nuts
1/2 cup (1 stick) butter or margarine, melted
1 cup NESTLÉ® CARNATION® Evaporated Milk, *divided*
35 (10-ounce package) caramels, unwrapped
2 cups (12-ounce package) NESTLÉ® TOLL HOUSE® Semi-Sweet Chocolate Morsels

PREHEAT oven to 350°F.

COMBINE cake mix and nuts in large bowl. Stir in butter and *2/3 cup* evaporated milk (batter will be thick). Spread *half* of batter into greased 13×9-inch baking pan.

BAKE for 15 minutes.

HEAT caramels and *remaining* evaporated milk in small saucepan over low heat, stirring constantly, until caramels are melted. Sprinkle morsels over brownie; drizzle with caramel mixture.

DROP *remaining* batter by heaping teaspoon over caramel mixture.

BAKE for 25 to 30 minutes or until center is set. Cool in pan on wire rack.   *Makes 24 brownies*

Banana Cream and Chocolate Pie

Chocolate Shortcakes

(pictured at right)

1-1/4 cups all-purpose flour
1/2 cup unsweetened cocoa powder
2/3 cup granulated sugar, divided
1 tablespoon baking powder
1/8 teaspoon salt
1/2 cup (1 stick) cold butter
1/2 cup milk
1 teaspoon vanilla extract
1-1/4 cups "M&M's"® Milk Chocolate
    Mini Baking Bits, divided
1 large egg
1 teaspoon water
1/2 cup cold whipping cream
2 cups sliced strawberries
1/3 cup chocolate syrup

Preheat oven to 425°F. In medium bowl combine flour, cocoa powder, 1/3 cup sugar, baking powder and salt. Cut in butter with pastry blender or two knives until mixture resembles coarse crumbs. Add milk and vanilla; mix just until dry ingredients are moistened. On lightly floured surface gently knead 3/4 cup "M&M's"® Milk Chocolate Mini Baking Bits into dough until evenly dispersed. Roll or pat out to 1/2-inch thickness. Cut with 3-inch round biscuit cutter; place on ungreased cookie sheet. If necessary, reroll scraps of dough in order to make six shortcakes. In small bowl combine egg and water; brush lightly over dough. Bake 12 to 14 minutes. Cool on pan 1 minute. Remove to wire racks; cool completely. In large bowl beat whipping cream until soft peaks form. Add remaining 1/3 cup sugar; beat until stiff peaks form. Reserve 1/2 cup whipped cream. Split shortcakes and place bottom of each on plate; divide strawberries evenly among shortcakes. Top with remaining whipped cream; sprinkle with 1/4 cup "M&M's"® Milk Chocolate Mini Baking Bits. Replace tops of shortcakes; drizzle with chocolate syrup. Garnish with reserved whipped cream and remaining 1/4 cup "M&M's"® Milk Chocolate Mini Baking Bits. Serve immediately.

Makes 6 servings

Helpful Hint

When you're in a hurry, choose desserts you can make ahead of time. Breads and cookies will keep at room temperature up to 3 days or frozen up to 3 months if wrapped tightly.

Peanutty Crisscrosses

3/4 cup (1-1/2 sticks) margarine or butter,
    softened
1 cup peanut butter
1-1/2 cups firmly packed brown sugar
1/3 cup water
1 egg
1 teaspoon vanilla
3 cups QUAKER® Oats (quick or old fashioned,
    uncooked)
1-1/2 cups all-purpose flour
1/2 teaspoon baking soda
    Granulated sugar

Beat margarine, peanut butter and sugar until creamy. Add water, egg and vanilla; beat well. Add combined oats, flour and baking soda. Cover; chill about 1 hour.

Heat oven to 350°F. Shape dough into 1-inch balls. Place on ungreased cookie sheets; flatten with tines of fork, dipped in granulated sugar, to form crisscross pattern. Bake 9 to 10 minutes or until edges are golden brown. Cool 2 minutes on cookie sheets; remove to wire racks. Cool completely. Store tightly covered.   *Makes about 7 dozen cookies*

Mini Custard Fruit Tarts

1 package (3 ounces) vanilla pudding and pie
    filling mix (*not instant*)
1/3 cup water
1 can (12 fluid ounces) NESTLÉ® CARNATION®
    Evaporated Lowfat 2% Milk
1 teaspoon grated lemon peel
6 *prepared* single-serving graham cracker crumb
    crusts
    Sliced fresh strawberries, kiwi, blueberries,
    raspberries, or orange sections (optional)
Mint leaves (optional)

COMBINE pudding mix and water in small saucepan. Add evaporated milk and lemon peel; stir until smooth. Cook over medium-low heat, stirring constantly, until mixture comes to a boil and thickens.

POUR into crusts; refrigerate for 1 hour or until set. Top with fruit and mint leaves before serving.

Makes 6 servings

Chocolate Shortcake

Peanut Butter Chip Pineapple Drops

(pictured at right)

1/4 cup (1/2 stick) butter or margarine, softened
1/4 cup shortening
  1 cup packed light brown sugar
  1 egg
  1 teaspoon vanilla extract
  2 cups all-purpose flour
  1 teaspoon baking powder
1/2 teaspoon baking soda
1/2 teaspoon salt
  1 can (8 ounces) crushed pineapple, drained
  1 cup REESE'S® Peanut Butter Chips
1/2 cup chopped nuts (optional)
    Red candied cherries, halved

1. Heat oven to 375°F.

2. Beat butter and shortening in large bowl until blended. Add sugar, egg and vanilla; beat until fluffy. Stir together flour, baking powder, baking soda and salt; add to butter mixture, beating until well blended. Stir in pineapple, peanut butter chips and nuts, if desired. Drop by teaspoons onto ungreased cookie sheet. Lightly press cherry half in center of each cookie.

3. Bake 10 to 12 minutes or until lightly browned. Remove from cookie sheet to wire rack. Cool completely. *Makes about 42 cookies*

Creamy Lemon Cake

CAKE
  2 cups cake flour
  2 teaspoons baking powder
1/4 teaspoon salt
2/3 cup butter, softened
  1 cup granulated sugar
  4 egg whites, room temperature
  1 teaspoon vanilla extract
3/4 cup buttermilk

TOPPING
1-1/4 cups whipping cream
1/2 cup confectioners' sugar
1-1/2 teaspoons grated lemon peel
3/4 cup prepared lemon curd

1. Preheat oven to 350°F. Grease two 8-inch round cake pans. Set aside.

2. Sift flour, baking powder and salt together in medium bowl. Set aside.

3. Beat butter and granulated sugar in large bowl with electric mixer at medium speed until creamy and light in color. Gradually beat in egg whites and vanilla. Increase mixer speed to high; beat 2 minutes. Reduce speed to low; add flour mixture alternately with buttermilk. Divide batter between prepared pans.

4. Bake 23 to 25 minutes or until toothpick inserted into centers comes out clean. Cool in pans on wire racks 15 minutes. Remove from pans to racks; cool completely.

5. To prepare frosting, whip cream until thickened. Add confectioners' sugar and lemon peel; beat until stiff peaks form. Refrigerate until ready to use.

6. To assemble cake, spread lemon curd evenly between 2 cake layers. Frost top and sides with frosting. Refrigerate until frosting is set.

Makes 8 servings

Oatmeal Hermits

  3 cups QUAKER® Oats (quick or old fashioned, uncooked)
  1 cup all-purpose flour
  1 cup (2 sticks) butter or margarine, melted
  1 cup firmly packed brown sugar
  1 cup raisins
1/2 cup chopped nuts
  1 egg
1/4 cup milk
  1 teaspoon ground cinnamon
  1 teaspoon vanilla
1/2 teaspoon baking soda
1/2 teaspoon salt (optional)
1/4 teaspoon ground nutmeg

Heat oven to 375°F. In large bowl, combine all ingredients; mix well. Drop dough by rounded tablespoonfuls onto ungreased cookie sheets. Bake 8 to 10 minutes. Cool 1 minute on cookie sheets; remove to wire racks. Cool completely. Store tightly covered. *Makes about 36 cookies*

For Bar Cookies: Press dough into ungreased 15×10-inch jelly-roll pan. Bake about 17 minutes or until golden brown. Cool completely; cut into bars.

Peanut Butter Chip Pineapple Drops

Best-Ever Short Cake

(pictured at right)

2 cups all-purpose flour
2 tablespoons sugar
1 tablespoon baking powder
1 teaspoon salt
3/4 cup shortening
1 cup milk
2 boxes (10 ounces each) BIRDS EYE® frozen
    Strawberries, thawed
    Whipped topping (optional)

• Preheat oven to 450°F. Combine flour, sugar, baking powder and salt.

• Cut shortening into flour mixture until mixture resembles coarse cornmeal.

• Blend in milk; mix well. Spread dough in 9×9-inch baking pan.

• Bake 15 minutes. Serve warm or let cool; top with strawberries before serving. Garnish with whipped topping, if desired.   *Makes 6 to 9 servings*

Hummingbird Cake

1 can (8 ounces) crushed pineapple, drained,
    juice reserved
1 package (18-1/4 ounces) white cake mix
3 eggs
1/3 cup vegetable oil
1/2 teaspoon ground cinnamon
1/4 teaspoon *each* almond, coconut and vanilla
    extracts
1/2 cup chopped pecans, toasted
1/2 cup flaked coconut
2 small bananas, chopped into small pieces

FROSTING:
    1 can (16 ounces) cream cheese frosting
1/2 cup flaked coconut, toasted
1/2 cup finely chopped pecans, toasted

1. Preheat oven to 350°F. Grease two 9-inch round cake pans; set aside. Add enough water to reserved pineapple juice to make 1 cup.

2. Beat cake mix, pineapple juice mixture, eggs, oil, cinnamon and extracts in large bowl with electric mixer at medium speed until light and fluffy. Fold in pineapple, 1/2 cup chopped pecans, 1/2 cup coconut and bananas. Divide batter evenly between prepared pans. Bake 30 minutes or until golden brown and toothpick inserted into centers comes

out clean. Cool in pans on wire racks 10 minutes. Remove cakes from pans to racks; cool completely.

3. Frost 1 cake layer with cream cheese frosting. Top with the remaining layer. Frost sides and then top of cake. Press toasted coconut and finely chopped pecans onto sides of frosted cake. Refrigerate 1 hour or until frosting is set.
   Makes 10 servings

Maple Pumpkin Cheesecake

1-1/4 cups graham cracker crumbs
1/4 cup sugar
1/4 cup (1/2 stick) butter or margarine, melted
3 (8-ounce) packages cream cheese, softened
1 (14-ounce) can EAGLE BRAND® Sweetened
    Condensed Milk (NOT evaporated milk)
1 (15-ounce) can pumpkin (2 cups)
3 eggs
1/4 cup pure maple syrup
1-1/2 teaspoons ground cinnamon
1 teaspoon ground nutmeg
1/2 teaspoon salt
    Maple Pecan Glaze (recipe follows)

1. Preheat oven to 325°F. Combine graham cracker crumbs, sugar and butter; press firmly on bottom of ungreased 9-inch springform pan.

2. In large bowl, beat cream cheese until fluffy. Gradually beat in EAGLE BRAND® until smooth. Add pumpkin, eggs, maple syrup, cinnamon, nutmeg and salt; mix well. Pour into crust.

3. Bake 1 hour 15 minutes or until center appears nearly set when shaken. Cool 1 hour. Cover and chill at least 4 hours. Top with chilled Maple Pecan Glaze. Store leftovers covered in refrigerator.
   Makes one (9-inch) cheesecake

Maple Pecan Glaze: In medium saucepan over medium-high heat, combine 1 cup (1/2 pint) whipping cream and 3/4 cup pure maple syrup; bring to a boil. Boil rapidly 15 to 20 minutes or until thickened, stir occasionally. Add 1/2 cup chopped pecans. Cover and chill. Stir before using.

Best-Ever Short Cake

Banana Split
Ice Cream Sandwiches

(pictured at right)

> 1 package (18 ounces) refrigerated chocolate chip cookie dough
> 2 ripe bananas, mashed
> 1/2 cup strawberry jam, divided
> 4 cups strawberry ice cream (or any flavor), softened
> Hot fudge topping and whipped cream (optional)
> 9 maraschino cherries (optional)

1. Preheat oven to 350°F. Lightly grease 13×9-inch baking pan. Let dough stand at room temperature about 15 minutes.

2. Beat dough and bananas in large bowl until well blended. Spread dough evenly in prepared pan and smooth top. Bake about 22 minutes or until edges are light brown. Cool completely in pan on wire rack.

3. Line 8-inch square baking pan with foil or plastic wrap, allowing some to hang over edges of pan. Remove cooled cookie from pan; cut in half widthwise. Place 1 cookie half, top side down, in prepared pan, trimming edges to fit, if necessary. Spread 1/4 cup jam evenly over cookie in pan. Spread ice cream evenly over jam. Spread remaining 1/4 cup jam over bottom of remaining cookie half; place jam side down over ice cream. Wrap tightly with foil; freeze at least 2 hours or overnight.

4. Cut into bars and top with hot fudge sauce, whipped cream and cherries, if desired.

Makes 9 servings

Apple Butterscotch Tart

> Pastry for single-crust pie
> 5 cups (about 5 medium) peeled and thinly sliced tart green apples
> 1 cup (6 ounces) NESTLÉ® TOLL HOUSE® Butterscotch Flavored Morsels
> 3/4 cup all-purpose flour
> 1/2 cup packed brown sugar
> 1/2 teaspoon ground cinnamon
> 1/4 cup (1/2 stick) chilled butter or margarine
> Ice cream or sweetened whipped cream

PREHEAT oven to 375°F.

LINE 9-inch tart pan with removable bottom with pastry; trim away excess pastry. Arrange apples in pastry shell; sprinkle morsels over apples. Combine flour, sugar and cinnamon in medium bowl. Cut in butter with pastry blender or two knives until mixture resembles coarse crumbs. Sprinkle mixture over filling.

BAKE for 40 to 45 minutes or until apples are tender when pierced with sharp knife. Remove side of tart pan. Serve warm with ice cream.

Makes 8 servings

Rich Heath® Bits Cheesecake

> Vanilla Wafer Crust (recipe follows)
> 3 packages (8 ounces each) cream cheese, softened
> 1 cup sugar
> 3 eggs
> 1 container (8 ounces) sour cream
> 1/2 teaspoon vanilla extract
> 1-1/3 cups (8-ounce package) HEATH® Milk Chocolate Toffee Bits, divided

1. Prepare crust. Heat oven to 350°F.

2. Beat cream cheese and sugar in large bowl on medium speed of mixer until well blended. Add eggs, one at a time, beating well after each addition. Add sour cream and vanilla; beat on low speed until blended.

3. Pour half of cheese mixture into crust. Reserve 1/4 cup toffee bits for topping; sprinkle remaining toffee bits over cheese mixture in pan. Spoon in remaining cheese mixture.

4. Bake 1 hour or until filling is set. Cool 15 minutes. Sprinkle reserved toffee bits over top; with knife, loosen cake from side of pan. Cool completely; remove side of pan. Cover, refrigerate at least 4 hours before serving. Cover; refrigerate leftover cheesecake. *Makes 12 to 16 servings*

Vanilla Wafer Crust: Combine 1-3/4 cups vanilla wafer crumbs (about 55 wafers) and 2 tablespoons sugar; stir in 1/4 cup (1/2 stick) melted butter or margarine. Press onto bottom and 1 inch up side of 9-inch springform pan. Refrigerate about 30 minutes.

The publisher would like to thank the companies and organizations listed below for the use of their recipes and photographs in this publication.

ACH Food Companies, Inc.

Allen Canning Company

Alouette® Spreadable Cheese, Alouette® Baby Brie®, Alouette® Crème de Brie, Chavrie®, Saladena®, Montrachet®

Bays English Muffin Corporation

Courtesy of The Beef Checkoff

BelGioioso® Cheese Inc.

Birds Eye Foods

Bob Evans®

Cabot® Creamery Cooperative

Campbell Soup Company

Cherry Marketing Institute

Delmarva Poultry Industry, Inc.

Del Monte Corporation

Dole Food Company, Inc.

Duncan Hines® and Moist Deluxe® are registered trademarks of Pinnacle Foods Corp.

EAGLE BRAND®

Filippo Berio® Olive Oil

Grandma's®, A Division of B&G Foods, Inc.

The Hershey Company

Hormel Foods, LLC

Johnsonville Sausage, LLC

© Mars, Incorporated 2008

MASTERFOODS USA

Mott's® is a registered trademark of Mott's, LLP

National Honey Board

National Pork Board

Nestlé USA

Ortega®, A Division of B&G Foods, Inc.

The Quaker® Oatmeal Kitchens

Reckitt Benckiser Inc.

Riviana Foods Inc.

Sargento® Foods Inc.

Sonoma® Dried Tomatoes

StarKist® Tuna

Sun•Maid® Growers of California

Unilever

Veg•All®

Watkins Incorporated

General Index

Alphabetical Index

METRIC CONVERSION CHART

VOLUME MEASUREMENTS (dry)

1/8 teaspoon = 0.5 mL
1/4 teaspoon = 1 mL
1/2 teaspoon = 2 mL
3/4 teaspoon = 4 mL
1 teaspoon = 5 mL
1 tablespoon = 15 mL
2 tablespoons = 30 mL
1/4 cup = 60 mL
1/3 cup = 75 mL
1/2 cup = 125 mL
2/3 cup = 150 mL
3/4 cup = 175 mL
1 cup = 250 mL
2 cups = 1 pint = 500 mL
3 cups = 750 mL
4 cups = 1 quart = 1 L

VOLUME MEASUREMENTS (fluid)

1 fluid ounce (2 tablespoons) = 30 mL
4 fluid ounces (1/2 cup) = 125 mL
8 fluid ounces (1 cup) = 250 mL
12 fluid ounces (1 1/2 cups) = 375 mL
16 fluid ounces (2 cups) = 500 mL

WEIGHTS (mass)

1/2 ounce = 15 g
1 ounce = 30 g
3 ounces = 90 g
4 ounces = 120 g
8 ounces = 225 g
10 ounces = 285 g
12 ounces = 360 g
16 ounces = 1 pound = 455 g

DIMENSIONS

1/16 inch = 2 mm
1/8 inch = 3 mm
1/4 inch = 6 mm
1/2 inch = 1.5 cm
3/4 inch = 2 cm
1 inch = 2.5 cm

OVEN TEMPERATURES

250°F = 120°C
275°F = 140°C
300°F = 150°C
325°F = 160°C
350°F = 180°C
375°F = 190°C
400°F = 200°C
425°F = 220°C
450°F = 230°C

BAKING PAN SIZES

Utensil	Size in Inches/Quarts	Metric Volume	Size in Centimeters
Baking or Cake Pan (square or rectangular)	8×8×2	2 L	20×20×5
	9×9×2	2.5 L	23×23×5
	12×8×2	3 L	30×20×5
	13×9×2	3.5 L	33×23×5
Loaf Pan	8×4×3	1.5 L	20×10×7
	9×5×3	2 L	23×13×7
Round Layer Cake Pan	8×1½	1.2 L	20×4
	9×1½	1.5 L	23×4
Pie Plate	8×1¼	750 mL	20×3
	9×1¼	1 L	23×3
Baking Dish or Casserole	1 quart	1 L	—
	1½ quart	1.5 L	—
	2 quart	2 L	—